W9-CBP-027

AUG 26 2019

Chester
Library

DISCARD

250 West Main Street
Chester, NJ 07930

Searching for

BLACK CONFEDERATES

CIVIL WAR AMERICA

Peter S. Carmichael, Caroline E. Janney,
and Aaron Sheehan-Dean, editors

This landmark series interprets broadly the history and culture
of the Civil War era through the long nineteenth century and
beyond. Drawing on diverse approaches and methods, the
series publishes historical works that explore all aspects of
the war, biographies of leading commanders, and tactical and
campaign studies, along with select editions of primary sources.
Together, these books shed new light on an era that remains
central to our understanding of American and world history.

Searching for
BLACK CONFEDERATES

The Civil War's
Most Persistent Myth

KEVIN M. LEVIN

THE UNIVERSITY OF NORTH CAROLINA PRESS

Chapel Hill

This book was published with the assistance of the Fred W. Morrison Fund
of the University of North Carolina Press.

© 2019 Kevin M. Levin

All rights reserved

Designed by Jamison Cockerham
Set in Arno, Scala Sans, Fell DW Pica, and Irby
by Tseng Information Systems, Inc.

Manufactured in the United States of America

The University of North Carolina Press has been a member
of the Green Press Initiative since 2003.

Jacket illustrations: (front) Sergeant Andrew M. Chandler of the 44th
Mississippi Infantry Regiment, Co. F., and Silas Chandler, family slave,
ca. 1861; (back) *"Confederate Camp" during the Late American War*, ca. 1871.
Both courtesy of Library of Congress Prints and Photographs Division.

LIBRARY OF CONGRESS CATALOGING-IN-PUBLICATION DATA
Names: Levin, Kevin M., 1969– author.
Title: Searching for black Confederates : the Civil War's most persistent myth /
    Kevin M. Levin.
Other titles: Civil War America (Series)
Description: Chapel Hill : The University of North Carolina Press, [2019] |
    Series: Civil War America | Includes bibliographical references and index.
Identifiers: LCCN 2019002919 | ISBN 9781469653266 (cloth : alk. paper) |
    ISBN 9781469653273 (ebook)
Subjects: LCSH: African Americans—Confederate States of America. | Confederate
    States of America. Army—African American troops. | Slaves—Confederate States
    of America. | African American soldiers—History—19th century. | United States—
    History—Civil War, 1861–1865—Participation, African American.
Classification: LCC E585.A35 L48 2019 | DDC 973.7/415—dc23 LC record available at
    https://lccn.loc.gov/2019002919

FOR MY PARENTS

with love and gratitude

Contents

Figures

Searching for

BLACK CONFEDERATES

Introduction

Virginian Edmund Ruffin had grown weary of waiting for disunion and an independent Confederate nation by the end of the 1850s. A well-known "fire-eater," Ruffin spent much of the decade advocating for secession and states' rights as a bulwark to protect the institution of slavery. As a way of pressing for Southern independence as a reality, Ruffin's writings imagined a new Southern nation fighting against Northern vandals. His book *Anticipations of the Future, to Serve as Lessons for the Present Time* was published in 1860, just shy of the presidential election that placed the Republican candidate Abraham Lincoln in the White House. Ruffin, like others who entertained visions of an imagined Confederacy, hoped to form and strengthen bonds of nationalism that, in the event of actual secession and war, would bring disparate groups closer together and carry the nascent nation through a lengthy and costly civil war.[1]

In Ruffin's fictional rendering of the coming war, the conflict between North and South begins not in 1861 but on Christmas Eve 1868, following the election of William Seward to the presidency. According to the narrative, Abraham Lincoln's first and only term proves to be uneventful, but abolitionists in Congress gradually erode Southern rights through the passage of tariffs and the appointment of Supreme Court nominees who are friendly to Northern interests. Seward's administration exacerbates the problem by abolishing slavery in the District of Columbia and by refusing to enforce the Fugitive Slave Act. In response, six slave states in the Deep South, including South Carolina, finally secede and subsequently seize Fort Sumter. None other than John Brown's son General Owen Brown leads the Northern invasion of abolitionists and black recruits that ensues. Once in Kentucky, however, their plans run afoul. According to Ruffin's vision, the enslaved people of Kentucky have no interest in being freed; those who join Brown do so only for the opportunity to rejoin their old masters. Eventually Brown is captured, and "from the different spreading branches of one gigantic oak" he is hung along "with twenty-seven of his subordinate white officers."[2] The war

1

comes to an end with a truce that all but guarantees Southern independence. The victorious South emerges economically dominant and stands poised to absorb the Northwestern states as well as those on the upper Mississippi and the Middle Atlantic states. These states join, agreeing to the condition that they accept the institution of slavery, in large part because they have grown weary of the fanaticism of New England abolitionists.

Beyond the seizure of Fort Sumter, very little of Ruffin's narrative proved accurate, but his observations concerning how the Southern states utilized their enslaved population deserves a closer look. According to Ruffin, "the numerous slaves has not produced the anticipated dangers and evils to the South, it has been found in other respects a most valuable aid to military strength." In Ruffin's imagined civil war, the South's use of its enslaved population to construct fortifications and "other labors . . . served to leave all the soldiers for military services only." Maximizing the use of slave labor on a wide range of military-related projects allowed "the dominant class of whites" to "go abroad to repel invasion, and thereby scarcely cause any of the labor of the country to be abstracted, or the superintendence and direction of the negro laborers to be greatly lessened or impaired." Whites could leave their homes and families without worrying about their safety or the loyalty of their slaves.[3]

At no point in Ruffin's fiction did slaves present a threat to the war effort or race relations in the South. In so writing, he clearly hoped to assuage the concerns of those who believed that the slave states would be unable to engage in a protracted war against the North and at the same time maintain vigilant oversight of the region's enslaved population. Rather than a weakness, Ruffin believed that the South's enslaved population constituted one of its greatest strengths.

That said, importantly, there is no hint at any point in his narrative that Ruffin ever imagined the possibility that slaves could or should be utilized as soldiers. Instead, the roles assigned to the South's enslaved population in Ruffin's fictional world followed deeply embedded assumptions about race and white supremacy that could never be overturned, even in the heat of war and with independence on the line.

Ruffin accurately predicted how the Confederacy chose to utilize its enslaved population from the time war broke out in the spring of 1861 until just a few weeks before its collapse four years later. Reality must have proven much stranger than fiction during the war's final days for Ruffin. Following a lengthy and divisive public debate, the Confederate Congress passed legislation in the last weeks of the war that allowed for the enlistment of slaves as soldiers. Like others, Ruffin supported enlistment with deep reservations but maintained that he did not believe that slaves or free blacks could make good soldiers. He did, however, believe, as he had argued in *Anticipations*, that they were loyal. For those slaves who fell short, Ruffin called for their execution as traitors to the government.[4] But the vision he had conceived was already crumbling around him. Black troops—loyal to the Union rather than the Confederacy—had contributed in crucial ways to the Union war effort and the capture of plantations Ruffin had owned. The surrender of Confederate armies that began on April 9, 1865, at Appomattox Court House only confirmed Ruffin's worst fears of Yankee domination. With his aspirations for an independent Southern nation and its racial order dashed, he saw only one thing left to do. On June 18 he committed suicide by gunshot.

Ruffin may have lived to read about the recruitment of a small handful of black men into the military just days before the fall of the Confederacy in April 1865, but I believe he would be utterly perplexed by the current debate and fascination with the supposed prevalence of black Confederate soldiers. Over the past few decades, claims to the existence of anywhere between 500 and 100,000 black Confederate soldiers, fighting in racially integrated units, have become increasingly common. Proponents assert that entire companies and regiments served under Robert E. Lee's command as well as in other theaters of war. One can find hundreds of websites telling stories of these men coming to the aid of their white comrades on the battlefield and standing firm on the firing line. Taken together, this picture of the Confederacy would be completely foreign to Ruffin and his Confederate comrades.

As this book will argue, claims that the Confederate government recruited significant numbers of black men into the army first emerged within the Confederate heritage community in the late 1970s in response to the gradual shift in popular memory of the Civil War following the civil rights movement. During this period, historians placed increasing emphasis on slavery as a cause of secession and war; its maintenance as central to the Confederate war effort; and emancipation as one of the war's most significant results, along with the preservation of the Union. Scholars and public historians during this period devoted more effort to uncovering the contributions and personal stories of former slaves and free blacks who volunteered to serve in the U.S. Colored Troops. This work contributed to a broader effort to recover the role of enslaved people in their own emancipation.

The Sons of Confederate Veterans (scv) was the first organization to promote stories of black Confederate soldiers, beginning in the late 1970s. Evidence shows that the group meant to counter the growing acceptance that slavery was the cause of the Civil War; that emancipation was central to what the war accomplished; and that former slaves and free blacks were instrumental in bringing about the Confederacy's demise. They hoped to demonstrate that if free and enslaved black men fought in Confederate ranks, the war could not have been fought to abolish slavery. Stories of armed black men marching and fighting would make it easier for the descendants of Confederate soldiers and those who celebrate Confederate heritage to embrace their Lost Cause unapologetically without running the risk of being viewed as racially insensitive or worse.

The black Confederate narrative emerged to perform a specific function, but many people today who accept the existence of black men in Confederate ranks are unaware that this mythical narrative does not date to the war years or even to the postwar period extending well into the twentieth century.

The origins of this myth do have roots in the war itself. Much of the confusion today centers on the failure to understand with precision the critical roles African Americans occupied in the Confederate war effort. The Confederate government utilized enslaved and free blacks for a wide range of activities to help offset significant disadvantages with regard to the Union army in manpower and war matériel. Tens of thousands of slaves were impressed by the government, often against the will of their owners, to help with the construction of earthworks around the cities of Richmond, Petersburg, and Atlanta. Slaves were also assigned to the construction and repair of rail lines and as workers in iron foundries and other factories producing war matériel. In service to the armies, thousands worked as teamsters, cooks, and musicians. And Confederate officers from the slaveholding class often brought their slaves from home to serve as "body servants" or "manservants." But critically, none of these roles included service on the battlefield as enlisted soldiers. Apart from the small number of black men who were recruited in the last days of the war, the Confederate bid for independence was fought by white men in the name of a government pledged to maintain white supremacy.

S earching for Black Confederates begins by guiding readers through the complex relationships that evolved over the course of the war between masters and slaves in camp, on the march, and on the battlefield. The vast majority of accounts interpreted today as evidence of significant numbers of loyal black Confederate soldiers rely overwhelmingly on this specific group—men who will often be described as "camp slaves" throughout this book so as not to confuse their legal status.[5] These men served their masters by performing a wide range of tasks related to the maintenance of an efficient campsite. Masters assumed their slaves were loyal to them and to the Confederate cause, which can be seen in their letters and diaries as well as in the photographs taken with uniformed slaves. Confederate officers expected unquestioned obedience from their slaves as they did back home, but the exigencies of war quickly undermined these assumptions. Camp slaves challenged their masters' authority by pushing for increased privileges in camp, such as the ability to earn extra money and the right to travel more freely. They also challenged that authority more directly by running away, especially when in close proximity to the Union army.

Focusing specifically on these men not only provides much-needed historical context to the current debate but also broadens our understanding of how the institution of slavery functioned in the army and how it unraveled over the course of the war. Historians have explored how the movement of the Union army into the deepest corners of the Confederacy proved to be a crucial factor in providing the space for enslaved people on the home front to assert themselves by sabotaging the Confederate war effort in various ways and by running away. The gradual erosion of slavery can also be seen in the army itself as body servants challenged well-established boundaries in camp, on long marches, during battle, and following the wounding or deaths of their masters. Although camp slaves remained in the army until the very end of the war, by the middle of 1863 it grew increasingly clear to many that the master-slave relationship in camp could not be maintained as prospects for a Confederate victory grew more doubtful.[6]

It was in this atmosphere of a looming defeat and the unraveling of slavery throughout the Confederacy that congressional approval for the enlistment of slaves as soldiers was passed in March 1865. For many the question forced a reckoning with what was identified as the central purpose of the Confederacy, namely the protection of slavery. Ruffin clearly understood this as a dangerous step forward whose only saving grace was that it might forestall or delay defeat, but he would have also been aware of another factor in this deliberation that is all too often ignored by those who accept the black Confederate narrative today: at no point during the debate over enlistment was it ever revealed that black men were already serving in the Confederate army as soldiers.

The story then shifts to how camp slaves were remembered during different periods after the war, beginning with the veterans themselves and with former slaves who also inserted their own memories into the historical record. As a way to cope with military defeat and the end of slavery, ex-Confederates insisted that their slaves had remained fiercely loyal until the bitter end. Accounts of faithful slaves on the home front and in the army published in the immediate postwar period reassured white Southerners that their cause remained righteous. These narratives also supported efforts in Southern states to roll back federal Reconstruction legislation meant to protect the rights of formerly enslaved people and to protect them from vengeful whites. Camp slaves became central to the story that white Southerners told themselves about their defeat. These men appeared at local and national Confederate veterans' reunions, in parades, in the records of soldiers' homes, and on monuments, as well as in countless works of literature, soldiers' memoirs, newspapers, and even state government records. But in this early postwar period, Lost Cause writers were careful to distinguish camp slaves from soldiers; most Confederate veterans pushed back vigorously against any suggestion that camp slaves had fought as soldiers on the battlefield. Instead, the Lost Cause highlighted the bravery of the rank and file and their officers, who were always assumed to be white. There was no push on the part of Confederate veterans during the postwar period to honor former slaves as soldiers or to recognize their participation in the war as anything comparable to the service and sacrifice of white men who served in the ranks. Conjuring up black soldiers neither corroborated the memories of the generation that fought in the war nor helped to vindicate the veterans' cause.

During this same period a relatively small number of former camp slaves took advantage of state pensions that were issued in the former Confederate states of Mississippi, South Carolina, Tennessee, Virginia, and North Carolina. Today these documents remain widely misunderstood and are often presented as indisputable evidence that black and white men were issued pensions for their service as Confederate soldiers. A closer look at the documents themselves reveals a very different story. These five states did indeed extend their pension programs to include former camp servants, but these pensions were clearly earmarked for former slaves and not soldiers. The title of the form used by the state of Mississippi, which reads in part "Application of Indigent Servants of Soldier or Sailor of the Late Confederacy," bears this out. These documents also offer important insights into the lives of these former slaves, who had to demonstrate loyalty to their former masters and the Confederate cause as part of their applications. Pensions reinforced the expectation that black Americans would remain subservient to the dominant white political hierarchy at a time of racial unrest during the Jim Crow era. But the pension applications also demonstrate that former camp slaves understood that loyalty to their former masters and the Confederate cause was necessary to secure financial assistance at a time when it was desperately needed. These men also used the application process to assert their own understanding of the war and laid claim to a martial manhood that was often out of reach during and after the war.

This select group of veteran camp slaves lived out their final days on modest pensions that once again confirmed their wartime legal status as slaves. It would take decades more before these stories of loyal slaves were transformed into stories of the loyal black Confederate soldier. A number of factors help to explain why this myth has grown since the SCV first popularized it and why many people continue to find it difficult to properly distinguish between history and myth. It is impossible to minimize the importance of the most vocal proponents of this myth within the SCV, the United Daughters of the Confederacy, and other heritage organizations who remain committed to promoting the black Confederate narrative as a means of defending the legacy of the Confederacy and the "honor" of their ancestors who served in the rank and file. Social media pages of individual SCV camps as well as an entire webpage devoted to black Confederates on the SCV's national website attest to the narrative's overall importance and acceptance within the organization. Members' conviction that the former Confederacy is under assault has only grown stronger in recent years in the face of an emancipationist narrative of the war that is now reflected in history textbooks, Hollywood movies, museum exhibits, and historic site interpretation and especially in the ongoing debate about the display of Confederate battle flags and monuments in public spaces throughout the United States.

It continues to matter deeply that we narrate this history accurately and use evidence that separates myth from reality. In a Pew Research Center poll from 2011, only 38 percent of participants identified slavery as a central cause of the Civil War, and nearly half of the white respondents pointed to states' rights as its cause.[7] A more recent McClatchy-Marist poll showed that a little over half of Americans believe that slavery was the main cause of the war, which suggests that the needle has not moved significantly in recent years.[8] In early 2018 the Southern Poverty Law Center issued a report that concluded that "[schools] are not adequately teaching the history of American slavery, educators are not prepared to teach it, textbooks do not have enough material about it, and — as a result — students lack a basic knowledge of the important role it played in shaping the United States" and its continued impact on "race relations in America" today.[9]

The widespread misunderstanding and confusion surrounding the history of slavery and more specifically the ways in which the Confederacy utilized black labor, from the first days of the war to the very last in the spring of 1865, opens up just enough room to interpret the historical record as supporting the existence of hundreds if not thousands of loyal black Confederate soldiers. Wartime and postwar reports of armed black men in Confederate ranks along with photographs of uniformed black men posing alongside their masters or attending Confederate veterans' reunions, accompanied with very little interpretation, are often viewed as requiring no interpretation. One especially prominent example is the popular photograph of Andrew and Silas Chandler, which can be found on numerous book and magazine covers as well as on T-shirts. For many, the image represents undeniable evidence that the Confederacy armed black men beginning in 1861. It is easy to see why. Both men are wearing uniforms and are armed to the teeth. At first glance they appear to be comrades at the beginning of a great adventure, not master and slave but men of different races united in a cause. But master and slave is exactly the relationship represented in the photograph. Silas Chandler never served as a soldier in the Confederate army. He was an enslaved body servant, and his legal status did not change until the Confederacy was defeated.

The widespread embrace of the Internet, coupled with an inability to properly interpret historical sources—and the desire to mold evidence for political and social purposes—has exacerbated the spread and continued acceptance of the mythical black Confederate narrative. The photograph of Andrew and Silas Chandler, along with numerous other primary sources, can now be found on thousands of websites, social media pages, and discussion boards masquerading as places that welcome serious debate and discussion. Some of these historical sources have been intentionally manipulated, such as a photograph purporting to be Confederate soldiers who served in the Louisiana Native Guard in 1861–62. This photo is, in fact, a manipulated image of black Union soldiers taken in 1864 in a Philadelphia studio. The pervasiveness of this photograph and its unquestioning acceptance by many suggests that few approach these sources with a critical eye or can place them in proper historical context that reflects the latest scholarship on the Confederacy and slavery.

Even more problematic is the failure to evaluate the veracity of the many websites that feature these sources as proof of the existence of black Confederate soldiers. If one spends enough time online, it becomes clear that much of the content found on these sites is simply copied and pasted from one website to another. The lack of education in the area of digital media literacy was highlighted in 2010 when the state of Virginia issued a new history textbook to its fourth graders. In the chapter on the Civil War, author Joy Masoff included a statement claiming that thousands of black men fought as soldiers with Stonewall Jackson in the Shenandoah Valley. It was later revealed that, in an attempt to be inclusive and satisfy the state's Standards of Learning, the author discovered the information on an scv website and accepted its claims without question. Access to primary sources and the ease with which it takes to build a personal website allows anyone today to be his or her "own historian," even if the result is an alternative historical universe that would be unrecognizable to real Confederates like Edmund Ruffin.

In addition to history textbooks, over the past two decades stories of black Confederate soldiers have found their way into museum exhibits, including those maintained by the National Park Service, and even popular television shows such as *Antiques Roadshow* and *Finding Your Roots*. Finally, a small but vocal number of African Americans have accepted the black Confederate narrative. The scv and other heritage groups have embraced these African Americans, who support the narrative itself as vindication of their broader agenda to drive a wedge between the history of the Confederacy and their ancestors and the history of slavery and white supremacy. Indeed, as will be discussed throughout this book, African Americans have helped to promote the loyal slave narrative stretching back to the war itself.

Academic historians have been anything but silent on this subject in recent years. In a 2014 interview, historian Gary Gallagher described the black Confederate movement as "demented."[10] Indeed, the scholarship produced over the past twenty years has helped to clarify how the war transformed the master-slave relationship; the many vital and dangerous roles performed by free and enslaved blacks in connection to the Confederate war effort; and the eventual bitter debate in 1864–65 over the enlistment of blacks into the army. Their efforts, however, have made few if any inroads in challenging the public's acceptance of the black Confederate narrative. More problematic is the increased politicization of history that has made it easier to dismiss the work of academic historians. Black Confederate websites routinely accuse historians of intentionally ignoring the subject for political and other nefarious reasons.[11]

Ultimately, this book will argue that stories of black Confederate soldiers and loyal slaves were embraced as a means to defend the memory of the Confederacy as well as in response to deteriorating race relations at the end of the twentieth century and beginning of the twenty-first. It is no accident that the black Confederate narrative thrived during a period that witnessed both a transformation in how Americans remembered and commemorated the Civil War and renewed debate on a wide range of hot-button political issues with race at the center.

The black Confederate narrative was challenged most strenuously between 2011 and 2015, during the 150th anniversary of the Civil War. Famous battlefields operated by the National Park Service and other historic sites, along with museums across the country, presented the general public with a narrative of the Civil War that directly challenged the foundation on which the black Confederate narrative rests. The only black soldiers recognized at sesquicentennial events throughout the country wore Union blue uniforms. In addition, Hollywood films like *Lincoln* and *12 Years a Slave* reached large audiences with dramatic stories about the politics of emancipation and the violence of slavery. Nevertheless, Confederate heritage advocates found other ways to promote their preferred narrative of the war. They unveiled new monuments and held elaborate ceremonies to honor black Confederates that included the dedication of military-style grave markers. Many of these events garnered local and sometimes national media attention that often did little more than present to their audiences the historical understanding of these organizations without questioning the veracity of their claims.

One of the most important ways in which the SCV and the United Daughters of the Confederacy have defended the integrity of the black Confederate narrative in recent years is the appropriation of what they believe to be evidence of black Confederates offered by prominent African Americans in the past. There is no better example than the frequency of references on websites and in other publications to the famed black abolitionist Frederick Douglass, who early in the war published reports in his own newspaper of armed black men in Confederate ranks. What is often overlooked is that Douglass took these steps as a means to convince the Lincoln administration to accept black men as soldiers in the Union army. Decades after the war, some black leaders such as Booker T. Washington also assuaged concerns about black uplift by reminding the white community of the loyalty of slaves to the Confederate war effort and their former masters. In the hands of neo-Confederates, this evidence confirms their own self-serving conclusions, but the results are no less damaging for countless others who are unable to interpret the evidence within a broader historical context.

Ultimately, the black Confederate narrative failed to halt or even slow down the nation's shifting Civil War memory that found its clearest expression during the sesquicentennial, including the growing acceptance that the Confederacy's central goal was the establishment of a slaveholding republic built on white supremacy. It still, however, resonates with the faithful, who show no signs of accepting defeat. In fact, recent events have reinvigorated the Confederate heritage community in the wake of the horrific murder of nine churchgoers during a prayer service by Dylann Roof at the Emanuel African Methodist Episcopal Church in Charleston, South Carolina, on June 17, 2015. In response to subsequent calls to remove the battle flag that had flown on the statehouse grounds since 1962, the South Carolina division of the SCV reminded the nation of the service of black Confederate soldiers.[12] Its attempt to convince the nation that Confederate symbols do not represent a racist past ultimately proved unsuccessful. The removal of the Confederate flag in Columbia, as well as in other cities and towns across the South, was followed by several announcements by corporations that they would no longer sell merchandise that featured the battle flag in their stores or on their websites.

A renewed call to remove Confederate monuments from public spaces ensued as well. Over the past three years, monuments and memorials have been taken down in New Orleans, Dallas, Orlando, Baltimore, and Louisville, as well as in a host of smaller towns across the country. In August 2017 a violent white nationalist rally in Charlottesville, Virginia, in defense of a monument to Robert E. Lee — which left one young woman dead — revealed that Americans remain deeply divided over how to remember the Civil War.

The ongoing debate about Confederate monuments at a time of increased racial tension points to the need for an honest national conversation about the history and legacy of slavery. That conversation can happen only if we put aside the myths and self-serving narratives of loyal slaves and brave black Confederate soldiers that have long played a role in maintaining the color line in American life. Understanding how these myths evolved and were perpetuated over time is the first step in that process.

Chapter One

THE CAMP SLAVES' WAR

In August 1861, Andrew Chandler enlisted as a private in the Palo Alto Guards, which eventually became Company F of the 44th Mississippi Infantry of the Army of Tennessee. Once enlisted, Andrew made time to stop at a studio to sit for a photograph. Like countless others, Andrew hoped to capture the confidence and excitement that went into his new identity as a soldier of the Confederacy. Just as importantly, he wanted his loved ones back home to remember him as a brave young man who answered his nation's call to military service and who would bring honor to his family. Unlike the vast majority of his fellow volunteers, Andrew did not enter the studio to pose alone.

Andrew left his home in West Point, Mississippi, accompanied by a slave who had been with his family since birth. Silas Chandler served as Andrew's body servant or camp slave through the battle of Chickamauga in September 1863 before accompanying Andrew's brother for the remainder of the war. Unlike other photographs of Confederate soldiers and slaves that place the former in a clear position of authority, Andrew and Silas sat side by side, both brandishing weapons and both wearing Confederate uniforms.[1] Andrew wore a typical private's jacket and held a pinfire pistol; a revolver was also nestled in his belt. Silas tucked a pepperbox conspicuously into his short shell artillerist's jacket, which left his left hand free to grip a rifle across his lap. To complete this unusual scene, both men wielded large bowie knives in their right hands.

There is an almost comic element in Andrew's attempt to cram in as many weapons — very likely studio props[2] — into the photograph. One can easily imagine an excited Andrew requesting each weapon in an attempt to complete the scene and satisfy his own ideas of martial manhood on the eve of war. Andrew, who was seventeen years old in 1861, did his best to strike

This photograph of Sergeant Andrew M. Chandler of the 44th Mississippi Infantry Regiment, Co. F., and Silas Chandler, family slave, was likely taken in 1861 when the two went off to war. The weapons are probably studio props. (Library of Congress)

the pose of a young Southern gentleman going off to war, but the naïveté of youth is still clearly visible in both his facial expression and body language. Seven years his senior, Silas sits more comfortably, even slightly slouched next to Andrew's stiff frame. Neither individual likely had any notion of the challenges and dangers that awaited them. Despite the military uniforms and weapons in this image, by the time this photograph was taken the nature of the relationship between Andrew and Silas had been clearly established legally and socially.

Twenty-two years earlier, at the age of two, Silas had traveled from Virginia to Mississippi as one of fifteen slaves owned by Andrew's father, Gilderoy "Roy" Chandler. Roy Chandler joined a wave of Americans from the Upper South and other parts of the nation looking to reap the profits from a rapidly expanding cotton economy in one of the southwestern states of western Georgia, Alabama, Mississippi, and Louisiana. Shortly after arriving, Chandler purchased 320 acres in Oktibbeha County in the northeast section of Mississippi. As Silas grew, so did the Chandler family's wealth, including their holdings in land and slaves. By the time of Andrew's birth on April 3, 1844, Silas likely had already been exposed to the backbreaking tasks and violence necessary to make cotton king. Silas was trained as a carpenter, a skill that singled him out from the rest of the slave population and that may have resulted in closer interaction with the white Chandlers, including Andrew.

We do not know the extent and nature of the contact between Andrew and Silas. Certainly as the two matured, their lives became defined by their respective roles as the eldest son of a wealthy slave owner and his slave. For Andrew, the death of his father in 1854 solidified his future as the eventual head of household. On the eve of the Civil War, the Chandler estate included thirty-five slaves plus land valued at $24,000 and a personal estate valued at $40,000.[3]

Andrew and Silas left West Point and their respective families as master and slave. For Andrew, the relationship between the two embodied a set of assumptions and expectations that had been reinforced over the previous decades. Slaveholding families expected absolute obedience and fidelity from their chattel in exchange for what they believed was a gentle, paternalist hand that offered both guidance and discipline as part of an extended family. Andrew could not know in the summer of 1861 whether this relationship could be uprooted from the confines of the plantation and transferred to a military setting. The photographs that Andrew and other young Southern men posed for during the early rush to enlist embodied their untested assumptions about honor and commitment to the new Confederate nation. But Andrew also wanted to be remembered as a slaveholder going to war. It is unlikely that Andrew questioned Silas's loyalty, but outfitting him in a uniform for the purposes of a photograph may have reassured him that the cause of the Confederacy united both men.

The true story of Andrew and Silas has been all but lost in our popular memory of the Civil War. After the war, the relationships between Confederate officers and their slaves were transformed into stories of loyal or faithful slaves that functioned as one of the central pillars of the Lost Cause narrative. The image of the camp slave alongside his benevolent master emboldened white Southerners through the years of Reconstruction and beyond. Confederates may have been thoroughly defeated on the battlefield, but they held tightly to the conviction that their slaves remained steadfast to the end and to the cause for which so many white men gave their lives. In more recent years, the narrative of the faithful slave has been transformed once again into countless Internet stories that wrongly claim thousands of loyal black Confederate soldiers fought willingly alongside their masters and for an independent Confederate nation. Such stories have moved us further away from understanding the relationship of Andrew and Silas as master and slave as well as the central place that the preservation of slavery occupied in the Confederate war effort.

The photograph of Andrew and Silas highlights the confidence with which the slaveholding class went to war and the place of slavery in the formation of Confederate national identity. Confederates believed that disadvantages in every aspect of war making and the population imbalance in 1861 could be overcome by the bravery and commitment of the South's male population of military age and with the support of its enslaved people. Slavery was embraced as a source of moral and military strength, not internal weakness or vulnerability.[4]

In the final years of slavery, the relationship between master and camp slave was tested to meet the demands and exigencies of war. Masters clearly articulated daily responsibilities and expectations to their servants and considered even the smallest behaviors as a reflection of their continued obedience, but extended stays in camp offered slaves numerous opportunities to earn extra money and interact with other slaves. Slave owners did their best to accommodate their servants and at the same time maintain their absolute authority, but this became more and more difficult as the war progressed. Long marches and the confusion that accompanied major battles and their immediate aftermath offered camp slaves frequent chances to run away, which they did. Photographs of master and slave reveal glimmers of Confederate optimism early on and the bonds that held them together. They also point to the long unraveling of slavery that took place within the army as well as on the home front in the face of invading Union armies between 1861 and 1865.

The inclusion of camp slaves in the army constituted a small part of a broader attempt to mobilize as much of the enslaved population as possible in a war against an enemy whose material and human resources appeared to be limitless. In 1861 slave owners, caught up in strong feelings of nationalism, volunteered their slaves to work for the Confederate war effort. That proved to be only a temporary solution. Once military operations commenced, Confederate officers in the field routinely issued orders to take every able-bodied slave within the boundaries of their command and sometimes even beyond it.[5] Beginning in March 1863 the government took steps to mobilize tens of thousands of free and enslaved blacks to work on various

Thousands of slaves were impressed by the Confederate government throughout the war to assist in the construction of earthworks and other projects. In this illustration, impressed slaves work on James Island, near Charleston, South Carolina, in 1863. (Library of Congress)

public and private military-related sites, such as the construction of earthworks and the maintenance of railroads and other roads. Enslaved people worked at the Griswold Pistol Factory in Georgia and Richmond's Tredegar Iron Works, producing arms and ammunition, as well as the lead mines and saltpeter caves managed by the War Department's Niter and Mining Bureau. It was not uncommon for impressed slaves to return home sick or not at all. Following the outbreak of a smallpox epidemic in Richmond, slave owners demanded the return of their impressed slaves working at a hospital. These steps to mobilize the enslaved population undermined the sovereignty of slaveholders and led to increased complaints that their property rights were being violated.[6]

Tens of thousands of impressed slaves were also assigned to Confederate armies throughout the war and in every theater of operation. The use of enslaved people as teamsters, cooks, butchers, blacksmiths, and hospital attendants allowed most white men to shoulder a rifle on the battlefield, where they were needed the most. Robert E. Lee's Army of Northern Virginia may have included as many as 6,000 to 10,000 impressed slaves as it moved into southern Pennsylvania in the summer of 1863. Enslaved labor performed crucial functions for Confederate armies while in camp, on the march, and, most importantly, on the battlefield. The sight of thousands of slaves in the military served as a constant reminder that the "peculiar institution" was an integral component of a slaveholding nation at war.[7]

In contrast with this large-scale mobilization of black bodies through government impressment, camp slaves occupied a unique place in a slave society at war. The most obvious difference between free blacks hired to perform a specific task within the army and those impressed by the government was that camp slaves answered directly to their masters. The relationship between the two was defined outside of the Confederate military hierarchy. Many camp slaves had already demonstrated their worth through the possession of a specific skill—as was the case for Silas Chandler—or through behavior that was understood as demonstrating unquestioning fidelity and trust. The families of both Andrew and Silas shared the fears that attended their departure and, even if they did not acknowledge it to one another, understood that the safe return of one depended on the other. Similarly, after learning of his decision to join the Hampton Legion, Harry Ford's mother insisted that he bring a servant with him into the army. Harry admitted that "a private with a servant seems an anomaly," but he agreed to do so if it helped to ease his mother's anxiety. The post of honor went to a trusted slave by the name of Kent.[8] It is likely that Harry's mother implored Kent to both obey and watch over her young son before they departed.

Some of these slave-owning families may have heard stories of "trusted" slaves accompanying family members in earlier wars. Both the British and Continental armies made use of personal servants or "waiters" during the American Revolution, though the practice was regulated. Camp servants served officers in camp or garrison as well as on the battlefield. Through the Mexican-American War, Southern slave owners continued the practice of utilizing slave labor in camp. During the battle of Buena Vista, two camp slaves, one of whom was wounded in the process, recovered the body of Kentucky colonel Henry Clay Jr. Slaves faced many of the same dangers on the battlefields of Mexico that would come to define their experience during the Civil War.[9]

The vast majority of camp servants accompanied Confederate officers, but the presence of Silas and Kent proves that slaves attended privates as well. The presence of camp slaves reminded both those who owned slaves and those who did not of what Confederate vice president Alexander Stephens referred to as the "cornerstone of the Confederacy." Their presence also reminded slave owners of the importance of maintaining control back home, where they no longer exercised direct oversight of their enslaved populations. Fears of slave unrest was likely a serious concern as they moved farther away from home and later as Yankee armies penetrated into Confederate territory. Confederates balanced these dark scenes by embracing a sense of collective purpose with their camp slaves. Mississippians such as Andrew Chandler and others from states in the Deep South did not have to be reminded that their states' secession conventions identified the defense of slavery as their primary reason for Southern independence.[10] Others in the military turned to religious leaders to reassure them that their slaves stood with them in defense of their homes. "I am looking to the poor despised slaves," Bishop Stephen Elliott intoned, "as the source of our security, because I firmly believe God will not permit his purposes to be overthrown or his arrangements to be interfered with."[11] Reverend Thomas Verner Moore implored his flock in Richmond "to trust the black face of the honest servant who fears God and loves his master."[12] For others it was simply necessary to glance nearby: "I think he is a great Negro," wrote James Adams Tillman about his camp slave, "and feel assured he will stick with me to the last."[13]

While few doubted which side God was on in the early months of the war or questioned the loyalty of their slaves, more immediate questions and challenges demanded attention. Armies of citizens-turned-soldiers needed to be properly trained and disciplined by officers, who themselves often had no prior military experience. As uniforms, weapons, and other essentials were distributed, enlisted men adjusted to a strict chain of command, the demands of daily drilling, and life in close quarters. Preparation for war and the acclimation to soldier life generally necessitated that enlisted men and junior grade officers learned their place within the military hierarchy and exercised control over their own impulses to independent behavior.[14]

The sights, smells, and sounds that awaited Andrew, Silas, Henry, and Kent as they arrived in camp for the first time must have been overwhelming. Row upon row of tents often stretched for miles and quickly came to resemble and function as small towns. For recruits from rural areas, it was likely the first time they had been exposed to large numbers of people, but the close quarters provided an opportunity to interact with comrades from different parts of the Confederacy, which in turn encouraged strong bonds of nationalism and esprit de corps.

It is likely that few Confederates worried about the risks of bringing slaves to camp, given the stability that characterized the armies early on and even during extended periods after major battles. An exception was Charles Lieberman, who served in the 13th North Carolina. He reported home at the end of August 1861 that his camp had "lost some 20 odd negroes for the last 5 days." Lieberman worried specifically about one black man who entered "camp in a suspicious way" but was confident "that death will be his doom if he is one of this [sic] negrostealers."[15]

Masters may have believed that their slaves were safer in camp, where oversight was more direct, than they were back at home. One historian has concluded that, in what would soon be known as the Army of Northern Virginia, "one in twenty or one in thirty soldiers" brought a servant, and "in rare instances the ratio was closer to one in ten or twelve."[16] Such numbers early on were likely found in the Army of Tennessee and other armies as well. Henry Ford's slave Kent was one of twenty-five camp slaves in the 3rd Alabama Regiment, which left home with "a thousand strong in rank and file and several hundred strong in Negro servants." The presence of large numbers of slaves in camp not only served as reminders of home and helped to ease the transition from civilian to military life for their owners but also helped to define a slaveholding community at war.[17] It did not take long, however, for many to agree with one Confederate who was forced to admit that "the army is a bad place for a young negroe."[18]

Days after the bombardment and surrender of Fort Sumter in April 1861, John Christopher Winsmith traveled from Spartanburg to Columbia to take command of Company G of the 5th South Carolina Volunteer Infantry. Accompanying him was his slave Spencer. While Winsmith learned the art of command, Spencer familiarized himself with his role as Winsmith's camp servant. The work was demanding, beginning before dawn and often extending well into the evening. Cooking breakfast, brushing uniforms, preparing hot water for shaving and bathing, and polishing swords and pistols occupied the attention of most camp slaves. Other duties depended on the specific needs of their masters and may have included providing entertainment, foraging, and carrying messages within camp and to loved ones back home. Though enslaved people took on a wide range of tasks back home, few were likely prepared for all the responsibilities that they were expected to manage in camp, nor could their owners anticipate how their needs would change given the uncertainty of war. These essential tasks reinforced the antebellum racial and social hierarchy within the military, which in turn strengthened the master's military rank as well as his position in a society that measured power and influence based on slave ownership.

Christopher and Spencer both adjusted to their respective positions and to army life. In letters home Winsmith praised Spencer's performance, noting that despite feeling "home-sick for the first few days," Spencer "has proved himself an excellent cook." Nothing was more important to an officer than his slave's ability to cook a good meal, made more challenging by often limited rations. Resourceful servants managed to forage and trade for the necessary ingredients, and Winsmith likely acknowledged that Spencer's acquisitions were not always appropriate. Within a few months Winsmith proudly reported to his sister back home that Spencer "is invaluable to me. I do not believe there is a better servant in the Army than he is, and I do not have any fears of his being deceived by the Yankees."[19]

Confederate officers who did not own slaves or chose to leave them home with family often hired free blacks as servants. At some point during the winter lull of 1861–62 and after receiving two promotions, Lieutenant Colonel Edward Porter Alexander "acquired two appendages": a "very pretty bay mare with a roan spot on one hip" and "a 15 year old darkey named Charley—a medium tall & slender, ginger-cake colored, & well behaved & good dispositioned boy." The reference to both as "appendages" and Alexander's mere physical comparison of horse and servant suggests that he initially viewed the latter in purely functional terms. Charley followed Alexander through the most important campaigns of the Eastern theater, from the Seven Days to Appomattox, as Alexander himself rose in the ranks from colonel to brigadier general of artillery.[20]

The presence of camp slaves did not preclude their masters from having to pitch in and perform necessary tasks, but it did narrow what they were willing to take on based on their social rank. Lieutenant William C. Nelson, who served in the 9th Mississippi, had no problem performing certain tasks when necessary, "but I can't see the use or the philosophy of a person's doing work when he has a servant who [is] more fitted for the business." His preoccupation with appearances and social rank, however, did not prevent Nelson from constructing what he believed to be a better cot than the one provided by his servant. Even though Nelson's comrades deemed the finished product to be "the best of the two," he reiterated, "A man can do everything that a soldier has to do, but it is needlessly making a slave of himself if he can get some one else to do it for him."[21] George C. Eggleston recalled that "whenever a detail was made for the purpose of cleaning the camp-ground the men detailed regarded themselves as responsible for the proper performance of the task by their servants, and uncomplainingly took upon themselves the duty of sitting on the fence and superintending the work."[22] Lieutenant Robert T. Hubard acknowledged early on in the war that his servant made it possible for him to "live in [a] very aristocratic style."[23] Confederates from the slave-

Camp slaves performed vital functions for their masters in camp, on the march, and on the battlefield. They also provided entertainment, as depicted in this 1862 drawing by Frank Vizetelly. (Illustration courtesy of Houghton Library, Harvard University, MS Am 1585 1)

holding class expected to be able to shift as much of the lifestyle that they enjoyed before the war into the military, and that entailed placing the burden of work on their slaves.

For the men of the Charleston Light Dragoons, the presence of camp servants allowed the men to maintain a lifestyle that was appropriate to their social rank. "We are not obliged to do our cooking, washing, or to attend, except when on picket, to our horses," wrote Private Edward L. Wells, "there being a sufficient number of negroes in camp to attend to these things." Private Frank Middleton advised other recruits that they "should by all means bring a servant with him, he could not do without one."[24] During moments of inactivity in camp, slaves provided much-needed entertainment. Lieutenant Samuel Lowry, who served in the 17th South Carolina, recalled that camp slaves "added a great deal to our amusement by telling their wonderful tales, and singing songs around the camp fires at night."[25] A British journalist visiting the Army of Northern Virginia in 1863 reported that in his camp, whenever there was music, "some nigger is sure to 'wade' in and put his legs through a series of marvellous gyrations, to the delight of the sympathetic lookers-on, who beat time for him."[26]

Roughly twenty years after the war, a soldier who served in the 3rd Tennessee remembered an "amusing" moment involving two camp servants, Ned and Major Pointer, who decided to resolve a quarrel by engaging in a duel. White officers provided instruction and acted as seconds to the two slaves. Both were armed with navy pistols, but unbeknownst to them the weapons were loaded with blank cartridges. The countdown proceeded in view of much of the camp, but at the last moment "both the dusky heroes started to run." The men positioned themselves two more times, but both ended with the same result, leaving the two "everafterwards good friends."[27] For the white observers, the humor in this faux duel came from having two camp servants, far removed in status from white Southern gentlemen, being egged on to fight a duel and depicted as simple and pretentious enough to carry it out, almost right to the deadly end. Ultimately, their courage failed them on the gentleman's field of honor.

It was not uncommon for officers with servants to organize messes to more effectively pool their resources and benefit from the skills of others. William Miller Owen of the Washington Artillery of New Orleans recalled that the "negro cooks in the Battalion were an institution unto themselves." The servants in his mess "were expected to black the shoes, forage for provisions at times, rub down private horses, etc. Many were accomplished body-servants, good barbers, and the like."[28] Robert Wallace Shand, who served in the 2nd South Carolina Volunteer Infantry, fondly recalled his mess's servant Mander, whose responsibilities included cooking breakfast for the group, thus affording a few extra minutes of sleep following roll call.[29] "We have a great comfort in Jim," noted a soldier in the 9th Virginia Infantry. "He cooks our dinner, waits on us . . . makes our bed, cuts my hair, builds our kitchen . . . can make our cartridges, mend or make our bridles & groom our horses."[30]

The presence of camp slaves, especially those who accompanied the rank and file, likely stirred some class resentment. All white men in Confederate ranks were united around the same cause, and Yankee bullets did not distinguish between military or social rank. Increased complaints in one Mississippi company that the use of servants to complete camp chores was unfair forced the captain to "order slaves to cook for the entire company." The owners of these men responded swiftly by threatening to "send their negroes home first" rather than tolerate having their authority undercut by anyone, including their commander.[31] On occasion soldiers kidnapped slaves during military campaigns from area farms. Former slave Gus Smith recalled after the war that following the battle of Wilson's Creek in August 1861, Confederate soldiers "stole all de niggers dey could, running dem down not want to go into de army."[32] Perry McGee recalled the harrowing moment when Confederates carried him off "to wait on de captain." "I had to clean off de horse, and played marbles and turned handsprings and dey had me for a monkey."[33] In these cases strong feelings of entitlement were given priority over the property rights of others, though it is unclear how pervasive this practice was during the war.

Camp slaves were expected to respond to the demands made by their masters, but they were also forced to fend for themselves rather than rely on the Quartermaster Department for food, shelter, and clothing. Officers depended heavily on loved ones back home to supplement their diets and provide necessary items like clothing, which entailed trusting servants to travel between home and camp. Among the items that James Tillman, who served in the 24th South Carolina Volunteers, requested from home included a "blanket, good oilcloth," and "some socks, a coat and pr of pants" for his servant Pete.[34] Colonel Thomas Henry Carter, who raised an artillery battery early in the war, relied on his slaves Harrison and Charles to travel fairly regularly between the army and his plantation home of Pampatike, located in Prince William County, Virginia. They routinely relayed letters to home and returned with food and clothing. Silas Chandler also traveled between Tennessee and Mississippi to transport items requested by Andrew. Writing from Chattanooga at the end of August 1862, Andrew requested his mother send butter, socks, and a new jacket. Silas was to provide the "brass buttons." As a warning, Andrew instructed his mother to "start Silas back" in response to any news of patrolling federal cavalry. Attesting to Silas's importance, Andrew acknowledged, "I don't want him caught."[35] Such a service was essential during those times when supplies and furloughs were in short supply.

Not every master, however, benefited from competent camp servants. Just as new recruits struggled to adjust to the routines of military life, so did their camp slaves, who in many cases were required to learn new tasks often under stressful circumstances. One Virginia soldier declared his servant Jack to be "as worthless a negroe as I ever have seen." "If I give him anything to carry he will loose it. The boys are afraid to give him any thing to wash[.] The first lot of cloths he had to wash, and he is not fit for nothing at all."[36] It took only a short time for Thomas Carter to candidly admit that his camp slave "is truly indifferent[,] lazy, & dirty & requires constant watching & scolding &

pushing to get anything out of him."[37] The frustration expressed by Carter and others was not simply in response to their slaves' inability to carry out assigned tasks; such perceived incompetence also prevented officers from assuming the rank and lifestyle that they believed their position as master entitled them to. The inability to manage their own personal slaves may have threatened to undermine their ability to maintain discipline among the men under their command.

Masters framed even the most routine tasks such as cooking and cleaning as a reflection of their slaves' fidelity. One Georgia officer wrote home flatteringly of his servant, Cyrus, by acknowledging that "he gives me no trouble at all. Attends well to my horse and things general." According to this officer, when asked if he did not want to go home, Cyrus reaffirmed his loyalty by responding, "not without [the officer] I go." In language that both praised his work and pointed to the vast gulf between master and slave that still existed at the end of the war, one South Carolina officer both asked and exclaimed, "Why weren't you white! Why weren't you white! Why weren't you white!" Writing after the war, Carlton McCarthy held tightly to the language of paternalism by concluding that the routine work of camp slaves represented "admiration . . . for their masters."[38] Masters may have experienced a heightened sense of paternalism given their close connection to one slave stretching over an extended period of time.

This one-dimensional and self-serving portrait tells us a great deal about how masters perceived their slaves but very little about how body servants experienced camp life and the meaning they attached to their time away from loved ones. Letters penned by slaves are exceedingly rare, given the high rates of illiteracy due to Southern law forbidding masters to teach slaves how to read and write. One notable exception is a brief letter from Franklin Scott to his wife, Fanny, back in Georgia, which was likely written in the early summer of 1863. Though there is a good chance that the letter was written by his master, Scott's voice comes through clearly. He was upbeat and healthy and missed his family. He encouraged his wife "to take care of my children, and kiss them both for me." Before closing, he promised to write again and asked her to "accept my love for yourself and my children."[39] Few slaves enjoyed the opportunity to communicate directly to their loved ones back home. The vast majority relied on the goodwill of their masters to pen a simple greeting or brief addendum at the end of a personal letter.

Camp slaves adjusted to the expectations of their masters (as they had always done) even as they confronted a new environment filled with opportunity and temptation. The carrying out of routine duties brought camp slaves into contact with other slaves in camp. They collected information by listening to soldiers, read newspapers, and gauged morale by probing rebel troops' thoughts about the progress of the war. Camp life also provided an occasion for servants to congregate, share stories about loved ones back home, and discuss their own understanding of what the war was about away from the gaze of their masters. It was likely a welcome escape from their daily responsibilities, even if their masters viewed it as a potential threat to their authority. Camp slaves took full advantage of the prospects that army life offered and leveraged them by negotiating and testing new boundaries with their masters, who in turn were forced to consider the limits of those boundaries and where and how to push back when necessary.

One of the most common ways that slaves took advantage of opportunities in camp was in performing various tasks for payment during their free time. For many, the practice was a continuation of the privileges enjoyed back home on plantations where the task system was utilized or on designated days off, such as Sundays and Christmas. The money earned by camp slaves was sometimes sent home to their families.[40] A flat charge of ten cents for a wide range of services earned Bill Yopp, a camp slave in the 14th Georgia Regiment, the sobriquet of "Ten-Cent Bill"—a name that he later leveraged for his own benefit at more than one reunion of Confederate veterans (though he himself was not a veteran). One Alabama slave familiar with horses purchased worn-out horses from cavalrymen and nurtured them back to full strength at a profit.[41]

John Winsmith's servant Spencer took advantage of his increased privileges by washing and cleaning for others while encamped in the relatively peaceful setting of Sullivan's Island, near Charleston, in the spring of 1861. He soon earned enough money to catch the attention of his owner, who noted that "he is making more money than any of us."[42] There is no indication that Winsmith viewed these increased privileges as a threat to his own authority or to Spencer's loyalty.

First Lieutenant Irby G. Scott, who served in the 12th Georgia Volunteer Infantry, came up with an arrangement that benefited both slave and master. On the one hand Franklin was encouraged to bring from home "several good razors, shaving brush &c. if he wants to make a few dimes he can get fifty cts a head for shaving." Scott's plan was to hire his camp slave out and "let the boys pay an equal portion of Franklin's time" and use the income to "pay for the negroes which wait on me."[43] Under this arrangement, Franklin earned a small income while the bulk of what he made paid for additional servants hired by Scott.

In the case of Sergeant Edwin Fay, who entered service in the spring of 1862 with the Louisiana Minden Rangers, the increased privileges granted to Rich caused him nothing but frustration. Over a two-year period, Rich challenged his master's authority by running off for days at a time and by maintaining a lucrative business cooking and cleaning for other men in the unit. In a letter home, Fay reported, "Rich has sent home 2½ [dollars] by Capt. Wimberly $2 another time and 4¼ by Linn Watkin." Rich's unwillingness to entrust his owner with his earnings likely contributed to his own sense of self-worth and autonomy. Even a "good whipping" on at least one occasion failed to yield the desired changes in Rich's behavior.[44] Fay was not alone in his attempt to find the right balance between maintaining his authority and granting certain privileges to his servant. An officer in the 51st Georgia Infantry granted his servant permission to attend "three negro Balls" but noted that even more often "he would go off without first asking permission."[45]

The willingness to negotiate more flexible boundaries stemmed from a number of factors, including the conviction that the war and even its ultimate goal created a shared experience between master and slave. Some trusted their camp slaves' ability to prioritize the personal obligations of their masters over any arrangement made with additional third parties. Others likely acknowledged a difficult reality that, as the war progressed and their slaves came into closer contact with the enemy or entered United States territory, opportunities to escape increased. Ultimately, the willingness to grant their slaves additional privileges reflected both a conviction about their fidelity and practical considerations that few could have anticipated at the war's outset.

Those slaves who pushed too far often faced a violent response by their masters in an attempt to reassert white authority. While the disciplining of soldiers in the ranks functioned to maintain order within a clearly delineated military hierarchy, officers who disciplined their servants did so as a reminder of their ultimate authority. Confederate general Edward Porter Alexander recalled giving Charley "a little licking but twice — once for robbing a pear tree in the garden of the Keach house, in which we were staying on the outskirts of Richmond below Rocketts, & once in Pa. just before Gettysburg, for stealing apple-brandy & getting tight on it."[46] It is impossible to know whether Charley judged his punishment as constituting a "little licking." A soldier in the 40th Alabama relayed the story of a servant who "got hold of some liquor, got drunk, stole and wasted a good deal of lard belonging" to another officer. When confronted, he "cursed and sauced" his master. The beating that this servant received was so severe that it resulted in his death.[47] The often violent disciplining of a servant not only functioned as a reminder of a master's authority in an environment that differed significantly from the plantation but also likely reflected a servant's willingness to challenge those strictly defined boundaries if there was a chance that it might lead to increased privileges in camp.

William Dorsey Pender's difficulties with one of two camp servants point to a more complicated relationship between master and slave. A little over a week after the bloody fight at Sharpsburg, Maryland, in September 1862 and just three days after Abraham Lincoln's issuance of the preliminary emancipation proclamation, Pender admitted to his wife that in reading Harriet Beecher Stowe's *Uncle Tom's Cabin* he found himself in agreement with the author on the subject of slavery. Yet in the very next sentence he reported that "I tried to whip Joe the other day but could go only three stripes." Whether his inability to apply additional "stripes" was the direct result of having read Stowe is unclear. Regardless of the reason, a month later he apparently had no difficulty meting out a "tremendous whipping" to Joe, which he "had been promising [for] some time and finally he got it." "He is a good and smart boy," admitted Pender, "but like most young negroes needs correction badly." Whatever impact *Uncle Tom's Cabin* may have had on Pender's beliefs concerning the morality of slavery, it did not have any lasting impact on what he considered to be appropriate and even necessary punishment for one of his own slaves.[48]

One of the more violent encounters between master and camp slave occurred while in winter quarters in December 1864. In a letter home to his wife, Mollie, Lieutenant John B. Evans of the 53rd Georgia described "whipping Joe" with "about four hundred lashes." Evans methodically described having Joe "pull off all his clothes," tying "his hands and feet," and stretching "him out full length" before laying it on hard—not out in the open for others to see but in what was likely his personal quarters. "I whipped him," Evans explained, "for carrying off our meat to the soldiers," which suggests that Joe may have sold the provisions for extra money. He closed by admitting that "I tore his back and legs all to pieces. I was mad enough to kill him."[49] The severity of the punishment and Evans's eagerness to teach Joe a lesson and to reassert his authority was likely exacerbated by the limited amount of food and other supplies that was available to Confederate soldiers by the end of 1864.[50] Evans may have chosen to share such stark details with his wife and other family members in part to remind them of the importance of maintaining discipline among the enslaved population back home, especially as Union armies penetrated farther into the Confederacy and threatened the stability of the home front.

Captain Ujanirtus Allen faced the dual challenge of having to keep in line both his own camp slaves and those left at home under the oversight of his wife. Lengthy periods away from home made it much more difficult for slave owners like Allen to maintain discipline among their slaves and more likely that those slaves would test well-established boundaries. In April 1862 Allen instructed his wife to "give Jim a severe whipping" for continuing to disobey his orders that he not visit with his wife. "Not a little one," Allen instructed, "but whip him from head to foot; not less than two or three hundred." Allen specifically requested that Jim be told "that I am the one that is having it done." Failure to carry out this punishment on Jim, as far as Allen was concerned, would lead to additional disciplinary problems among his enslaved population. "If he is not whipped you might as well set them all free."[51]

After the war, Confederate veterans often singled out their former camp slaves in their memoirs and other published accounts for their devotion to their masters' every need, but the violent encounters such as those sketched above serve as an important reminder that masters' authority was absolute and could be manifested forcefully at any time and for any reason. Whatever else was experienced while in camp, on the march, and even on the battle-field, the boundaries of the relationship between master and slave was built on and reinforced over time through violence. However, even within a relationship that was defined through coercion, moments of mutual affection and caring were possible. Master and slave experienced many of the same challenges and dangers of camp life. They inhaled the same dust during long marches over dry roads; were exposed to drenching downpours, snow, and freezing temperatures; were prone to the same infections and diseases; and were forced to deal with periods of malnutrition. Most importantly, both yearned for word from loved ones back home and looked forward to the day when they would return to their familiar embrace.

Undoubtedly, the shared experience of being away from home and having to face the many challenges of military life brought master and slave closer together. Letters home from Confederates routinely included brief well wishes from their camp slaves to their own families. News from home likely also created moments of shared celebration. In March 1863 Silas Chandler learned of the birth of his first son: "I think I ought to tell Silas that Lucy has a fine boy," Andrew said. "They call him General Bragg."[52] It is likely that Andrew shared Silas's joy upon hearing the good news.

Master and slave also shared news about the health of family members. Only a few months after leaving home in November 1861, it fell to General James Cantey to inform Sam of the death of his baby back home in South Carolina.[53] Upon returning to camp in March 1863, Pete relayed word to James Tillman that his sister "Fannie is growing better daily." A few months later, it was Tillman who was forced to share the sad news with Pete of the death of his child. Tillman's diary entry for September 27, 1864, simply noted, "Poor Negro, he is truly unfortunate."[54]

Disease often ravaged Confederate ranks and directly threatened the relationship between master and slave. In some instances, it may have brought the two closer together. James Tillman suffered repeated bouts of diarrhea, as did Pete. This shared experience that often forced the two into close quarters may explain his sharing with his wife that he regarded Pete not only as "a very faithful Negro" but "almost as a brother." "If I am killed," he reminded his wife shortly thereafter, "I want this Negro treated with uncommon kindness for he has served me faithfully."[55] While some officers replaced slaves who died in camp with little difficulty, for others the loss was felt on a personal level. "Our mess has met with a great loss in Mr. Kirkland's boy Tomson," admitted Frank Middleton of the Charleston Light Dragoons. The boy died "in the greatest of agony" and was "one of the best and quickest servants I have ever known." Another officer's slave in the same unit died of typhoid fever even after being sent home for treatment. News of his death, admitted his owner, "grieved him much."[56] Disease cut down soldiers and slaves indiscriminately, but there can be little doubt that it led to moments of genuine concern between the two.

Personal moments that reminded master and slave of a shared experience may have brought them closer together, but officers and enlisted men also operated under the assumption that their slaves supported and identified with the army and the broader Confederate cause. One of the ways in which they may have encouraged this among their camp slaves is by outfitting them in or permitting them to purchase military uniforms. Today, photographs of uniformed camp slaves alongside their masters can be found on numerous websites and are used as supposedly indisputable proof that large numbers of black men fought as soldiers in the Confederate army. Such an interpretation would strike actual Confederates as absurd and speaks to the need to understand the outfitting of slaves in uniforms within the historical context of the master-slave relationship.

Though it is impossible to gauge their frequency, the outfitting of camp servants in Confederate uniforms constituted a powerful visual reminder for the entire army of a shared purpose between master and slave. The practice was already common in the United States and elsewhere by the Civil War. Officers may have assumed that in wearing a uniform, their servants might come to identify more closely with the units in which they labored. While the *Regulations for the Army of the Confederate States*, published in 1862, stated clearly that "servants . . . will not be allowed to wear the uniform of any corps of the army," numerous photographs taken of master and slave during the war demonstrates that this regulation was not strictly enforced.[57] Confederate officers and enlisted men viewed the practice as a means of reinforcing their own military rank or social position. Photographs of camp slaves standing rigid with eyes forward reflected their masters' moral character and ability to maintain discipline and their own sense of honor.

Some slaves who were not provided uniforms were permitted to purchase their own with money earned carrying out jobs in camp during their free time. William Dorsey Pender's servant Joe "managed to dress himself in a nice gray uniform, french bosom linen shirt—for which he paid $4" and "two pairs new shoes." Pender marveled at Joe's "trades" and predicted that "his clothing will never cost me anything." The opportunity to discard clothing worn back home and instead don uniforms may have given slaves like Silas Chandler, Joe, and Marlboro Jones[58] (whose owner served in the 7th Georgia Regiment) a sense of their own self-worth as men and may even have helped to distinguish them from the large number of impressed slaves who performed numerous roles in the army. James H. Langhorne of the 4th Virginia Infantry gifted his "old uniform overcoat" to his camp slave, who in turn planned to have his photograph taken and sent to his family and other slaves back home. For this particular slave, the uniform came to signify more than a new set of clothes.[59] For others, whether the uniform was gray or blue was irrelevant. One Virginia camp slave bragged that he would soon discard his old clothing for the uniform of the first dead Union soldier he came across on the battlefield.[60] Enemy soldiers did not, however, have to be killed in action to be relieved of their clothing. During his visit with the Army of Northern Virginia, Lieutenant Colonel Arthur J. L. Fremantle, a British army officer, recalled a conversation with a camp slave "dressed in full Yankee uniform" escorting a prisoner shortly after the battle of Gettysburg "with whom he had evidently changed clothes."[61] Even if their legal status did not change as a result of wearing a military uniform, they could at least imagine a new identity that transcended their legal status and that might even earn respect from loved ones back home.

Slaves in uniform may have experienced a certain esprit de corps when

Lieutenant J. Wallace Comer of the 57th Alabama and his camp slave, identified only as Burrell. Like other camp slaves, Burrell may have been outfitted in a uniform by his master or may have paid for it with money earned in camp. (Photograph courtesy Southern Historical Collection, Wilson Library, University of North Carolina at Chapel Hill, P-167/1)

gathered together, especially on long marches. English-born Confederate artilleryman Thomas Caffey took time to comment on large numbers of servants marching together "some fifty yards in front of the band, whistling and singing, forming in regular or irregular files, commanded by some big black rogue who, with a stick and a loud voice, enforces discipline, among his

heavy-heeled corps." Caffey also related the story of a camp servant in an Alabama regiment who "had the reputation of a saint among the colored boys of
the brigade; and as he could read the Bible, and was given to preaching, he
invariably assembled the darkeys on Sunday afternoon, and held meetings in
the woods."[62] One Virginia officer enjoyed the service of a "bright mulatto"
by the name of Napoleon Bonaparte and Solomon, who was described "as
black as tar." Bonaparte assumed a position of authority over Solomon, perhaps because of the latter's dark skin color as well as Bonaparte's belief that
"he was nothin' but a free nigger nohow." It is possible that the officer was
unaware of this arrangement. Napoleon had successfully "feathered his own
nest and worked things," according to one writer after the war, "so that the
major was really paying two men to do the work of one."[63] These stories suggest that slaves organized themselves within an informal hierarchy while in
camp and, when on the march, around individuals who had demonstrated
certain leadership skills and were in good standing with their masters.[64]

Camp slaves may have been permitted and even encouraged to march
together, which fostered stronger bonds and was an efficient way to ensure
their continued presence with the army while on the move, especially in hostile territory. Marching slaves did not pass without notice. During the Confederate invasion of Pennsylvania in late June 1863, Fremantle observed that
following "each regiment were from twenty to thirty negro slaves." Nine
months earlier Dr. Lewis Steiner of the U.S. Sanitary Commission left a
detailed account of the Army of Northern Virginia's entry into Frederick,
Maryland, during the Antietam campaign of September 1862. This particular report remains one of the more popular references for those who believe
that significant numbers of black men fought as soldiers in the Confederate army. Steiner's account can be found on hundreds of websites today, including the national website for the Sons of Confederate Veterans, which
includes it as evidence "that over 65,000 Southern blacks were in the Confederate ranks."[65]

In judging the size of the invading force, Steiner estimated that "over
3,000 Negroes must be included in this number." According to Steiner, they
"were clad in all kinds of uniforms, not only in cast-off or captured United
States uniforms, but in coats with Southern buttons, State buttons, etc."[66]
In addition to the uniforms, the author noticed that the black men carried
"rifles, muskets, sabers," and other assorted weapons. Even with the greatly
reduced size of the army that Robert E. Lee brought into Maryland, owing
to the continuous fighting throughout the summer, it is possible that Steiner
correctly gauged the number of African Americans with the army. In addition

to camp slaves, the army utilized a significant number of impressed slaves in a wide range of roles, which included driving wagons. It is also likely that many of the black men observed by Steiner were carrying weapons. Camp slaves were responsible for lightening their masters' load as much as possible during long marches, and this most certainly would have included weapons. What Steiner observed was one small aspect of the crucial role that the labor of enslaved people played in supporting the Confederate military.

Regardless of the dynamics of the relationship that masters believed they had established with servants, little could prepare them for the moment when slaves chose to run off to embrace their freedom. Slaves who abandoned their former masters forced them to deal with the evidence that their servants' loyalty was not unconditional. How they dealt with missing servants reflected the ambivalence that underlay the master-slave relationship at war. For some the moment passed with little comment and concern, but for others the realization that their slaves would never return brought about a profound existential crisis.

The problem was especially acute when Union and Confederate armies were in close proximity to one another or during marches into Northern territory, but the publication of runaway notices in newspapers throughout the Confederacy and for the duration of the war suggests that the problem was more pervasive.[67] A camp slave present at the battle of Antietam secured a horse to bring his master to safety and then proceeded to remount the horse and rode over to the enemy.[68] Stephen Moore reported that upon entering Maryland, his camp slave was "greatly dissatisfied and wants to get home." "While I was sick he started to run away from the army but some one saw him and persuaded him to come back." Moore was convinced that "if we ever go into Maryland again he will be sure to leave."[69] For those masters who believed they had established a bond long before the war commenced, the shock of realizing their camp slaves had run off was difficult to accept. One Alabamian claimed to have shared "every article of food and clothing," and yet his slave "seized the first opportunity which presented of deserting him and joining the Yankees."[70] Albert T. Sharp offered a twenty-dollar reward for the return of Calvin ("about five feet nine inches high, not very dark, weights about 175 pounds"), who was left behind in Petersburg to recover from an illness and who was expected to return once he was well enough to travel.[71]

While John Claiborne's servants appeared to still be "very loyal" in the spring of 1864, hearing from one directly that "he knows which side his bread is buttered" likely assuaged any lingering concerns.[72] Declarations of fidelity did not, however, always stand the test. A year into the war, John Winsmith was forced to come to terms with Spencer's disappearance while he was away from camp on assignment. Winsmith struggled to acknowledge even the possibility that Spencer escaped to the Union navy, which was now patrolling off the coast near Charleston. Upon his return to James Island, Winsmith suggested or more likely hoped that his trusted servant had been kidnapped by the enemy or had been influenced by "a free boy from the city who was hired as a cook" by a fellow officer. Apparently, he never seriously considered the possibility that Spencer desired to be free or that he may have exploited the trust placed in him with earlier displays of loyal behavior; rather, Winsmith fell back on the observation that "negroes are very uncertain and tricky creatures so it is difficult to tell what is the real truth in this case."[73] Spencer was never heard from again.

The personal struggle of coming to terms with the disappearance of camp slaves was compounded by word from home and the occasional news that slaves had run off. For William Nelson the news of the disappearance of a family slave was nothing less than a test of the Confederacy's legitimacy. "I have thought that this war was ordered by Providence, as a means of settling definitely and conclusively the question of slavery," asserted Nelson. "If slavery is a divine institution," he continued, "I believe we will be successful, that our independence will be recognized and the Southern Confederacy will be established as a government with slavery as its great distinctive feature." If not, Nelson was convinced that God would use the war as "the means of abolishing it from the face of the earth."[74]

Winsmith was far from alone in his struggle to come to terms with the loss of his servant. Even early in the war, news of runaway or missing slaves filtered through camp, but with the movement of armies into enemy territory and the confusion of battle, Confederates were forced to explain increased rates of flight. In early January 1862 a Virginia soldier wrote home with news of the disappearance of Dick. He was convinced, however, that Dick would not "stay with the Yankees unless forced to do so." During Jubal Early's raid near Washington, D.C., in the summer of 1864, Captain Robert E. Park likely gave little thought to the order for Charles to stay behind "to cook a chicken and some biscuits." That was the last time he saw Charles, but like the others, Park was unable to consider any other explanation than that he had been "enticed away or forcibly detained by some negro worshipper, as he had always been prompt and faithful, and seemed much attached to me."[75] To even consider otherwise was to question the very foundation of the bond that masters believed governed the relationship with their slaves.

The historical record is also filled with stories of servants who refused to abandon their masters. Returning to Silas Chandler can help researchers begin to piece together the many factors that may have determined whether a camp slave chose to remain with his master or seek his freedom. Silas rescued his master, Andrew, on the Chickamauga battlefield after he was severely wounded in the leg. Rather than abandon him, Silas brought Andrew to a hospital in Atlanta, where he likely worked to ensure that his leg was not amputated. From there he escorted Andrew home to West Point, Mississippi. Many of the one-dimensional accounts of Andrew and Silas that can now be found on the Internet reduce Silas's decision to an unquestioned and transparent loyalty to Andrew. Such self-serving accounts do little to help us to understand how Silas may have viewed the situation.

Silas may have felt other concerns for his master that were the result of a shared experience, but what is often ignored is that, along with Andrew, Silas also had a family waiting for him in Mississippi, including a wife and newborn child. In escorting Andrew, whom he was still legally bound to, Silas also brought himself one step closer to a reunion with his own family. Any consideration of abandoning Andrew was tantamount to abandoning his family as well. Slaves may also have considered their failure to return (with or without their masters) a threat to the safety of their loved ones.[76]

The transition from slavery to freedom is often told through the words and actions of enslaved people rushing into the Union army to do battle with their former masters or in the form of long lines of people pushing relentlessly with their belongings in wagons toward "a new birth of freedom." For many, the choices may have been more difficult. Returning home may also have been the result of a simple calculation between a familiar world with all its dangers and an unknown future filled with strangers who may or may not have their best interests in mind. Others may have heard stories about the threat of disease in contraband camps or the racial discrimination that awaited them as servants in Union camps.[77]

Secessionists argued in 1861 that the institution of slavery was safer outside the Union than as part of a nation now under the control of Abraham Lincoln and the "black Republicans." Confederates marched off to war alongside their slaves in full confidence that the cause of Southern independence united them. The assumptions underlying this conviction were soon tested. Slave owners attributed the actions of their camp slaves as a reflection of their devotion and commitment to putting their masters' needs before their own, but as the war progressed this relationship was severely tried. Few Confederates who were accompanied by a camp slave anticipated the many ways in which life in the army would challenge the fundamental assumptions that governed the master-slave relationship. Slaveholding Confederates did their best to manage their property in a military landscape that shifted dramatically over the course of the war.

The slaves themselves did their part to challenge long-standing boundaries that had governed their lives before the war. Some pushed for additional privileges, failed to carry out responsibilities to the satisfaction of their masters, or voiced their displeasure by running off to the enemy. As a result, camp slaves compelled their masters to adjust their expectations and question long-held assumptions about the loyalty of their bondmen— expectations that helped to prop up their slaveholding culture. By the middle of the war, that ideological foundation appeared to many slave owners in the army and on the home front to be less secure than in 1861. Whatever challenges masters faced maintaining control of their camp slaves in camp and on the march paled in comparison to what they faced both during and in the wake of battles and extended military campaigns.

The Camp Slaves' War

Chapter Two

CAMP SLAVES ON THE BATTLEFIELD

Over the course of two days in September 1863, Union and Confederate forces faced off in northwest Georgia along Chickamauga Creek in a battle that would come to determine control of the strategically vital city of Chattanooga, Tennessee. Union major general William Rosecrans and the Army of the Cumberland proved victorious over General Braxton Bragg's Army of Tennessee, but not before the two armies suffered roughly 35,000 casualties—the most of any battle after the three days of fighting at Gettysburg just two months earlier. After the war Andrew Chandler recalled in the pages of *Confederate Veteran* the 44th Mississippi's role in a charge on the second day of fighting that "broke the Federal line and drove them nearly one mile," only to be "recalled and reformed, and marched back to the old field, which was literally covered with dead and wounded Yankees." Later that same day, the regiment was "ordered to the foot of a long ridge, heavily wooded," to meet a "Yankee" countercharge.[1]

The regiment went into battle with 272 officers and enlisted men on September 19 and came out having suffered 81 casualties, one of whom was Andrew Chandler. A bullet had torn into Andrew's right leg and ankle, a near-crippling injury that took him out of action.[2] What happened next is not entirely clear, but it is likely that Silas Chandler came to Andrew's assistance on the battlefield during or shortly after the fighting had ceased. Today websites are filled with colorful stories about Silas's bravery on the battlefield and the escorting of his master to a military hospital for treatment. According to one website, when the doctor advised amputation, "Silas pulled out a gold coin that the boys were saving to buy some whiskey. Bribing the doctors to let Chandler go, he then carried the injured boy on his back to the nearest train."[3] Other accounts claim that the coin had been sewn into his coat to be used in case of an emergency, but there is no wartime evidence to confirm any of these stories. Questions about these reports are compounded by the fact that Andrew failed to mention Silas in his description of the battle for a publication that was brimming with stories of loyal slaves who risked their lives to come to the aid of their masters. What is known is that Andrew left the hospital with both of his legs and that the two returned to West Point, Mississippi.

Confederates filled their letters and diaries with accounts of camp slaves, like Silas, who placed their own lives at risk to aid their wounded masters on the battlefield. Others told of the emotional response of slaves to the sight of their masters' lifeless bodies and the commitment to fulfill their final responsibility to transport personal effects or the remains home to their families for a proper burial. The narrative of the loyal slave that would become so prevalent in the postwar period and that served as the foundation of the Lost Cause was rooted in these wartime stories. Observers also acknowledged camp slaves who marched into battle alongside white soldiers or who even picked up a rifle and shot at charging Yankee soldiers. Such accounts are almost indistinguishable except for the battle in question and the names of the principals involved. For each author, however, these moments of unquestioned slave fidelity pointed to masters' moral character and constituted indispensable proof of the special bond that was believed to connect master and slave even in the most harrowing moments.

Reports of armed slaves marching into battle alongside masters and assisting them on the battlefield remain the most contentious aspect of the memory of these men. Many in the Confederate heritage community today insist that these stories demonstrate that the army recruited blacks as soldiers into integrated units long before the Confederate Congress authorized slave enlistment in March 1865. For others who approach the subject with a sincere interest in understanding how enslaved people and free blacks functioned in the Confederate army, the historical record can be difficult to penetrate. Company cooks, for example, were occasionally listed on muster rolls and paid between ten and twenty dollars a month. The goal of honoring these so-called black men in gray, however, results in little more than a simplistic and self-serving picture that ignores the impact of extended military operations that both challenged and stretched the master-slave relationship to the breaking point. It also ultimately fails to acknowledge the extent to which slaveholders themselves struggled with the implications of their servants setting foot on the battlefield. Masters praised their slaves for their

Camp Slaves on the Battlefield

loyalty in the midst of shot and shell, but their presence on the battlefield challenged their understanding of masculinity and Southern honor. White Southern men believed that the battlefield was a testing ground on which they were expected to demonstrate their manhood to their comrades, family, and community. The presence of camp slaves on the field of battle tested these assumptions. Confederates remained deeply ambivalent when confronted with stories about slave heroics that potentially collapsed this crucial distinction between master and slave.

The eventual debate that took place throughout the Confederacy beginning in mid-1864 about whether slaves should be enlisted as soldiers further complicated matters. Confederates on the home front and in the military were forced to consider whether slaves should be recruited into the army as soldiers as well as various emancipation policies that covered their extended families, all in the desperate hope of preventing defeat and keeping the hope of independence alive. For many Confederates, the proposal to enlist slaves accompanied by limited emancipation undercut the very rationale for waging war, namely the protection of slavery and white supremacy. "If we offer the slaves freedom as a boon," said one Virginia congressman, "we confess that we are insincere and hypocritical in saying that slavery was the best state for the negroes themselves."[4] Today, Confederate heritage advocates, who interpret colorful stories of camp slaves coming to the aid of their masters on the battlefield or firing a weapon at a Yankee as evidence of blacks serving as soldiers as early as 1861, conveniently ignore or are unaware that a debate over the enlistment of slaves ever took place. In doing so they overlook a crucial moment in which Confederate officers and the rank and file were forced to consider whether camp slaves could or should be turned into soldiers. More importantly, they fail to acknowledge that none of the actions performed by enslaved people attached to the army on the battlefield were understood as those of a soldier or rendered them equal to whites as a result.

What has gone entirely unnoticed by the Confederate heritage community is that in all the records produced by the slave enlistment debate, including letters, diaries, and literally thousands of newspaper articles, not a single officer or soldier suggested that slaves were already serving as soldiers in the Confederate army. No newspaper ran an editorial with tales of camp slaves stepping onto the battlefield and proving that they were already serving as equals among the rank and file. The very question of whether enslaved people could be made into soldiers serves as a reminder that camp servants, cooks, musicians, or others attached to the army were not recognized as such. This must be the starting point if we are to have any chance of understanding the multiple and often conflicting meanings that Confederates and later veterans attached to these men and the relationships they forged on numerous battlefields throughout the Civil War.

Neither the Confederacy nor the United States was committed to recruiting black men into its armies in 1861. President Lincoln was constrained by the necessity of maintaining the allegiance of the four border slave states (Maryland, Kentucky, Delaware, and Missouri) that remained in the Union as well as the vast majority of the loyal white citizenry who were willing to volunteer to fight to put down an illegal rebellion and save the nation but not to liberate four million enslaved people.[5] The Confederate government in Richmond was constrained by its very purpose — the creation of an independent slaveholding nation built on white supremacy. Echoing Vice President Alexander Stephens's "Cornerstone Speech," Secretary of War James A. Seddon insisted that "the foundation of the Southern theory of the racial superiority of whites would crumble if blacks were allowed to enlist."[6] The government opposed enrolling blacks in the army except as servants and laborers. Many officials anticipated a relatively short war and believed that there was a sufficient number of white men available to defeat the enemy. For both nations, this was to be a white man's war.

Black Southerners, however, were essential to the ability of Confederate armies to carry out even the most basic functions. As a result, their presence on the battlefield was unavoidable. Enslaved people were found on every major battlefield in both the Eastern and Western theaters of operation between 1861 and 1865. Confederates do not, however, appear to have expected their servants to follow them into the heat of battle. Wartime accounts indicate that servants were often assigned to the rear to guard wagon trains and personal effects and to look after the wounded. Confederates likely worried about the physical safety of their slaves and the dangers of their being captured or running off to the enemy. However, the constant movement of troops, the unexpected breakdown of unit cohesion, the desperate need for additional manpower, and mere curiosity all but guaranteed that enslaved people attached to the army would experience some aspect of the battlefield.

Any thoughts that camp slaves could be protected from the dangers of the battlefield were shattered early on in the war. The first major battle at Bull Run, or Manassas, on July 21, 1861, fought just outside of Washington, D.C., in Virginia, exposed some of the challenges of maintaining a strict separation between the relative safety behind the lines and the front. At the height of the fighting on Henry Hill, a soldier in the 5th Massachusetts recalled coming upon a "rifle pit which was filled with negroes, some of the[m] armed with battle axes." The presence of axes suggests that these men were either impressed slaves or servants assigned to the construction of earthworks who were unable to avoid the Union advance. At least one soldier resisted firing into these men, urging his comrades to save their ammunition for their "masters." Another Bay Stater "pinned" a black man to the ground with his bayonet before declaring, "'Here goes a thousand dollars; I wish it was his master!'" The soldier walked off with the slave's ax, which suggests that this man was killed. As the men marched forward they saw "darkies flying in all directions."[7]

The report of "darkies" fleeing reinforced the racial assumptions of their Union pursuers on that hot July day, but the sight of these men running scared into the Confederate rear also confirmed deeply seated beliefs about the moral character of African Americans and likely influenced the roles they would be assigned by their masters in the future. Despite the need to control the movements of camp slaves and other enslaved people, the battle near Manassas demonstrated that the boundary between the battlefield and the safety of the rear would be difficult, if not impossible, to maintain.

Slaves moved freely onto the battlefield for a host of different reasons. William Coleman, along with twelve other camp servants, was required to transport wounded from the battlefield to hospitals. He recalled that "while part of us seen after the wounded," others "would have to go and dig out a long ditch, roll the dead ones in and cover them over." This was certainly dangerous and even shocking work for a twelve-year-old boy.[8] A Texas slave described his role in the hospital as an "official lugger-in of men that got wounded." Throughout the postwar years, former slaves shared stories about their various experiences on or near the battlefield that comported with the expectations of their largely white audiences, but these men also wanted to convey a sense of their own bravery in the face of conditions that few could fathom. Amos Gadsen "held arms and legs while" the surgeon "cut them off," but he also made it a point to stipulate that "after a while I didn't mind." Similarly, a former slave from Alabama explained his assignment at a battlefield hospital, "caze dey knowed I warn't afeered of nothin."[9] With these personal accounts that were often interpreted as loyalty to the Confederacy, their authors also hoped to demonstrate their bravery and steadfastness under difficult conditions.

The task of guarding wagons was equally dangerous, given the continuous movement of soldiers and cavalry. Just before the battle of Antietam on September 17, 1862, a camp slave found himself under attack by Union cavalry while guarding wagons. He remained a prisoner for a short time before escaping and making his way back to the unit in Sharpsburg.[10]

Slaves bled on many, if not all, of the major battlefields of the Civil War. Henry Neal, a slave from Tennessee, recalled that "both of my masters were killed in the Battle of Shiloh and I was shot in my left leg." Another camp servant from Tennessee was shot in the arm in the same battle, while another slave retold the story of his wounding at the battles of Murfreesboro and Chattanooga and may have even shown the "holes in [his] body" as part of his application for a servant's pension after the war. Monroe Jones's service to his master ended at Vicksburg in July 1863 when he "had both legs shot off at the knees."[11] Reports of slaves engaged in combat were almost always accompanied by an explanation that framed their actions as integral to an army fighting for its independence against an evil invader. Readers of the *Daily Sun* in Columbus, Georgia, learned of the "heroic" acts of Jack, who accompanied his master on the battlefield "to drive back the insolent invaders." Jack was reported to have fired his weapon twenty-seven times and was severely wounded as a result. He was "taken from the field in great pain" and "bore his sufferings with great fortitude."[12] The sight of wounded and disfigured camp slaves in the heat of battle was embraced as clear evidence of a willingness to risk their own lives for the benefit of their masters.

Confederates interpreted the actions of their camp slaves on the battlefield as a reflection of their own moral character and as an extension of their own motivation. Servants, it was assumed, risked their own lives on or near the battlefield to protect and aid their masters and the Confederate cause. A closer look, however, suggests that camp slaves may have had their own agenda. In the summer of 1862 Stephen Moore wrote home to inform his family of his first experience of battle: "Tell them all I have been on the Battlefield where the Yankees was slain." This was news that Stephen wanted conveyed to everyone back home, beginning with his family and extending to the rest of the enslaved community. His reference to "slain Yankees" suggests that he wanted his first battlefield experience to confirm some level of identification with his master and the rest of the unit, but there is no indication that Stephen viewed his battlefield exploits as reflective of any kind of loyalty to the Confederacy or unwavering fidelity to his master. Neither is there any indication that he fired a weapon at Union soldiers. It is possible that Stephen did not set foot on the field until after the fighting had ceased, but even this much exposure would have been sufficient to demonstrate his bravery to loved ones back home and to enhance his own self-worth.[13]

Stephen Moore's account of being on the battlefield was also likely intended to enhance his reputation at home as someone who stood out from the rest of the enslaved community based on a wholly unique set of experiences that tested his courage and manhood. Former camp slave Jacob Stroyer suggests as much when he recalled that, "having spent a little time at these war points, we had gained some knowledge which would put us beyond our fellow negroes at home on the plantations, while they would increase our pride by crediting us with far more knowledge than it was possible for us to have gained."[14] The camp slave of one Confederate general informed his family that he had also experienced battle "and heard the bullets whiz." The retreat of the enemy provided an opportunity to collect discarded "clothes, blankets, overcoats, and razors," but he chose to close by inquiring, "How other niggers do to stay at home, while we soldiers are havin' sucha good time is more than I can tell."[15] The reference to himself as a "soldier" may also have been intended as a way to enhance his reputation back home as well as his own sense of self-worth and purpose while attached to the army.

Long marches that culminated in bloody fighting helped to redefine the master-slave relationship, but they also fueled speculation among Union soldiers that the Confederacy was already utilizing slaves as soldiers. General George B. McClellan's slow and methodical march up the Virginia Peninsula toward the Confederate capital of Richmond beginning in April 1862 placed the armies in close proximity with one another for an extended period of time. Numerous sightings of blacks constructing earthworks, guarding wagon trains, and even manning artillery and firing rifles at Yankees were communicated from the army to numerous newspapers throughout the North. The *New York Times* reported on April 22 that Confederate artillery "are manned altogether by negroes, or at least all the work of swabbing, loading, and shifting is done by them, with white men to oversee and direct them." Hundreds of uniformed black men made the news in the *Boston Daily Advertiser*: "Any one who doubts that the Rebels are fighting side by side with their slaves can be convinced at any hour of the day by going up to the edge of the woods, about twelve hundred yards in front of their works. With the aid of an ordinary glass the matter can be put beyond room for doubt."[16] A slow trickle of escaped slaves to Union lines throughout the campaign confirmed the use of camp servants and impressed slaves — or as they were now called by the Union, "contraband" — in more direct military roles and made clear to some officers and politicians the necessity of tougher legislation in connection with their capture.

While few Northerners believed that these men were serving with the army voluntarily, their presence proved to be politically useful for Radical

Republicans and others who were pushing the Lincoln administration to recruit African Americans into the United States Army. As early as September 1861, Frederick Douglass reported in his own newspaper that "it is now pretty well established, that there are at the present moment many colored men in the Confederate army doing duty . . . as real soldiers. There were such soldiers at Manassas, and they are probably still there."[17] Douglass believed that reports of black men under arms and assisting in other capacities would force a fundamental choice on Washington politicians and the military: they could do nothing and continue to allow the Confederacy to utilize its valuable slave labor, or they could undercut the South's war effort by encouraging these men to escape to Union lines.[18] Whatever influence Douglass had on the Lincoln administration's decision to recruit black men into the army may have been rooted in his use of battlefield reports of armed black Confederates for propaganda purposes.

Douglass traveled widely early in the war to promote black recruitment and even featured an escaped slave from the battle of First Bull Run. John Parker—an impressed slave who in the spring of 1861 had helped construct earthworks near Winchester, Fredericksburg, and Richmond, Virginia—manned a Confederate artillery piece with three other slaves at Bull Run. Later, after fleeing to the Union army, Parker characterized his presence with the army as having been forced: "We wish[ed] to our hearts that the Yankees would whip, and we would have run over to their side but our officers would have shot us if we had made the attempt."[19] Parker went on to give numerous interviews with Northern newspapers, which were reprinted across the country, and on at least one occasion he spoke alongside Frederick Douglass, who was more interested in his expressions of loyalty to the United States and the political weight of his observations than in their accuracy.[20]

It is difficult to determine the number of slaves utilized by Confederates during the Peninsula campaign, given the nature of the reports, many of which went unconfirmed or were related secondhand. Certainly the close proximity of the two armies to one another over an extended period of time played a role in the frequency of sightings and the necessity on the part of Confederates to utilize slaves more directly on the front lines. There can be little doubt that slaves did man artillery and perform as sharpshooters on occasion. Confederate commanders such as General John Bankhead Magruder used his authority during the campaign to call up large numbers of slaves from surrounding plantations to assist the army at a moment when the Confederate capital of Richmond was threatened. Their contributions certainly resulted in the deaths of Union soldiers, but their motivation (beyond the coercive nature of slavery) is difficult to discern. Escaped slaves provided vital intelligence to the Army of the Potomac as it edged closer to Richmond, but it proved insufficient to propel the army farther than the city's outskirts. Confederate general Robert E. Lee's assumption of command in late May, following the wounding of General Joseph Johnston at the battle of Fair Oaks, and his decision to go on the offensive in what became known as the Seven Days campaign ultimately unraveled McClellan's plans. Reports of the use of slaves as soldiers in the Confederate army helped to push the United States closer to emancipation and black recruitment into the army out of military necessity.[21]

Those looking today to prove that the Confederacy preceded the United States in recruiting black soldiers eagerly embrace Northern newspaper reports of armed black men. But accounts of significant numbers, even entire regiments, of black soldiers would have come as a surprise to the Confederate government and even to many of the soldiers in the ranks. Throughout the first year of the war, the government maintained its policy of barring blacks from serving as soldiers in the army. African Americans challenged this policy, most notably by free blacks in New Orleans who hoped to protect their property and social rank by demonstrating their loyalty to the Confederacy. Just ten days after the bombardment of Fort Sumter, roughly 1,500 free men of color offered their services to Louisiana's governor, Thomas O. Moore. These men eventually formed the 1st Louisiana Native Guard on May 29, 1861, but despite parading through the streets with weapons and uniforms that they secured with personal funds, their service proved to be short-lived owing to legislation that limited membership in the state militia to "free white males capable of bearing arms." The unit disbanded but was reformed in response to the presence of United States naval forces under the command of Admiral David G. Farragut, which appeared at the mouth of the Mississippi River in April 1862. The Native Guard found itself alone in defending the Crescent City but failed to muster any resistance before it was captured. The unit was once again ordered disbanded by General John L. Lewis of the Louisiana state militia. Although the story of the Native Guard is often cited as evidence of loyal black soldiers, the unit was never accepted into Confederate service, and by September 1862 many of its former members were wearing blue uniforms as members of the U.S. Corps d'Afrique, organized by General Benjamin Butler.[22]

Other free black communities offered to serve in the army, but the Confederate response was consistent in maintaining the ranks for white men, even as casualties continued to accrue.[23] In addition to implementing the first national conscription policy in April 1862, the Confederate government also clarified and expanded its military policies related to slaves and free blacks. Noncombatant roles such as blacksmiths, musicians, teamsters, and cooks that were filled by white soldiers early in the war were gradually opened to blacks. The government's provisions authorized regimental and company officers to employ "colored persons" as army musicians, who were entitled to the same pay as their white counterparts. Additional measures authorized commanding officers to enlist at least four cooks for each company, who could be "white, slave, or a free person of color." Slaves could be utilized only with the written consent of their masters. Company cooks were to "be defined as enlisted personnel and placed on the muster rolls with their pay put between ten and twenty dollars a month."[24]

Despite claims that persist to this day, the men who appeared on company muster rolls and received pay for their services were usually not acknowledged as Confederate soldiers with military rank. Many of the wartime accounts that surfaced during the first half of the war purporting to demonstrate the use of large numbers of slaves as soldiers in the army continue to be embraced by modern-day neo-Confederates, who see them as indisputable proof of black soldiers' existence. These accounts are almost always offered without any historical context, however, and what they fail to acknowledge is that Confederates not only did not confirm the use of slaves as soldiers (beyond the presence of camp servants, cooks, musicians, and impressed slaves) but also often flatly denied their presence in the army. There were few people who had a better grasp of what was happening in the Confederate army on the racial front than John B. Jones. Jones, who worked in the Confederate War Department throughout the war, wrote and read reams of correspondence every day, met with the secretary of war nearly every day, and frequently spoke with Jefferson Davis. In his diary entry for March 20, 1863, Jones denied reports in Northern newspapers that the Confederacy had recruited black soldiers: "This is utterly untrue. We have no armed slaves to fight for us, nor do we fear a servile insurrection." Jones had already commented on the Emancipation Proclamation and the Union's own recently approved policy to allow blacks to serve, both of which he understood as dastardly attempts to stimulate a Southern slave uprising. According to Jones, these reports were nothing more than lies. The United States may have stooped to such nefarious tactics, but the Confederacy had not. Jones closed his diary entry for the day by questioning the "value the negro regiments employed against us will be to the invader."[25]

Jones and others would soon learn just how valuable African American soldiers proved to be to the Union war effort, but for now Confederates remained confident that independence could be achieved with an army of white soldiers alone. While Confederate armies in the Western theater had experienced military setbacks early in the war, the Army of Northern Virginia had achieved an impressive number of victories under the command of Robert E. Lee. After pushing McClellan away from the very gates of Richmond, he assumed the offensive and achieved a decisive tactical victory at Second Manassas at the end of August 1862 before pushing into Maryland, which culminated in the battle of Antietam on September 17, 1862. Although Lee failed to achieve most of his goals, he managed to bring the war out of the Confederacy and pose a political threat to the Republicans just weeks before congressional elections. In December Lee decisively turned back a Union advance under the command of General Ambrose Burnside at a high cost along the Rappahannock River at Fredericksburg. Five months later he prevented a new offensive under a new U.S. commander at Chancellorsville in early May 1863.

The victory at Chancellorsville provided Lee another opportunity to threaten the North and bring the war out of Virginia. These bold offensives into the United States were intended to strike at Northern morale and produce a speedy end to the war. The Army of Northern Virginia was in a much better position for an extended campaign north compared with the previous September, but the long marches into unknown territory, along with the other dangers once in enemy territory, forced masters to redouble their efforts to keep their camp slaves in line.

The battle of Gettysburg has long been remembered as the turning point of the war, but while its significance as the "high-water mark of the Confederacy" has been challenged in recent years, it may have been a watershed moment for the place of camp slaves within the ranks. The three-day fight in the small south-central Pennsylvania town during the first three days of July 1863 placed camp slaves in the Army of Northern Virginia at the center of some of the bloodiest fighting of the war and for the first time on free soil.

Even if taken at face value, the number of black men observed by Dr. Lewis Steiner in September 1862 paled in comparison to the number who accompanied the Army of Northern Virginia north the following year. Such a move was fraught with danger for masters who continued to worry about the fidelity of their slaves, given the dramatic shift in Union policy since the beginning of 1863. On the first of the new year, Lincoln had signed the Emancipation Proclamation, news of which quickly filtered through Confederate ranks and was certainly discussed among the slaves. The proclamation in effect turned Union armies into armies of liberation that functioned as a funnel through which freed slaves could enlist in one of the new black regiments that were quickly filled throughout the North as well as in occupied parts of the South. But the army that Lee brought north was in much better condition than it had been in the earlier campaign in 1862. According to one historian, anywhere between 6,000 and 10,000 slaves, including camp servants and those assigned to the reserve train, quartermaster department, and medical wagons, accompanied an army that hovered around 70,000.[26]

As Lee's columns pushed north with the Union army in close pursuit, Confederate officers likely gave some thought to crossing into Pennsylvania. Camp servants probably marched in column as they had in earlier campaigns. On June 25, British observer Lieutenant Colonel Arthur Fremantle noted the passing of Georgians, Mississippians, and South Carolinians in Lafayette McClaws's division, which unlike other units "marched very well." "In the rear of each regiment," reported Fremantle, "were from twenty to thirty Negro slaves, and a certain number of unarmed men carrying stretchers and wearing in their hats the red badges of the ambulance corps."[27] Though unintended, it is likely that Confederates approved of such a formation as they stepped closer to Pennsylvania, which unlike Maryland was a free state.

There were a number of signs that Lee's three corps of infantry had crossed the Mason-Dixon Line. South Carolinians in James Longstreet's First Corps listened as the women of Chambersburg, Pennsylvania, appealed to the army's slaves to run off and seize their freedom.[28] The rich bounty of food, livestock, horses, and other resources on farms that had yet to experience the "hard hand of war" also impressed the men under Lee's command. If he worried about his camp servant, William Dorsey Pender did not share it in what would prove to be his final letter home to his wife. "Joe enters into the invasion with much gusto," he noted, "and is quite active in looking up hidden property."[29] It is unclear whether Joe and the rest of the slaves accompanying the army were aware of orders issued throughout the army to remove other "hidden property" in the form of escaped slaves living in southern Pennsylvania. Free African Americans and fugitive slaves in Adams County (including Gettysburg) and surrounding counties fled with the news of Lee's advance. While there is no evidence that the army's slaves assisted in the pursuit that took place in towns such as Chambersburg, McConnellsburg, Mercersberg, and Greencastle on the eve of the famous battle, it is very likely that some of those kidnapped and led south passed camp servants and other slaves whose very presence helped to make their capture possible.[30]

The battle that commenced west and north of Gettysburg on July 1, 1863, expanded gradually as the two armies shifted units along the roads leading to the small town. By the end of the first day, Confederates had achieved a decisive victory as the Union army established a new defensive line along Cemetery Ridge south of the town, with Confederates taking up a position opposite along Seminary Ridge. Lee went on the offensive for the following two days but failed to crack the Union defenses.

Unlike the previous summer on the Virginia Peninsula, where the two armies were in close proximity to one another for an extended period of time, there are very few accounts of black men marching with Confederates in the heat of battle at Gettysburg. Camp slaves remained in the rear, prepared to perform various support roles. As units readied for battle, a member of the 24th Georgia recalled, "The Colonels sent back their horses by their servants."[31] On the afternoon of July 1, Captain Alfred Lee of the 82nd Ohio found himself wounded and behind enemy lines. A number of rebels passed by until a "young man of benevolent expression" attempted to locate a surgeon. Failing this he "directed some negroes to go and gather" items that "might improve our comfort."[32] Matt Butler, assistant surgeon of the 37th Virginia, had a horse shot out from under him and was wounded in the foot on July 2 as he tended to fallen Confederates. He managed to "limp" off the field with the help of a camp servant by the name of Jim.[33] Just as the firing ceased at the Peach Orchard late on July 2, Edward Porter Alexander was pleasantly surprised to see his servant Charley "on my spare horse Meg & with very affectionate greetings & a good haversack of rations." Alexander recalled, "Negro servants hunting for their masters were a feature of the landscape that night."[34]

Lee's failure to dislodge the Union army from its position along Cemetery Ridge led him to order one final assault on the afternoon of July 3, utilizing the men under the command of Generals George Pickett and James Johnston Pettigrew. As the remnants of their shattered command fell back following their repulse, it is likely that scores of camp slaves made their way out from the cover and protection of Spangler's Woods in search of their masters. Removal of the wounded took on a renewed urgency through the late afternoon and evening of July 3, following the final assault along the center of the Union line as the army made preparations to disengage and move south. The Army of Northern Virginia's ability to safely cross the Potomac with the Union army in pursuit depended in large part on camp servants, who cared for their wounded masters, and the great numbers of slaves assigned to ordnance trains, wagons, and ambulances, all of which extended for miles.[35]

In the immediate aftermath of the battle, as it became clear just how badly the army had been defeated, slaves began to abandon their posts. This continued throughout the army's retreat to Virginia. A quartermaster in John Bell Hood's division observed that "a great many Negroes have gone to the Yankees." Union cavalry raids, such as the one led by Judson Kilpatrick at Monterey Pass on July 5, hampered the retreat of tired Confederates and resulted in additional prisoners being taken, including the camp servants attached to the Richmond Howitzers as well as Major William H. Chamberlain's servant, horse, and personal equipment. On that same day, the 1st Vermont Cavalry intercepted part of a reserve train in Leitersburg, Maryland. As in other raids, likely among the roughly 100 seized were camp slaves.

Numerous civilians observed long columns of black men being marched off as prisoners to Frederick, Maryland.[36] The question of how to treat and classify black prisoners taken at Gettysburg and elsewhere occupied the attention of officials at places like Fort McHenry in Baltimore. Prisoners were soon given the opportunity to work as cooks for Union regiments, join new black Union regiments, or work as laborers and teamsters for the government. Many took advantage of these opportunities, though six black prisoners managed to escape from Fort McHenry.[37]

For many Confederate officers who were separated from their servants as a result of the battle or the confusion of the retreat, disappointment awaited them as it did Captain Waddell of the 12th Virginia, who rejoined his unit on July 8 only to learn that his servant Willis had run off with his personal baggage.[38] But the extraordinary steps taken by servants to accompany their wounded masters from the battlefield or escort their bodies, along with personal possessions, home quickly supplanted stories of abandonment. These stories survived the war and became the centerpiece of the Lost Cause movement, which stressed unwavering and unquestioning obedience of slaves to their masters.

Sidney Carter's wounding at Gettysburg cut his life short, but before his death he requested that Dave "take everything he had and bring it home," where each item would be offered as a parting gift to specific family members. More important than the transportation of personal possessions, however, Dave also conveyed the final thoughts of his master to loved ones. Carter wanted it known that "he was willing to die" and that he "talked to the clergyman about dying . . . tho so weak he could hardly be understood."[39] He assured his family that they would meet again in heaven. Absent the body, news that a soldier had been comforted in his final hours and had prepared himself for death reassured family members that their loved one experienced what nineteenth-century Americans understood as a "Good Death."[40]

Sergeant Major C. C. Cummings of the 17th Mississippi relied heavily on George who tended to him along the retreat route after his wounding on July 2. As Cummings's condition deteriorated, George learned that approaching Union cavalry was likely to separate "black folks from dar masters." Rather than risk permanent separation, George chose to leave his master's side but promised to rejoin him across the Potomac opposite Williamsport. "A canteen of water and some hard tack was the last token of kindly care for me," Cummings later recalled. While Cummings eventually fell into Union hands, George met with an even more unfortunate end. While making his way along an escape route, he was mistakenly identified as a Confederate soldier and shot by a Yankee patrol, perhaps because he was wearing a uniform.[41]

The loss of Colonel Henry King Burgwyn Jr., killed along Willoughby Run on the first day of fighting at Gettysburg, was a devastating loss not only to the 26th North Carolina but also reportedly to Kincien who "takes it bitterly enough." Once Burgwyn's body was given an appropriate burial, Kincien proposed transporting the young colonel's personal items home along with information about his death that he knew his family craved. The regiment's quartermaster reassured the family that the colonel's items, including spyglasses, watch, toothbrush, and various memoranda books plus ninety-five dollars, were all safe under Kincien's care. "I never saw fidelity stronger in any one," he noted. Four years later Burgwyn's body was reinterred in Oakwood Cemetery in Raleigh, North Carolina.[42]

For one major from South Carolina, his war ended along the difficult retreat route from Gettysburg, forcing his servant to take steps to properly bury the body. The servant eventually made his way home and remembered enough information about the burial site to escort family members there to disinter the body for transport home shortly after the war. Captain William McLeod of the 38th Georgia expired before the retreat, but Moses took steps to bury his master on a farm owned by Jacob Keim. Moses followed the rest of John Gordon's brigade to Winchester, Virginia, before heading home with McLeod's personal effects to Swainsboro, Georgia. In 1865 Moses made the long journey back to Gettysburg with McLeod's brother-in-law to bring the body home.[43]

It is unlikely that many bodies were escorted home by camp servants, given the quick departure made by the army from Gettysburg on July 4, the challenges faced on the retreat routes, the pursuit of Union cavalry and infantry, and a swollen Potomac River that had to be crossed to reach the safety of Virginia. Slaves like Moses who, for whatever reason, were committed to their masters made due with the limited resources available and resigned themselves in the end to passing on their masters' parting words to their grieving families. These men chose not to escape, and there can be little doubt that these stories convey evidence of strong bonds between master and slave, but the tendency to frame them around the narrow motif of unwavering loyalty fails to capture other factors that may have influenced their behavior. The reported tears of camp slaves like Kincien can certainly be interpreted as a sign of grief and loss, but it is unlikely that they were intended for his fallen master alone.

Whatever the case may be, Confederates remained committed to viewing those slaves who remained with the army as it crossed the Potomac River on July 13–14 as stalwart servants. But as the army reorganized in the weeks following the campaign, the thin ranks of many regiments were magnified by the absence of its slaves. Gettysburg may not have been the turning point of the war for Lee and the Army of Northern Virginia—the army would go on to fight for close to two more years—but the Gettysburg campaign did signal a crisis of confidence in soldiers' belief in their slaves' unwavering fidelity. Certainly this had been experienced on an individual basis, but the extent of flight at the moment when these slaves were needed most undercut a central tenet of a slaveholding society's belief in its loyal bondmen.[44]

For the remainder of the war, the Army of Northern Virginia relied more on the employment of free blacks—individuals who, it was believed, had fewer reasons to flee—to fill the support roles throughout the army. This process was likely repeated in other Confederate armies by the middle of the war. Logistical concerns also pushed many slaves out of the army for the remainder of the war as advancing Union armies cut off roads and railroads, which supplied Lee's army with important resources. The inherent dangers of army life experienced during the Gettysburg campaign influenced numerous officers to either send their servants home or resist requesting that additional slaves be directed to the army to replace those already lost. This became all the more apparent once the two armies locked horns with each other at the Wilderness on May 5–6, 1864, in what would prove to be an incredibly violent and costly campaign that stretched for close to a month from the Rappahannock River in central Virginia to the James River near Richmond.[45]

The experience of war shaped the master-slave relationship in ways that neither party could have anticipated in the spring of 1861. Masters interacted with their camp slaves in a completely new environment and witnessed behavior that both reaffirmed, for some, assumptions about slaves' loyalty and left others with profound doubts and questions. Camp slaves also adjusted their expectations based on their close contact with masters, who were challenged in ways that deviated greatly from the comforts and routine back home. Some Confederates came to terms with the extent to which the war undercut the relationship with their slaves or with beliefs that had never before been put to the test. Shepherd Pryor, who served in a Georgia regiment, admitted that Henry had provided "great help" during the first two years of war but had become "very trifling" since Gettysburg. He assumed that Henry's behavior would improve as the army moved "farther away from the free states." After spending a brief period with free blacks in Martinsburg, West Virginia, during the retreat, however, Pryor was forced to admit that he "isent the boy he was last year."[46] For Pryor and others, the line between unquestioned fidelity and betrayal became difficult to identify.

While the twin Confederate defeats at Gettysburg and Vicksburg in early July 1863 did not completely close the window on the Confederacy's bid for independence, they may have proved decisive among slaveholders as to whether it was wise to continue to use servants in the army. On July 4 an entire Confederate army surrendered at Vicksburg under the command of General John C. Pemberton, who requested that officers be allowed to "retain their private property," including "body servants." General Ulysses S. Grant permitted officers to keep their side arms, private baggage, and one horse but avoided a direct response regarding the status of slaves. Even without a clear statement by Grant, however, the presence of U.S. Colored Troops in Vicksburg encouraged former camp slaves and others to join the Union army and embrace the opportunity to fight their former masters. Evidence also suggests that some camp slaves remained with their masters, who were allowed to leave once paroled, though it is unlikely that the number of enslaved people attached to the armies achieved pre-1863 levels.[47] Doubts like those expressed by Pryor about slave loyalty and the impact of the Emancipation Proclamation and U.S. Colored Troops, as well as the heavy fighting that occurred beginning in 1864, all likely took a toll on the willingness of slave owners to bring servants into the army.

The experience of a servant running away from his Confederates master gave the lie to the assumptions many had about their bondmen's loyalty to them, but servants' actions on the battlefield also probably left masters with profound doubts and questions. The experience of seeing slaves braving the battlefield may have been comforting on one level, but it may just as likely have been perceived as a threat to their masters' cultural worldview, given the importance of Southern notions of honor and masculinity that white men took with them to war. White men were responsible for defending the safety of their families and enslaved communities. Servants accompanied Confederates not to fight as soldiers but to assist masters in fulfilling responsibilities as honorable Southern men who courageously led others and risked their own lives to defend home and nation. Observing their servants in uniform and on the battlefield engaged in actions that may have had no resemblance to anything witnessed back home threatened to collapse the slave owners' understanding of a racial hierarchy that they had been raised to uphold and defend.

This may be why Confederates took advantage of opportunities to ridicule slaves' behavior on the battlefield once the bullets started flying. The servant of one Alabama officer chose to send forward a meal to his master rather than risk bringing it onto the battlefield himself. His owner was likely comforted by his servant's admission that "minie balls and bomb shells are too thick for [me]."[48] Another slave admitted to being "terribly demoralized" in the face of enemy fire.[49] William Miller Owen praised his mess's servants for their work on preparing meals and bringing them to the front, "but let the guns open and they would make tracks to the rear in a hurry."[50] Edward Porter Alexander also recalled a moment during the battle of Chancellorsville in May 1863 when Charley got caught up in a particularly dangerous moment. While riding a horse toward Alexander's position to deliver news and food, "there came the crash of a volley of musketry." According to Alexander, "Charley disappeared in the direction from which he came so fast that nothing but a bullet could have caught him."[51] Masters and slaves all faced the possibility of death at the hands of enemy musketry and artillery. White Southerners from the slaveholding class, however, were expected to demonstrate their bravery under fire while leading men into the heat of battle. Descriptions of fleeing camp slaves helped to clarify their own social status and battlefield exploits that were often included alongside references to their servants in letters sent home to loved ones.

Others went even further and offered colorful descriptions of camp slaves' physical responses to the sounds and impact of artillery. Writing after

Camp Slaves on the Battlefield

the war, S. C. Mitchell, who served in the 3rd Tennessee, was still able to re-call "negro cooks of our regiment" who "dug themselves holes behind a log and got in them to protect themselves" in the face of a Union bombardment near Fort Donelson in early 1862. "They found out that there were more negroes than holes," wrote Mitchell, "so they piled up three or four deep in a hole." In response to the explosion of one shell, Mitchell recalled that one slave exclaimed, "'Unker Ike, if youse tired down dar you git up here and let me git down dar awhile.'"[52] During the battle of Val Verde in the far south-west New Mexico Territory, John Shophsire reported that in response to the explosion of an artillery shell close by, "Bob's eyes got a foot wide . . . and as far as we could see him he was making good time, the boys cheering him as he went."[53] Readers of the *Memphis Daily Appeal* in November 1863 must have been entertained by the description of slaves who "concealed them-selves behind trees and stumps; but which made the most noise, the shells, or the negroes, it was difficult to tell." The author gave voice to one slave who between "chattering teeth" exclaimed, "'Heyer she comes — get out de way, boys — look out all you t'ree thousand dollah negroes . . . ain't she got a noisy tail, etc.'"[54] These descriptions treated the battlefield as a stage on which slaves performed for their white audience, not unlike a minstrel show. Reduced to dim-witted, buffoonish, and childlike caricatures, they offered a moment of levity in an otherwise horrific experience that ultimately re-inforced the distinction between master and slave.

Masters found themselves in a difficult situation. On the one hand they needed to believe that their slaves were allies in a war against abolitionists, but their own words undercut the very actions their slaves offered as proof of such loyalty and commitment. The choice was between elevating their slaves and reinforcing their own authority as brave and honorable white men.[55] This tension was severely tested during the final year of the war when the question of whether slaves could be soldiers was taken up by the Confeder-ate government and its citizens serving in the army and on the home front, desperate for news that independence was still possible.

Whatever doubts masters harbored about the ability of their servants to fight or to conduct themselves as men, the growing likelihood of defeat led to increased calls to recruit slaves as soldiers beginning in mid-1864. Proposals to recruit slaves and free blacks into the army had been heard stretching back to the very beginning of the war, and concerns with such proposals echoed the debate about the use of free and enslaved African Americans going as far back as the American Revolution. General

George Washington rejected early attempts to recruit blacks into the Continental army based on the conviction that they could not be trained and that arming them raised an additional threat to Southern slaveholding interests. Only with Lord Dunmore's Proclamation in 1775, welcoming escaped fugitive slaves into the British army to fight for their freedom, did Washington and others accept that success in the war would come to whichever side could arm black men the fastest.[56]

Even as others were celebrating the Confederate victory at First Manassas, Confederate general Richard S. Ewell argued for the necessity of raising black troops. President Jefferson Davis, who had traveled from Richmond to visit the battlefield, flatly rejected Ewell's proposal as madness.[57] Early calls to broaden the racial profile of the Confederate rank and file fell on deaf ears and could be easily dismissed, especially following important victories and during periods of high national morale that reinforced the conviction that the current use of camp servants and impressed slaves provided the military with sufficient support.[58]

The process that led to this debate was gradual and was shaped, in large part, by the deteriorating military situation by the end of 1863. By October of that year, Confederate officers were authorized to impress slaves regardless of state laws but, owing to concerns about the deterioration of state power, were required to consult with governors in those areas where impressment occurred. Many planters resisted the government's encroachment on their property rights, which along with problems of enforcement convinced President Davis that additional legislation to employ more slaves and free blacks as teamsters, cooks, nurses, and "any other service for which the Negro may be found competent" would be necessary. For now Confederate policy remained focused on finding ways to maximize the number of white men in the rank and file.[59]

That was certainly Robert E. Lee's goal. For over a year he increasingly called for an end to class exemptions and other national policies that narrowed the pool of available labor. He encouraged the government to be more aggressive in impressing food and other resources for military use, while out in the Western theater of operations Confederate general William J. Hardee pushed for an enlistment policy that would place all men between the ages of fifteen and sixty, including black Southerners, under military authority.[60] Hardee's policy fell short of using slaves and free blacks as soldiers, but it was designed to increase their role as military support. President Davis echoed the concerns of his generals by appealing to Congress to "add largely to our effective forces as promptly as possible." He also called for utilizing black

Southerners with the objective of "placing in the ranks such of the able-bodied men now employed as wagoners, nurses, cooks, and other employees as are doing service for which the Negroes may be found competent."[61]

On February 17, 1864, President Davis pushed the Confederacy's impressment of slaves even further by signing into law legislation that authorized the secretary of war to employ up to 20,000 slaves and free blacks between the ages of eighteen to fifty for military purposes. The policy acknowledged a growing sense among Confederate citizens in the wake of Gettysburg and Vicksburg that the poor were being asked to sacrifice more than the slaveholding class. The masters of the slaves utilized under this legislation "earned such wages as may be agreed upon, and were entitled to proper rations and clothing." They were also entitled to compensation for the full value of those slaves who ran away; contracted disease while employed in Confederate service; died in the performance of their duties; or were captured, injured, or killed in battle. Once again, slave owners pushed back in defense of their property rights, as did governors who remained concerned about the federal government's continued encroachment on state power.[62]

Confederate policy governing the use of slaves for military purposes fit neatly into a broader national project that began out of fear that the election of the first Republican president constituted an immediate, existential threat to slaveholders. Slaves could be utilized to the extent that they advanced the goal of creating an independent slaveholding republic. Any consideration that they should serve as soldiers threatened the very foundation or "cornerstone" outlined by leaders such as Alexander Stephens. But by the end of 1864 it became increasingly clear to commanders in the field that the advantages gained by impressing slaves for various support roles was no longer sufficient to prevent defeat.

It was certainly clear to General Patrick Cleburne, a division commander in the Army of Tennessee, who witnessed the loss of Chattanooga and the stampede of Confederates along Missionary Ridge. Cleburne foresaw what would be the key weakness of the Confederate army in early 1864. Cleburne understood that the Confederacy's smaller population—eroded by years of fighting—was a clear disadvantage compared with the North's supply of fresh recruits. Many anticipated that Ulysses S. Grant would take full advantage of this discrepancy with coordinated offensives in the 1864 spring campaign. "Our soldiers can see no end to this state of affairs," observed Cleburne, "except in our own exhaustion; hence, instead of rising to the occasion, they are sinking into a fatal apathy."[63]

Patrick Cleburne believed that the reserves of available white men had been tapped and that the recruitment of slaves as soldiers, if it began promptly, would solve the Confederate army's manpower problem for 1864. The benefits of such a policy were plain:

> The measure will at one blow strip the enemy of foreign sympathy and assistance, and transfer them to the South; it will dry up two of his three sources of recruiting; it will take from his negro army the only motive it could have to fight against the South, and will probably cause much of it to desert over to us; it will deprive his cause of the powerful stimulus of fanaticism, and will enable him to see the rock on which his so called friends are now piloting him. The immediate effect of the emancipation and enrollment of negroes on the military strength of the South would be: To enable us to have armies numerically superior to those of the North, and a reserve of any size we might think necessary; to enable us to take the offensive, move forward, and forage on the enemy. It would open to us in prospective another and almost untouched source of supply, and furnish us with the means of preventing temporary disaster, and carrying on a protracted struggle. It would instantly remove all the vulnerability, embarrassment, and inherent weakness which result from slavery. The approach of the enemy would no longer find every household surrounded by spies; the fear that sealed the master's lips and the avarice that has, in so many cases, tempted him practically to desert us would alike be removed.[64]

Cleburne believed that the diplomatic value of Lincoln's Emancipation Proclamation would be undermined and military advantages gained if the Confederacy adopted a general slave emancipation policy that included those who served in the ranks as well as their families.[65]

The Irish-born Cleburne had arrived in America in the mid-1840s and never owned slaves, but for all his love of his adopted country, he had never fully appreciated the fear, racism, and greed of white Southerners that underlay their commitment to the "peculiar institution." As an acknowledgment of the limited number of white recruits that were still available to the army, his proposal made a great deal of sense, but for many it directly contradicted the very purpose of the war and the goals of the Confederate nation. His fellow officers in the Army of Tennessee listened to his proposal on the evening of January 2, 1864, before Joseph E. Johnston dismissed it and ordered

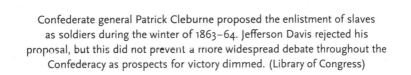

Confederate general Patrick Cleburne proposed the enlistment of slaves
as soldiers during the winter of 1863–64. Jefferson Davis rejected his
proposal, but this did not prevent a more widespread debate throughout the
Confederacy as prospects for victory dimmed. (Library of Congress)

Cleburne and his officers to cease with any further discussion. Cleburne followed Johnston's order; Johnston refused to send Cleburne's controversial proposal to Davis in Richmond, but Major General William H. T. Walker, who believed the proposal "would ruin the efficacy of our Army and involve our cause in ruin and disgrace," broke the chain of command and forwarded Cleburne's proposal to the Confederate president.[66] Davis also rejected it and ordered Walker and Johnston to keep the controversial document secret rather than risk what promised to be a divisive and heated public debate. Cleburne's assessment of how the Confederate citizenry would respond to such a drastic shift in policy was naive in retrospect, but for him it came down to choosing between one of two alternatives: "Between the loss of independence and the loss of slavery, we assume that every patriot will freely give up the latter—give up the negro slave rather than be a slave himself."[67]

It took President Davis close to a year to publicly embrace manumission as a war measure. Davis unveiled a surprise in his address to the Confederate Congress on November 7, 1864, the day before Lincoln was reelected president of the United States. In his address, Davis requested that the Confederate Congress approve 40,000 additional slaves for noncombat roles that might be utilized as soldiers in the event of future Confederate setbacks. Owners would once again be paid for their impressed bondsmen, but this time the president held out freedom in return for their service to the country. Even with the increased acknowledgment that defeat was likely, the Confederate Congress proved unwilling to follow Davis down the road to enlisting slaves as soldiers. Their failure to act pushed the debate into the armies still operating in the field as well as cities and towns throughout the Confederacy.[68]

For slaveholders and non-slaveholders alike, the question of whether to enlist slaves as soldiers as well as the question of whether they could make good soldiers cut to the core of why the war was being waged. What is important about this debate is that at no point did soldiers in the field report that blacks were already serving as soldiers. No tales of heroic acts by camp servants on the march or even on the battlefield surfaced demonstrating that slaves could make good soldiers or that they were already executing tactical orders within the command structure of an assault.[69] Regardless of whether camp servants fired a weapon in the heat of battle, manned artillery, or assisted fallen Confederates on the battlefield, the plan that Cleburne first proposed and that eventually became a topic of debate was seen by everyone engaged as a dangerous step in an entirely new direction for a nation committed to the protection of slavery and white supremacy.

Camp Slaves on the Battlefield

No one expressed this concern more forcefully than Howell Cobb, who in 1861 was president of the several sessions of the Confederate Provisional Congress. Early in the war he served as colonel of the 16th Georgia Infantry as well as of a brigade in the Army of Northern Virginia before being promoted to major general in September 1863 and placed in command of the District of Georgia and Florida. Cobb was well aware of the declining military situation by November 1864, his own plantation home having been burned to the ground by Union soldiers under the command of General William Tecumseh Sherman. Still, Cobb regarded the proposal to arm slaves as "the most pernicious idea that has been suggested since the war began." He believed that to make soldiers of slaves unsettled the very foundation of their slave society. In a letter to Secretary of War James Seddon, Cobb was adamant: "The moment you resort to negro soldiers your white soldiers will be lost to you. . . . The day you make soldiers of them is the beginning of the end of the revolution. If slaves will make good soldiers our whole theory of slavery is wrong." Cobb, however, was convinced that "they won't make soldiers." "As a class they are wanting in every qualification of a soldier."[70]

Cobb's position has been cited widely and for good reason. He articulated for many throughout the Confederacy the consequences of disrupting a racial hierarchy that the exigencies of war had already severely weakened. The enlistment of slaves as soldiers had the potential to bring about the leveling of Southern society and even more horrific scenes of miscegenation and violence that secession was originally intended to prevent. But there is another way to interpret Cobb's warning. Cobb commanded Confederate forces throughout the war, beginning with the Peninsula campaign, Seven Days Battles, and Antietam campaign before he was reassigned to the District of Georgia and Florida. Few people were better positioned to observe the use of blacks in the Confederate army throughout the South. What is often overlooked is that Dr. Lewis Steiner acknowledged Cobb's presence in the same account in which he described what he took to be thousands of armed black men in Confederate ranks before the battle of Antietam. At no time did Cobb ever admit that the men observed by Steiner or any other group of free or enslaved black men attached to the army were serving as soldiers during the war.[71]

The debate about whether to arm slaves as soldiers took place in communities throughout the Confederacy. For those regions under direct threat from the Union army, the call to arm slaves was made more forcefully, while in places such as Texas that had yet to feel the full brunt of war, a more cautious approach was voiced.[72] But even in individual communities, the issue proved to be contentious and often fell along political lines. The *Richmond Daily Examiner* spoke for many when it declared in November 1864 that "if a negro is fit to be a soldier he is not fit to be a slave." "The employment of negroes as soldiers in our armies, either with or without prospective emancipation," continued the editor, "would be the first step, but a step which would involve all the rest, to universal abolition."[73] On the other hand, the *Richmond Whig* hoped to delay what it called the "grand moral spectacle for as long as possible." Its editors "would not shrink from the use of black soldiers, if the situation called for it," but in early November 1864 the editors doubted "that such a measure would be necessary."[74] Readers of the *Richmond Sentinel* considered similar sentiments: "If ever it should become a practical question, it will be a plain one. At present, its discussion only arouses prejudices and passions and pride of opinion, which will be bad counselors." In response to the president's message of November 7, the *Sentinel* cautioned that "no such exigency as would justify it [the recruitment of slaves as soldiers], or render it judicious, has, however, arrived; and it is an improbable contingency that it ever will."[75] The reelection of Lincoln, news of Sherman's move through Georgia and the Carolinas, and additional military setbacks elsewhere as well as reports of desertion made it more and more difficult to avoid taking a stand on this momentous question, one way or the other.

In a letter printed in the *Galveston News*, Judge John T. Mills, a slave owner himself who had voted for secession in 1861, admitted that it was no longer possible to win independence without enlisting slaves: "The blood of our brave soldiers will not have been shed in vain, should we gain our independence and lose our slaves." Mills spoke for many in giving priority to independence over any desire to maintain the slave system. On the other hand, even defeat at the hands of Yankee soldiers could not bring one South Carolinian to abandon "God's institution of labor, and the primary political element of our Confederate form of Government. The arming of slaves," this writer insisted, "will destroy the household, disorganize the family, and annihilate our Government . . . and doom ourselves to utter humiliation, contempt and wretchedness as a people."[76]

For Confederate soldiers stationed in the trenches around Petersburg, Virginia, or the shattered remnants of the Army of Tennessee, the decision hinged on more immediate concerns of maintaining what was left of the army and a viable defense in the face of an enemy that appeared to have unlimited manpower reserves and matériel. A soldier in the Greensboro Guards of the 5th Alabama Infantry reported home that the men in his unit would agree to the arming of slaves if it prevented "subjugation by the Yankees, & they are willing to submit to any measures deemed necessary to prevent it." Major Thomas J. Goree, who served on General James Longstreet's staff, echoed this soldier's sentiments. "I say put the negroes in the ranks," Goree wrote to his sister, "and make soldiers of them—fight negro with negro. I believe they will fight as well or better for us than for the Yankees, and we had better even free the negroes to gain our own independence than be subjugated and lose slaves, liberty and all that makes life dear."[77] The choice between subjugation and independence was clear to Goree, who was willing to go as far as grant slaves freedom in return—a step that divided many Confederates in this debate.

Entire regiments made their voices heard, including the 56th Virginia Infantry Regiment, which expressed approval of enlisting slaves as soldiers if it would aid in the "successful resistance to our enemies, and to the maintenance of the integrity of our Government."[78] On February 15, 1865, the 1st Virginia Infantry resolved "that we would hail with acclamation the enrollment of our armies of negro troops."[79] One Confederate surgeon reported that in the Army of Northern Virginia, "almost to a man they favor it." W. A. Mallory offered his slaves to the government to be used as soldiers and requested that he be assigned to command what would hopefully be the "first Confederate Negro Regiment."[80]

Support for the enlistment of slaves as soldiers was certainly not universal, even in the ranks. Many of the same fears that were expressed on the home front surfaced among soldiers, numbers of whom had come face to face on the battlefield with black men wearing blue uniforms. Slave enlistment horrified Private Joseph Maides because "if they are put in the army the[y] will be on the same footing with the white man." "I did not volunteer my services," Maides shared with his mother, "to fight for A free Negroes free country, but to fight for a free white mans free country & I do not think I love my country well enough to fight with black soldiers." In contrast with other regiments that voted in favor of enlisting slaves, Maides reported that "it is pointedly against the wills of nearly all the soldiers" and may have led to increased desertion among his comrades.[81] South Carolinians used the *Charleston Mercury* to share their disgust with talk of making slaves soldiers. These men announced that they refused to "fight beside a nigger—to talk of emancipation is to disband our army. We are free men and we choose to fight for ourselves, we want no slaves to fight for us."[82]

By late 1864 and the beginning of 1865, Confederates had camped and marched among thousands of enslaved people, from camp servants to those impressed by the government, and yet they are decidedly absent from their letters and other published statements. Not once did a soldier in support of slave enlistment reference the courage of a servant, cook, or musician who braved the battlefield to rescue a master or pick up a rifle and fire in the direction of the enemy. Similarly, soldiers who stood steadfast against the policy failed to share stories of slaves who exhibited cowardice in the face of shot and shell and ran at the first opportunity for the safety of the rear.

Robert E. Lee's endorsement of slave enlistment in January 1865 gave the plan a giant boost and pushed in its favor many who were undecided, including the men under his command as well as those serving in the Confederate government.[83] Lee's backing cannot be understated and speaks to his role as a symbol of Confederate nationalism. Many throughout the Confederacy would have agreed with the editor of the *Richmond Daily Dispatch*'s assessment of the civilian embrace of Lee: "They are unwilling to believe, and cannot be taught to believe, that anything he undertakes will fail, that any course he recommends can be wrong, that any cause he may adopt can fail."[84] Lee was now convinced that slaves could "be made efficient soldiers" and advocated for their enlistment "without delay," but he did so on the condition that they be granted their freedom.[85] Continuing the policy of impressment or even drafting slaves into the army, according to Lee, would likely fail "to bring out the best class, and the use of coercion would make the measure distasteful to them and to their owners." More importantly, admitting that slaves would not fight without first being freed undercut a central tenet among slaveholders, which assumed that enslaved people were not interested in freedom.

With support from Lee and the Davis administration, Congressman Ethelbert Barksdale of Mississippi introduced a bill authorizing the military to accept black men as soldiers, but only with their masters' permission, on February 10, 1865. The bill reflected the influence of the slaveholding class over Robert E. Lee's recommendations by allowing masters to free their slaves following their terms of service, but they were not required to do so. Following bitter debate in the House of Representatives and with Lee's endorsement, the bill was passed on February 20 and sent to the Senate. By a one-vote margin, the Senate approved an amended version of the Barksdale bill on March 8, which Davis signed into law five days later. The War Department responded almost immediately with General Orders No. 14, authorizing the enlistment of free blacks as well as slaves who had already been emancipated by their masters before enlistment. As far as the army was concerned, no enslaved men would be accepted as Confederate soldiers.

With Union forces moving north through North Carolina to link up with the Army of the Potomac, which was still pressing Lee's army outside of Petersburg, the enlistment of slaves and free blacks commenced. In Richmond, Majors James W. Pegram and Thomas P. Turner took charge of recruiting efforts by running advertisements in the city's newspapers. The *Richmond Sentinel* reported on March 21, 1865, that the "brigade for whom, Majors Pegram, and Turner had organized was accepting recruits from all Negroes in the area, and the regiment was rapidly filled."[86] Reports of recruits enthusiastically joining the ranks proved to be premature as perhaps two dozen free blacks enlisted, only to be followed by news of these very same men abandoning their camp. Among the slaves who signed up were two men who had been sentenced to hang for the crime of burglary but were granted pardons by the governor on the condition that they join the new unit. As a sign of just how little faith was placed in this unusual project, recruits were quartered at a former tobacco factory that had been turned into a military prison and served their meals at the notorious Libby Prison.[87]

Two units were quickly organized in the Confederate capital. Winder and Jackson hospital supplied roughly sixty orderlies and nurses for the first, while the other numbered fewer than ten recruits. A local newspaper attempted to cast the recruitment and training in the best possible light. The *Daily Dispatch* assessed their efforts by admitting that it had "no hesitation saying that, for the time they [black recruits] have been at it, as much aptness and proficiency was displayed as is usually shown by any white troops we have ever seen." In its coverage of their drilling, another newspaper noted that "the knowledge of the military art they already exhibited was something remarkable. They moved with evident pride and satisfaction to themselves." Their quarters were reported to be "neat, clean, warm, and comfortable." The truth, however, was less than bright. The son of a Virginia legislator who supported slave enlistment observed the new recruits on parade in Richmond and concluded that "they appeared to regard [themselves] as isolated or out of place, as if engaged in a work not exactly in accord with their notions of self interest."[88]

Any opportunity to continue their training ended with the abandonment of Richmond by Confederates on April 2, 1865, and the subsequent entry of the Union army with black men in the vanguard. There is no conclusive evidence that these new Southern recruits marched with the Army of Northern Virginia out of the Petersburg trenches on the final retreat, which ended in surrender one week later at Appomattox Court House. The army that surrendered on April 9 likely included hundreds of camp servants and impressed slaves. In the end, the status of the army's enslaved population remained the same.

As the signatures were affixed to the surrender documents in Wilmer McLean's parlor room at Appomattox, Edward Porter Alexander shared with Charley that he was planning to offer his own services to the slave-owning nation of Brazil in its war against Paraguay. Alexander recalled that Charley "was very anxious to accompany me; & would have gone anywhere on earth."[89]

At the time of his purchase Alexander set up a bank account in Richmond from which Charley's owner could withdraw payment for his services. For reasons unknown, no withdrawals were made. It was this money that Alexander finally exchanged in the form of a ten-dollar gold piece that he gave to Charley. The two went their separate ways. Alexander never traveled to Brazil. By April 14 he was in Washington, D.C., the same day that President Lincoln was assassinated at Ford's Theatre.[90] Whether Alexander ever anticipated such an experience with a black man at the beginning of the war is unknown, and what Charley made of this gesture from a man whom he had spent much of the war with and who beat him on at least two occasions must also remain unknown.

The surrender of another Confederate in Columbia, Mississippi, brought to the surface what may have proven to be a moment of clarification between master and slave. Luke had served his master, John Andrew Wilson, for four years and may have believed that his experience in camp and perhaps even in battle rendered him as something other than a servant. The test came when he requested his own parole form. Wilson quickly responded by reminding his slave and the federal officer that "you don't need one. You never been a soldier." A Union officer granted Luke his parole, though it was likely intended as an insult to his master rather than as an acknowledgment of his service in Confederate ranks.[91]

The injuries sustained by Andrew Chandler at Chickamauga kept him from returning to his unit in 1864, but that did not prevent Silas from rejoining the war effort—this time as a servant to Andrew's brother, Benjamin, who joined the 9th Mississippi Cavalry in January. Silas's final role as a camp servant extended beyond Lee's surrender at Appomattox by close to one month. The 9th Mississippi Cavalry was given the responsibility of escorting President Jefferson Davis to safety after Richmond was abandoned on April 2. The troops' efforts came to an end when they were forced to surren-

Camp Slaves on the Battlefield

der on May 7 near Washington, Georgia, on the same day that Davis himself was captured. It is unknown whether Silas gave any thought on his journey home to his role in extending the very life of a government that, if successful, would have guaranteed his and his family's future enslavement.

Four years of close interaction left master and slave in a place that neither could have anticipated at the beginning of the war. Slaveholding Confederates did their best to manage their property on a military and political landscape that shifted dramatically over the course of the war. The slaves themselves also compelled their masters to adjust their expectations and question long-held assumptions about the loyalty of their bondmen — expectations that helped to prop up their slaveholding culture. Whatever bonds of affection existed between the two, they were part of a shifting master-slave hierarchy. Regardless of the relationship forged between master and slave, Confederate defeat meant that Luke, Silas, and countless others now had the freedom to build relationships on their own terms and for the benefit of themselves, their families, and the communities in which they chose to live. For now these men could rest contented that not only did they survive the war, they survived slavery.

Chapter Three

CAMP SLAVES AND
THE LOST CAUSE

On Tuesday, June 4, 1929, Steve Perry stepped off a segregated train car in Charlotte, North Carolina, to take part in the thirty-ninth annual reunion of the United Confederate Veterans (UCV). The city prepared for the four-day reunion and the large crowds that were expected by decorating buildings with red, white, and blue bunting and by cleaning streets and other public spaces. A variety of Confederate flags flew alongside the Stars and Stripes, while large images of Robert E. Lee, Stonewall Jackson, Jefferson Davis, and other Confederate luminaries adorned storefront windows. Organizers took the necessary steps to ensure that there was sufficient food for the veterans. Makeshift hospitals were constructed to handle any emergencies. Schools closed so that the city's youth had the opportunity to meet the veterans and hear their stories. For four days Charlotte's residents and visitors from around the country crowded into ballrooms and other public spaces to listen to leaders of various civic groups as well as local and state politicians, including Governor Oliver Max Gardner, who saluted the "magnificent remnant of the finest army that ever trod the earth."[1]

The sights and sounds of the reunion were all too familiar to Perry as he walked the city's streets and interacted with the crowds. By 1929, this "High Ranking Negro" had become a regular sight at these gatherings and always emerged as a crowd favorite.[2] Like the other Confederate veterans, Perry had plenty of stories to share about the war, but his reminiscences were those of a former camp slave, not of a soldier.

Little is known about Perry's life before 1865.[3] It was not until March 1863 that the son of his owner, Private Patrick S. Eberhart, enlisted in Tiller's Company, Georgia Light Artillery, in the county seat of Lexington. Perry was likely in his late teens when he accompanied Eberhart to war as his camp slave. Unfortunately, there are no surviving letters or diaries from Eberhart's military service that might shed light on the relationship that developed with his camp slave. In later years Perry regaled his audiences with stories that placed him and his master in some of the fiercest battles of the war, including Bull Run, Antietam, and Gettysburg, but this was little more than an attempt to tell a more compelling and entertaining story. Tiller's Company was stationed in the Departments of Georgia, South Carolina, and Florida, where the fighting failed to rise to the level of the more significant and costly battles in the Eastern theater. Eberhart and Perry saw limited action apart from the battle of Olustee, which took place in Florida on February 20, 1864. Perry may have caught a glimpse of the three black Union regiments, including the 54th Massachusetts Volunteer Infantry, which participated in the battle, though any evidence of what he thought about these men in uniform has been lost to history. Patrick Eberhart was paroled in April 1865 near Goldsboro, North Carolina. Master and slave likely traveled the relatively short distance back to Georgia together. Whatever Steve Perry had experienced during the war, by 1930 the stories he told about himself and his war service bore little resemblance to the historical record.

On the final day of the reunion in Charlotte, Perry marched alongside the *"bravest of the manhood of the South"* in front of a crowd that was estimated at 6,000.[4] Attendees of the Charlotte reunion who caught a glimpse of Perry witnessed him playing a role that he had perfected for the sole purpose of reminding the crowds of the undying loyalty of former camp slaves who stood by their masters from Bull Run to Appomattox. Perry's loyalty to the former Confederacy was evidenced by his ability to "speil [sic] off the causes of the war," which reinforced the pervasive belief that it was states' rights as opposed to the preservation of slavery and white supremacy. He invoked his role as a wartime forager by carrying a live chicken under each arm, but it was his attire that attracted the most attention. According to one reporter, Perry "displayed a high silk hat decorated with chicken feathers, Confederate flags on each shoulder, enough medals and badges to outfit two Central American generals, and a gray uniform embellished with every kind of ornament."[5] Perry's flamboyant attire suggests that at some level he understood the cultural and racial significance of the role he had perfected as a former camp slave.

A Charlotte newspaper reported that at least two other former camp slaves attended the reunion. "Uncle" Louis Nelson, who claimed to be a "bodyguard" of Confederate cavalryman Nathan Bedford Forrest, was described as a "well-preserved, erect, old-time darkey with short grizzled hair surmounting his grinning, dusky face." A photograph of former slave William Harrison standing next to his former master, A. S. Hughey, bore the title "COMRADES." The accompanying brief caption informed readers that "Harrison served Mr. Hughey as a slave before the War Between the States and followed him through the days of the sixties."[6] Perry very likely encamped together with Nelson and Hughey during the reunion and marched together in the final parade, but neither of these men could match Perry's ability to entertain the crowds as a representative of the onetime loyal slave.

By the early twentieth century, former camp slaves like Steve Perry, Louis Nelson, William Harrison, and others were regular attractions at public events involving Confederate veterans, including reunions, parades, and monument dedications. The roles that they perfected to different degrees were based on their ability and willingness to conform to a set of expectations among their largely white audiences to reenact the relationship between master and slave at war that developed throughout the postwar years. No one was confused about the status of these men. They returned year after year to reunions as former slaves and not as soldiers. Perry and other former camp slaves served as living reminders of the Lost Cause's central claim that enslaved people had always remained loyal to their masters on the home front and in the army right until the very end of the war and beyond. Their presence helped to bring the past to life and served as a living history lesson that slavery was a benign institution, that race relations remained peaceful during the war, and that slaves shared their masters' commitment to bringing about an independent slave nation. Most importantly, their participation in public events such as reunions also served as a model of deference to a new racial order that black Southerners were expected to adhere to following Reconstruction and through a period that was defined by continual political and economic uncertainty as well as racial and social unrest.

The crowds that eagerly greeted and embraced Steve Perry at the turn of the twentieth century did so under no illusions as to his status during the war. Perry would always be remembered and treated as a camp slave who obediently and in good cheer followed his master through the cauldron of war. This understanding of him and others like him as slaves, and not as men co-equal to the white soldiers in Confederate ranks, remained consistent throughout the postwar period. Former Confederates had little difficulty recalling the intense debates over whether slaves should be enlisted as soldiers or speculating about what might have been had that decision been

Camp Slaves and the Lost Cause

made earlier. As far as Richmond journalist Edward Pollard was concerned, "To suppose that it [the Confederacy] could accomplish with negro soldiers what it had totally failed to do with the white, who had a much greater interest in the issue, was supremely absurd."[7] Pollard's *The Lost Cause* (1867) may have offered his readers little reassurance that slaves could make competent soldiers, but he did begin to help craft a reinterpretation of the war that drew heavily on the memory of camp slaves and that turned battlefield defeat into a different sort of victory.

For white Southerners, Confederate defeat was a crippling blow to the most basic assumptions of life in the South. Cities such as Richmond, Atlanta, and Charleston lay partly in ruins, and large swaths of territory on which armies marched and fought over remained barren. Nineteen-year-old William Selwyn Ball rode home to his family's estate in Fairfax County, Virginia, only to find it completely destroyed. His brothers and cousins, who had also served in Lee's army, were "sprawled out on the lawn . . . dazed and unable to realize that actually all was lost." Ball was unable to regain his confidence and sense of purpose; with the loss of the war, "the world seemed to . . . come to an end," leaving him with "no ambition."[8] Beyond the physical transformation of the South was the reality of emancipation and the end of slavery.

Former camp slaves like Steve Perry embraced their freedom and built new lives or reunited families under the protection of new laws and, at least temporarily, the United States Army. They did so under the watchful eyes of their former masters and in the face of continual violence perpetrated by terrorist organizations such as the Ku Klux Klan throughout the era of Reconstruction and beyond. Those former slaves who chose to exercise their civil rights by voting or running for office likely experienced a violent backlash. Each small step taken by former slaves to give meaning to their lives as free citizens served as another reminder to former Confederates and white Southerners generally of defeat, emancipation, and a world that had been turned upside down.[9]

The goals of removing federal occupiers, limiting the freedoms of the formerly enslaved, and reestablishing white supremacy necessitated a need to explain and justify the cause and sacrifice that had led to Confederate defeat and emancipation in the first place. This reframing of the war and its outcome began almost immediately after the war with the establishment of cemeteries in communities across the former Confederacy, where the fallen could be honored.[10] But it soon blossomed into a full-blown reinterpretation of the war. Although there was never anything close to an official handbook, what eventually became known as the Lost Cause narrative of the war quickly coalesced around a set of assumptions about the war, including its causes and consequences. Among other things, Lost Cause writers insisted that the overwhelming resources of the North brought about defeat on the battlefield and not the failure of the South's generals or the wavering of support among the enlisted soldiers and broader populace. They also celebrated Generals Lee and Jackson and all Confederate soldiers as embodying the highest virtues of bravery, sacrifice, and Christian morality.[11]

Lost Cause writers asserted with the same confidence, as white Southerners had for decades, that slavery was a "positive good," benefiting the black race and serving as the foundation of a peaceful society before the war, as opposed to a violent and immigrant-ridden industrial North. In contrast with Confederate vice president Alexander Stephens, who spoke for many when he declared in 1861 that slavery constituted the "cornerstone" of their new government, Lost Cause writers now insisted that the Southern states seceded in defense of states' rights. Most importantly, they argued that African Americans showed unwavering support for the Confederacy on the home front and in their various capacities with the army through the very end.

Loyal slave narratives were certainly nothing new in the postwar period, but they took on a heightened importance and new urgency in the aftermath of emancipation and defeat and in the midst of black political action. Virginia veteran George Cary Eggleston asserted confidently that despite the understanding that a Union victory meant freedom, the newly freed people "remained quiet, faithful, and diligent throughout, very few of them giving trouble of any sort, even on plantations where only a few white women remained to control them."[12] Appeals to a nostalgic past filled with contented slaves functioned as both an emotional salve for some and as part of a gradually more vocal and aggressive critique of Radical Republican programs that called for social change and equality and as justification for a return to the antebellum racial status quo.

Former camp servants soon occupied a central place in a burgeoning Lost Cause revisionism. Their presence in the army made it easy to frame their experience as an extension of the loyal slave narrative. Paintings, popular prints, and stories of camp slaves found in magazines throughout the country, along with the published reminiscences of former Confederate soldiers, extended the notion of black loyalty, which was almost always located on the home front during the war. These accounts of faithful camp slaves offered evidence and reassurance to readers of a unified white and black population bravely resisting Yankee invaders both at home and in the army. Confederate veterans themselves led the way in shaping this narrative.

Most veterans would have had little difficulty recalling the presence of camp slaves in the army, especially early in the war, owing to their large numbers. Their temperament, unquestioning loyalty, and willingness to act on behalf of their masters' interests at a moment's notice were popular themes in postwar accounts. Carlton McCarthy's memoir, *Detailed Minutiae of Soldier Life in the Army of Northern Virginia, 1861–1865* (1882) is typical. "Never was there fonder admiration," asserted McCarthy, "than these darkies displayed for their master. . . . Their chief delight and glory was to praise the courage and good looks of 'Mahse Tom.'" Just a few short years after the war, Archibald McKinley lamented the death of Scott, in his personal journal. According to McKinley, Scott remained "true as steel" and "faithful to me and the Cause I fought for, until the day of his death." Scott's commitment to McKinley was no doubt reinforced when he recalled that he was reportedly "crying when he heard . . . that I had been killed" during the Vicksburg campaign, "but finding that I was only wounded he nursed me with the greatest care & tenderness until I recovered." For McKinley, the fact that Scott and his family remained on property given to him by his former owner solidified this narrative of boundless loyalty and proved that not even freedom could sever the bonds between former master and slave.[13] In 1900, A. B. Carter, who served as a captain in the 6th Virginia Cavalry, took out an advertisement in the *Alexandria Gazette* in search of information about Benjamin. Carter boasted of Benjamin as a "true and faithful servant of mine prior to the war between the States and my most trusted friend during the four years of the war." Benjamin never left his side and remained on the family's property for a year following the war. It apparently never occurred to Carter that his former slave may have had a different perception of their relationship and may not have been interested in a reunion, or that reasons other than simple personal loyalty may have caused Benjamin to remain on the Carter property for a time after the war.[14]

Former Confederates recalled their camp slaves' moral character and skill at carrying out even the most mundane tasks as evidence of unquestioning obedience and as a positive reflection of their benevolent masters' honor and character. General Richard Taylor remembered Tom Strother as a "model servant." "Tall, powerful, black as ebony, he was a mirror of truth and honesty. Always cheerful, I never heard him laugh, or knew of his speaking unless spoken to." As for Strother's work ethic, "He could light a fire in a minute under the most unfavorable conditions and with the most unpromising material."[15] The memories of veterans reinforced the assumptions among the slave-owning class that the camp slave's highest priority was in responding to his master's needs as if they were his own. Such expressions of paternalism on the part of former masters obscured the coercive nature of slavery, but it also smoothed over the rougher edges of the master-slave experience at war. Gone were any references to disobedient camp slaves who needed to be punished or to those who left their masters never to return.

Accounts of former camp slaves who resisted the opportunity to run away or seize their freedom in some other way proved to be very potent for a population that feared the implications of emancipation and that expected formerly enslaved people to acknowledge their subservient place in postwar Southern society. A Georgia volunteer insisted that he only "managed to get home again by the help of a negro servant, who was captured three times by the enemy but always managed to get away and come back to me."[16] Shortly after returning home John Dooley took the opportunity to revise his wartime journal and lavished praise on Ned, who "remained faithful during the whole [1862 Maryland] campaign, and there was nothing to prevent him from going to the Yankees had he such an idea."[17] The stories reassured white Southerners that emancipation had been forced on slaves by an invading army rather than embraced by the slaves themselves.

Confederate veterans recalled former camp slaves engaged in a wide range of activities and settings, but their presence before battle and the risks that some took to assist their masters in the midst of the fight occupied a central place in postwar accounts. Even the act of guarding the valuables of soldiers before going into battle merited recognition. A veteran of Parker's Battery, Virginia Light Artillery, singled out a camp slave who "took great pride in guarding" his master's "treasures." Another camp slave with the 15th Louisiana Infantry was singled out for his trustworthiness at what would have been a very tense moment for those about to face the enemy: "The officers and privates gave him their money and watches to keep until the fight was over, and the faithful old man proved true to the confidence reposed to him."[18] Such postwar reports of camp slaves guarding the personal possessions of Confederates before the soldiers went into battle complemented popular stories of slaves hiding valuable family possessions on the home front from unscrupulous Union soldiers, such as those in the path of Sherman's March in late 1864.[19]

Accounts of slaves coming to the rescue of their masters in the heat of battle or securing their bodies in death to be sent home for burial functioned as a central pillar of the Lost Cause mythos and were interpreted as indisputable proof of slave loyalty. Following the bloody fight at Chickamauga, Wilson Carter "made his way alone, recovered the lifeless body [of his master], prepared it with all the care and tenderness possible, wrapped it in his blanket . . . [and] marked the place" before walking "home to the stricken family."[20] A Tennessee camp slave carried the "dead body of his young master on his back" for over a mile, buried the body, and walked back home to "report the sad news."[21] The family of a fallen Confederate officer killed at Fredericksburg commemorated his former camp slave's loyalty with an inscription on his tombstone: "WHEN NIGHT FELL NEPTUNE WENT OUT ON THE BATTLEFIELD, FOUND THE BODY OF HIS MASTER AND BROUGHT IT HOME TO REST IN THE FAMILY BURYING GROUND."[22] Civil War veterans and their families on both sides of the conflict struggled to move beyond the horrors experienced on the battlefield. The physical and psychological wounds of battle left an indelible imprint on survivors. It is difficult to discern to what extent Confederate veterans assumed a shared experience with those former camp slaves who came to their assistance on the battlefield. For some the often confusing and painful personal narratives of battle that included a familiar face from home may have made the very act of remembering more accessible. For the families of the fallen, these stories likely brought some relief and reassurance that their son's or husband's last human contact was with a loving member of his "family."

Few ex-Confederates recounted the divisive slave enlistment debate in their memoirs, but in public it was occasionally raised. In 1872 John Bell Hood addressed the South Carolina State Survivors' Association meeting in Charleston. During his presentation Hood argued that the Confederacy could have staved off defeat if it had recruited its enslaved population into the ranks. "We could by emancipating the negro," Hood insisted, "have used him with greater efficiency even than the enemy, as he is naturally subordinate, and we better understand his characteristics and the manner to control him." Hood was convinced that blacks would not desert the army but would serve honorably. In considering this counterfactual imagining of black soldiers, Hood managed to reaffirm the central Lost Cause tenet that enslaved people were both "naturally subordinate" and loyal to the Confederacy.[23]

Even decades after the guns fell silent, Confederate veterans continued to lavish praise on their former servants. "The army negro, as we had among us," recalled one veteran, "gave every evidence of being pleased with the life that he then lived."[24] Robert Stiles reflected on the rarity of coming "in contact with relations more beautiful than existed in some cases between young Southern masters in the service and their slave attendants."[25] In 1905, G. Moxley Sorrel, who served on General James Longstreet's staff, could still easily recall a scene from the battle of Williamsburg in 1862. Following the fatal wounding of an officer, "his black servant in the rear immediately took a horse and went to the firing line for his master's body." "The devoted negro had straddled the stiffened limbs of his master on the saddle before him," recalled Sorrel, "covered his face with a handkerchief, and thus rescued his beloved master's body for interment with his fathers on the old Mississippi estate."[26] It is impossible to know whether these accounts had been embellished by this time. What is important to acknowledge is that in all of these postwar descriptions, Confederate veterans consistently referred to these men — regardless of their actions on and off the battlefield — not as soldiers serving their nation or state but as slaves serving their owners.

The presence of camp slaves in popular prints such as John Chester Buttre's *Prayer in "Stonewall" Jackson's Camp* (1866) reminded former Confederates that the war united both races even in the most intimate of settings, where God was invoked to deliver victory. Buttre's print was based on earlier sketches done by Peter Kramer and Adalbart Volck. A New York engraver, Buttre hoped to capitalize on Jackson's popularity and a reopened Southern market. Even though Jackson himself rarely led camp prayers, the scene serves as a reminder of the importance that he attached to religion in the larger Confederate cause. Buttre made a number of changes to the earlier versions of this scene, including adding the likenesses of Generals Richard S. Ewell and A. P. Hill, but he maintained Volck's emphasis on a band of Christian brothers with Jackson as a disciple of Christ in a holy cause. In this peaceful setting in which swords were now utilized as instruments for prayer, Buttre retained Jim Lewis, who was positioned just behind and to his right. The inclusion of Lewis reinforced Jackson's reputation as a benevolent slave owner even as it gave strength to defeated Southerners who insisted that the Confederacy rallied whites and blacks and that its demise had little to do with the preservation of slavery.[27]

Less dramatic though just as revealing is Conrad Wise Chapman's painting of *The Fifty-Ninth Virginia Infantry — Wise's Brigade* (1867), a unit in which the artist served beginning in July 1863 as an ordnance sergeant. Although not as popular as his paintings of wartime Charleston, Chapman's scene captured a peaceful moment that many veterans would have easily recognized. Apart from a small group of men drilling in the background, Chapman offered a picture of Confederates at rest among trees that had yet to be cut down for firewood or shelter. The scene stands in sharp contrast with the bloody and marred battlefield landscapes that many of the men had already experienced. Soldiers are huddled in small groups engaged in conversation or sharing a meal. Chapman included a number of what appear to be camp

Prayer in "Stonewall" Jackson's Camp, 1866. The image of the loyal camp slave
was a popular feature in soldiers' memoirs as well as in artwork. In this
peaceful scene, Confederate general "Stonewall" Jackson leads a religious
service that includes his camp slave to his right. (Library of Congress)

slaves in the background, all of whom work without supervision. One tends a
fire while the other approaches with a small stack of firewood. Another camp
slave in a red shirt and wide hat stands outside of a tent engaged in an unidentified activity. Chapman's painting did more than note the presence of
camp slaves in his own unit. Depicting slaves at work helped to draw a contrast with the rest of the men engaged in pursuits more appropriate to white
men, especially drilling. The resulting scene reinforced the racial hierarchy
at a time when many were witnessing its collapse.[28]

Chapman's painting served as the basis for a lithograph published in
London in 1871. In printers M. and N. Hanhart's *"Confederate Camp" during the Late American War,* the artist focused on the activity surrounding the
cluster of tents that served as Chapman's background. The print dispenses
with depicting a strict division of labor along racial lines. Two white men
prepare a meal while a camp slave is shown napping outside a tent. Three
black individuals, including one woman, can be seen in the background as
well, likely preparing food for the men. Both Chapman's original painting
and the Hanharts' print highlighted the roles camp slaves played even as

"Confederate Camp" during the Late American War, ca. 1871. Few people who lived during the war years were confused about the roles that enslaved people played in the Confederate army. They performed a wide range of roles, but they were not remembered as having served as soldiers. In this scene, camp slaves cook and clean, while another servant takes a nap next to a tent. (Library of Congress)

they once again ignored the coercive nature of slavery. Both reinforced for their audiences the central Lost Cause tenet that slaves knew their place in the army and were not the least bit concerned with opportunities to seize their freedom.

Stories of camp slaves also proved to be a very popular subject for fiction writers during the postwar period. By the 1880s a group of regional authors, led by Thomas Nelson Page and Joel Chandler Harris, author of the popular Uncle Remus series, generated an enormously popular literature devoted to moonlight and magnolias, cavaliers and fine ladies, and, of course, faithful slaves. In Harris's "An Ambuscade," a loyal camp slave named Plato carries his wounded master, Jack Kilpatrick, off the battlefield to the family plantation, thus reinforcing the all-too-prevalent theme of loyalty and love over emancipation and freedom. But no writer of the genre proved more popular than Page. Born on a Virginia Tidewater plantation, Page was twelve years old when the war ended. His writings, beginning with "Uncle Gabe's White Folks" (1873), reflect the Lost Cause's emphasis on a peaceful and pastoral Old South destroyed by invading Yankees and occupied by corrupt North-

Camp Slaves and the Lost Cause

ern "carpetbaggers" who remained ignorant of the true relationship between master and slave.

Page's most famous work, "Marse Chan," first published in *The Century's* April 1884 issue, was told in flashback from the perspective of Sam, a young slave in antebellum Virginia who is assigned as a camp slave to his master's son, Tom Channing. Sam follows his young master into the army, describing his role in the dialect style of writing commonly used by white authors of the period when creating dialogue for black characters: "An' I went wid Marse Chan an' clean he boots, an' look arfter de tent, an' tek keer o' him an' de hosses."[29] Sam recounts a romantic story of Master Tom Channing (Marse Chan), whose sweetheart, Anne, rejects him out of obedience to her father, who disapproves of their match owing to differing political views with Channing's father. After Channing's departure for the army, Anne fully acknowledges her love for him and her desire to marry him. Unbeknownst to her, however, Channing has fallen in battle. Sam escorts the body home: "Marse Chan-he-done got his furlough." Ann is left with a broken heart. The two are eventually buried together. Narrative in the voice of a former camp slave evokes nostalgia for the plantation era, and it suggests to readers that not even death and Confederate defeat could sever Sam's sense of loyalty to his former master and family. It is difficult to exaggerate the importance of "Marse Chan" in popularizing the narrative of the loyal camp slave. The story was read at meetings of the United Daughters of the Confederacy and, as will be seen later, inspired in part at least one monument to the Confederacy.

The image of the loyal camp slave, whether in the form of Page's fictional Sam or Taylor's personal memory of Tom Strother, came to embody many of the same characteristics popularized in stories about the popular and pervasive "Mammy."[30] Both offered the unconditional love and service that was central to the faithful slave narrative. The camp slave, however, demonstrated these qualities in the defining moment of the white South's military defense of the old order. This Lost Cause narrative certainly made it easier for ex-Confederates to approach the war as something other than a complete and humiliating defeat, but it did so at the price of distorting the violent nature of slavery. Each appearance of the loyal camp slave pushed the history further away from the slave in 1864 who was stretched out "full length" and given 400 lashes.[31] Stories of loyal camp slaves served both as a reminder of what white Southerners chose to believe about race relations before the war and as a lesson to newly freed people that they were expected to conform to a society still defined by white supremacy.

The memory of camp slaves also found expression among "New South" publicists like Henry W. Grady, who leveraged the Lost Cause to push the region to take its place at the forefront of an expanding and industrializing national economy. Grady, a prominent newspaper editor of several papers, including the *Atlanta Constitution,* joined others in the 1880s in encouraging the South to embrace industrial expansion and the national market economy. The pace of industrial development, including manufacturing and mining, grew considerably during this period in places like Atlanta, Richmond, Durham, and Birmingham. Large and small communities experienced an increase in population with the consolidation and development of rail lines. Industrial growth and market integration grew the middle class and transformed small-town culture in ways that few could have anticipated or fully embrace. Many encouraged and even celebrated these trends while others worried that they threatened an already fragile racial order along with the stability and traditional values of small communities.[32]

Grady and other New South boosters hoped to reassure Northern investors that race relations remained peaceful and his fellow Southerners that industrial development and economic change would not compromise the postbellum racial status quo. In regard to the latter, Grady ignored the racial violence of Reconstruction and appealed to the heart of the Lost Cause's emphasis on the "plantation darkey" as the "happiest laborer on all the earth." Grady accepted emancipation as a positive outcome of the war but worried that the nation was headed toward another crisis. In numerous speeches delivered to Northern audiences, Grady was confident that the bonds of affection that defined the relationship between master and slave would continue to guide the two races into the future as long as each acknowledged its "natural place" in the racial hierarchy. For Grady as for most white Southerners, that hierarchy was defined by black disenfranchisement and a "clear and unmistakable" belief in the "domination of the white race."[33]

Less than two weeks before his sudden death in December 1889, Grady delivered an address before the Boston Merchants Association in which he invoked his father's former camp slave as a way to tie together the Old and New South.

> I catch another vision: The crisis of battle — a soldier struck staggering fallen. I see a slave, scuffling through the smoke, winding his black arms about the fallen form, reckless of the hurtling death — bending his trusty face to catch the words that tremble on the stricken lips; so wrestling meantime with agony that he would lay down his life in his master's stead. I see him by the weary bedside

ministering with uncomplaining patience, praying with all his humble heart that God would lift his master up, until death comes in mercy and in honor to still the soldier's agony and seal the soldier's life. I see him by the open grave, mute, motionless, uncovered, suffering for the death of him who in life fought against his freedom. I see him, when the mound is heaped and the great drama of his life is closed, turn away and with downcast eyes and uncertain step start out into new and strange fields faltering, struggling, but moving on, till his shambling figure is lost in the light of this better and brighter day. And from the grave comes a voice saying: "Follow him! Put your arms about him in his need even as he put his arms about me. Be his friend as he was mine. And out into this new world—strange to me as to him, dazzling, bewildering both—I follow! And may God forget my people when they forget these."[34]

Grady left out the fact that his father lost his life on July 30, 1864, at Petersburg, Virginia, in what came to be known as the battle of the Crater— a battle that is best remembered for the early-morning detonation of explosives under a Confederate salient followed by a Union assault that included an entire division of U.S. Colored Troops. After surrendering, many of these black soldiers were executed by Confederates who viewed their participation as a slave rebellion.[35] It is entirely possible that a black soldier killed Grady's father. Yet Grady utilized the story of the death of his father to highlight the moral obligation incurred by white Southerners as a result of the camp slave's devoted service. With the end of slavery, Grady's camp servant is directionless after the war, but the love that bound slave to master survived and, according to Grady, deserved to be cultivated by members of the generation that fought the war along with their children. Grady hoped that the close race relations embodied in the connection between former master and camp slave that he described would convince Northern investors that the South was socially and economically stable and worth their investment.

Dr. Walter B. Hill, chancellor of the University of Georgia, may have harbored some of the same concerns as Grady when he addressed a conference, "Negro Education in the South," held at the University of Virginia in 1903. In his address, Hill related stories shared by Confederate veterans about the bravery and fidelity of their body servants. One such anecdote told of a servant "darting forward in the very crest of the battle and in the leaden hail of bullets bearing back the body of his wounded master, and afterwards nursing him into life." Hill recalled that one veteran pledged himself at the next veterans' reunion to "propose a monument . . . to be erected in honor of the Confederate nigger." According to Hill, white Southerners had an obligation to educate "the children and grandchildren of the Confederate negro," not only as an acknowledgment of their wartime sacrifice but as a recognition and maintenance of the old order. The call to educate the next generation of free blacks was in recognition of those who had chosen to remain in the South rather than seek employment in Northern cities. It could also be used to reinforce white home rule and promote the values of the New South.[36]

By the turn of the twentieth century, the memory of the camp slave, along with other popular images of faithful slavery, associated the African American's place in the New South with obedience and merriment. Former slave Nancy Green gave her first performance as "Aunt Jemima" at the World's Columbian Exposition in Chicago in 1893.[37] The success of the marketing campaign spoke to the popularity of nostalgic stories about the Old South that had filtered through the country in the decades since the end of the war.[38] Similarly, a small number of African Americans embraced their former roles as camp slaves in various public settings. Some hoped to win favors among whites in positions of power in their communities, while others sought financial gain and notoriety. "Ten-Cent Bill" Yopp — who earned his moniker after charging ten cents for various tasks in camp during the war — went to great lengths to cultivate favors and assistance by taking on the role of the loyal camp slave. Yopp gained attention for playing Santa Claus and organizing an annual fund-raising campaign to purchase Christmas presents for the veterans of Atlanta's Old Soldiers' Home. In 1920 the Georgia state legislature appropriated a special fund to continue his work, and Yopp was eventually allowed to take up residence at the home as a result of a special vote by the veterans.[39] South Carolina governor Wade Hampton appointed Billy Rose to the position of porter in the executive building in 1876 in recognition of his devotion after the war to the memory of Confederate general Maxcy Gregg, who was killed at the battle of Fredericksburg in December 1862. Rose remained in that position through subsequent administrations, and some speculated that "when he dies the Governor's Guards will build a monument to him after they have laid him to rest in his brilliant staff uniform with military honors."[40]

Yopp and Rose both cultivated a personal narrative that had taken hold in popular memory since the end of the war through veterans' accounts, visual culture, and literature. To different degrees, both men embodied the image of the faithful slave and impressed their white neighbors with their devotion to the Lost Cause and their deference to white authority. Their lives

Even national leaders like Booker T. Washington often embraced the Lost Cause to assuage concerns among whites and further their own personal and professional agendas. (Library of Congress)

embodied the memory of the faithful slave and served as evidence to whites that race relations could be peacefully managed as long as blacks acknowledged their proper place.

African American leaders like Booker T. Washington also took advantage of the faithful slave narrative to underscore the roles that they believed blacks should play in the progress toward regional prosperity in the new century. In front of a white audience at the Cotton States and International Exposition in Atlanta in 1895, Washington outlined his terms for racial peace in front of a segregated audience: "In all things that are purely social we can be as separate as the fingers, yet one as the hand in all things essential to mutual progress."[41] Agitation for social equality, according to Washington, was "folly." Instead, he called on blacks to seek training in industrial skills at places like his own Tuskegee Institute in Alabama. In support of this agenda, Washington took advantage of the memory of slave-owner paternalism and the loyalty of the enslaved during the war in support of his New South vision. In his biography of Frederick Douglass, published in 1907, Washington placed African Americans "on both sides of the firing line" during the war as "friends of the white race." "The armies on both sides of the conflict," according to Washington, "were indebted to the black man as friend and as fighter." Washington's referencing of blacks as "fighters" for the Confederacy and Union struck a decidedly reconciliationist tone and paved the way for him to declare that African Americans earned their freedom and "a share in the fruits of a reestablished peace, and in the goodwill of a reunited country."[42] It also reinforced Washington's insistence that blacks and whites could be "one as the hand" without disturbing the racial hierarchy that had taken hold in the Jim Crow South. White Southerners applauded Washington's acknowledgment that his fellow black citizens should respect white authority, but it was the visibility of former camp slaves at veterans' reunions who most clearly symbolized the long history of black compliance and acknowledgment of white rule and were offered as examples of simple, enduring fealty to white authority.

Confederate veterans' reunions, including the annual meeting of the UCV, provided the ideal stage on which to showcase the strong connections forged during the war between master and slave. Reunions also fulfilled multiple needs in a region beset with political unrest and economic change. The social aspect of these gatherings was paramount. Veterans delighted in assembling with their former comrades and relished the opportunity to showcase their acts of bravery and wartime stories with one another and the larger community. Reunions also helped communities preserve a collective memory of the past to be passed down to a younger generation and strengthen their Southern loyalties. Parading veterans in uniform down the main streets of cities such as Richmond, Atlanta, Houston, and Raleigh, with their camp servants in tow, offered a seamless blend of the Old and New South. The participation of former camp slaves reinforced political and racial orthodoxies that had taken hold long before the end of the war. In attending these reunions, former slaves modeled the kind of behavior and deference that their white audiences came to expect from African Americans by the turn of the twentieth century. For the editor of *Confederate Veteran* magazine, there was a "lesson in it for young negroes." The push for "social equality will ever be their calamity," but the "old-time negro lives in the South to-day faithful to white people who has not among them sustaining friends."[43] John W.

Former camp slaves attend a veterans' reunion in Tampa, Florida, in 1927. Steve Perry ("Uncle Steve Eberhart") is fifth from the left and holds a Confederate flag, while Louis Napoleon Nelson sits on the far right with his bugle. The individual in the center is wearing a white ribbon that says "Ex Slave." (Courtesy of the National Civil War Museum, Harrisburg, Penn.)

Stevens, a veteran of Hood's Texas Brigade, used the memory of loyal and upright former slaves to draw a sharp distinction with a younger generation of black Southerners. While "kindly feeling between the outgoing generation of slave-owners and of slaves is mutual the current generation of blacks is handicapped by illegitimate children, criminal activity, and venereal disease amongst one another."[44] Reunions and other public events involving veterans and their former camp servants were opportunities to showcase those members of the black community who acknowledged and even celebrated the racial status quo through their acknowledgment of the honor of their former masters and the Confederate cause itself.[45]

It should come as no surprise that camp slaves were welcomed at veterans' reunions. After all, many of these men spent significant time with the army and shared in a number of the hardships that came with military service. Forty "faithful old ex-Confederate negroes" from Mississippi marched together in a reunion in Memphis in 1902.[46] One newspaper reported the presence of twenty-five former camp slaves who attended the 1928 UCV reunion in Little Rock, Arkansas: "These grizzled old former slaves find their greatest pleasure in seeing . . . the officers they served during the war and of talking over old times with their buddies at the reunion."[47] This was undoubtedly true for the veterans as well.

The relative ease in which African Americans were integrated into the annual meetings of the UCV can be explained, in part, by the fact that these men were self-selected. Former camp slaves participated in reunions often under the patronage of their former masters or the surviving members of the unit in which they served. They had already demonstrated their good character within their communities and established close relations with local veterans. Many were welcomed as formal members of local veterans' organizations as camp "mascots," a reference that reflected their subordinate status. Joe Bloke and Andy Bailey, who attended a reunion in 1902, were characterized as "two old negro Confederate veterans, who are here as mascots for the Seventh Georgia Infantry."[48] Former camp slaves also relied financially on local veterans and the rest of the community to pay for travel and other costs of attending a reunion. Owen Snuffer, described as a "pet negro slave," earned financial support to attend a reunion owing to his behavior during the war and in recognition that he had "raised a most intelligent, honest industrious family."[49] "Uncle" Howard Divinity solicited funds from his "white friends" in Crystal Springs, Mississippi, to attend the 1910 meeting of the UCV in Mobile, Alabama. Divinity's reputation as a loyal servant was unassailable given the "silver plate" that was fitted to his skull, the result of a wound he claimed had occurred while rescuing his master in the heat of battle. Divinity attended numerous reunions and was one of a select few who played the role of camp forager. One year he managed to raise thirty dollars from "prominent white citizens" but failed to attend the reunion owing to his wife's health. Divinity returned the funds instead of using the "money for a purpose other than that for which it was intended." For one newspaper, "the simple honesty of the old negro soldier is indeed a refreshing thing to contemplate." This act likely secured his reputation within the community and allowed him to go on and request funds for future reunions, including the 1919 UCV meeting in Atlanta.[50]

Former camp slaves also secured their reputation and raised travel funds by speaking out in favor of the Democratic Party or against the Republican Party. Calvin Harper accompanied "the old soldiers" of Laurens, South Carolina, to a veterans' reunion in Mobile, Alabama, in 1910. He was remembered for tending to J. E. B. Stuart's horses, but what stood out in the newspaper coverage of Harper's trip was that "he has always voted with the Democrats and is a negro generally accepted."[51] The W. L. Moody Camp of Fairfield, Texas, presented "Uncle Nick" Blaine of Freestone County, Texas, with a certificate as a delegate to the UCV meeting in Nashville in 1904 after receiving a letter from a county judge who described Blaine as a "good citizen, good Confederate and a good Democrat."[52] This assessment sent a clear message that the individual in question knew his place in the community and reflected a biracial commitment to Democratic Party solidarity. One former Virginia camp slave was described favorably as "entirely unreconstructed" —

Camp Slaves and the Lost Cause

a shorthand way of stating that he never joined the Republican Party after the war and that he knew his place in society.[53] Steve Perry endeared himself to his fellow residents of Rome, Georgia, by thanking them directly for sending him to an annual UCV meeting. "I shall ever remain in my place," he reassured his fellow citizens, "and be obedient to all the white people. I pray that the angels may guard the homes of all Rome, and the light of God shine upon them."[54] The attention to selecting men of good character went far in minimizing any potential problems on the racial front for the duration of the reunion and served as a reminder to white audiences of the kind of behavior that should be demanded from all African Americans.

Former camp slaves organized their own reunions, though their frequency is not clear, at the turn of the twentieth century, which were encouraged by the white community for much the same reason that the former camp slaves were welcomed to veterans' reunions. In 1889 the "drivers, teamsters, servants and laborers connected with the Confederate army" in Georgia met and, according to local reports, "are worthy of praise for their devotion and faithfulness."[55] Reunions of former impressed slaves and camp servants took place alongside more general reunions of enslaved people. In North Carolina an estimated 400 "ex-slaves participated in a festival, which included plantation melodies . . . and reminiscences." These events were promoted throughout the South as a way to highlight "honest, peaceful and law-abiding citizens — a model for the younger negroes to follow."[56] A slave reunion held at the Griffin Ebenezer Baptist Church in 1913 attracted a reported 1,000 people. Local whites were likely encouraged by reports that they maintained "good order and enjoyable behavior."[57] Reunions for formerly enslaved people offered an opportunity to share experiences away from the gaze of the white community, but for those camp servants who attended veterans' reunions, their presence was highly regulated.

Reunion organizers, city officials, and the owners of private businesses reinforced accepted racial mores for the duration of the reunions. "A good many of the negro veterans have arrived," reported the organizers of the Seventeenth Annual Reunion in Birmingham in 1907, "and a special place has been set aside for them. . . . They are being well cared for and treated as their faithfulness deserves." Black participants ate their meals together but when seated with the veterans were often placed on the periphery. Separate housing proved to be the most pressing need for black attendees. Reunion organizers often provided tents, but at least one Birmingham hotel manager "prepared a special place for the old darkies, remnants of the faithful bodyguard that will come."[58] Individual acts of kindness also resulted in housing for black participants. One black attendee was welcomed into the private home of a white family after they learned that he had not secured housing and heard "the old-darky" recount a harrowing story of carrying Stonewall Jackson's body "to a place of safety" following his accidental shooting at the battle of Chancellorsville.[59] The veracity of the story likely mattered little. What secured this former camp slave a roof over his head for a few days was the expression of loyalty to the memory of a fallen Confederate chieftain, which in turn confirmed his own trustworthiness.

The history that was remembered and reenacted in veterans' camps and UCV meetings in cities across the South stood in sharp contrast with the reality of race relations at the turn of the twentieth century. African Americans continued to join interracial labor unions and push for civil rights in a much-weakened Republican Party and other political organizations. The editor of Nashville's *Fisk Herald* spoke for a new generation of blacks in 1889 when he proclaimed, "We are not the Negro from whom the chains of slavery fell a quarter of a century ago. . . . We are now qualified, and being the equal of whites, should be treated as such."[60] Whites countered black political action and other incursions against the new racial status quo with disenfranchisement and violence, most notably in the form of lynching. Prominent politicians like South Carolina's Ben Tillman publicly declared in 1892 that he would "willingly lead a mob in lynching a negro who had committed an assault upon a white woman." African Americans, according to Tillman, "must remain subordinate or be exterminated."[61] The behavior of former slaves at reunions contrasted with the more aggressive posture of some younger African Americans and likely reinforced the violent responses to the imagined specter of black violence that became a staple of the Jim Crow South.

Some former camp slaves remained little more than a curious sideshow at reunions. Crock Davis, who attended numerous reunions of Terry's Rangers in Texas, was reported as only "an interested and quiet spectator at all sessions" of the group, and "in the [formal] banquet he was not overlooked, but served at a side table along with 'his white folks.'" Other former camp slaves embraced their roles as servants or cooks, often in a highly caricatured and even comical way for the large crowds. African Americans who did so placed themselves in good stead with their former owners and the white community generally, who likely financed their trip. Jefferson Shields cultivated a very attractive wartime backstory that placed himself in the camps of both Generals Stonewall Jackson and J. E. B. Stuart as a cook. He even went as far as claiming in 1901 that he was the "only survivor of the class of nineteen negro scholars" who attended Jackson's Sunday school classes

The ribbons and medals worn by Jefferson Shields attest to the numerous veterans' reunions that he attended around the turn of the twentieth century. (Library of Congress)

in Lexington, Virginia, before the war. As in the case of the black attendee who secured housing in Birmingham after regaling his audience with stories about Jackson's wounding, the truth of Shields's stories was of little concern. Even those who doubted his stories likely appreciated their value as entertainment.[62]

Former slaves who dressed as foragers proved to be exceptionally popular with veterans and reunion crowds and usually received the most attention from local and national newspapers. One of the earliest references to these men appeared in the "Confederate Column" of the *Fort Worth Morning Register* in May 1902. A former Texas cavalryman, T. M. Presley, wrote, "I noticed while at the reunion that an old-time darky was in the grand parade bearing a chicken and a foraging outfit." For Presley, the sight of the man reinforced his belief "that there were negroes who were faithful and true to the white people."[63] A contingent of former camp slaves paraded down the streets of Mobile, Alabama, in 1910 during a reunion, including Jefferson Shields. His clothing was festooned with reunion badges, and he carried a live chicken under his arm. "When asked what he was doing with the chicken," noted a reporter, "he replied that he was just carrying his lunch."[64] Mississippian Howard Divinity, who was billed as the "Champion Chicken Thief of the Confederate Army," attended numerous reunions in the 1920s. A California newspaper left readers with this description of Divinity in 1923: "'Uncle' Howard, attired in a gray coat with a frazzled hem, an old gray cap, and with his coat and vest covered with reunion souvenirs, occupied the front seat of a big touring car. In his lap he held an old burlap sack and in the sack was a huge white hen, with her head and neck poked through a hole."[65] Foragers reminded veterans of the important role camp slaves played in securing what limited food was available to the army during difficult times. But they were also objects of ridicule and laughter. They reinforced the worst stereotypes of the happy slave, who enjoyed nothing more than entertaining white crowds. Onlookers likely cared little for the history embodied in these costumes and instead viewed the men in such clothing as a spectacle, not unlike popular minstrel shows. In addition and despite the uniforms, foragers drew a sharp contrast for reunion crowds between the memory of the brave Confederate soldier and the supporting role that only slaves could assume.

Arguably, the best-known former camp slave and forager was Steve Perry, who became a major attraction at Confederate reunions and other public events during the 1920s. He was easily singled out with his tall, feathered stovepipe hat, live hens, brightly colored sash embroidered with "ROME, GA," and tiny U.S. and Confederate flags pinned to his shoulder boards. In one local history, an image of Perry is captioned as "mascot of Floyd County Camp 368 of Confederate Veterans."[66]

One of the earliest references to Perry as a forager was published in the *Rome Tribune* in 1911, which placed him "on horseback, with a couple of chickens under his arm," at a gathering of Confederate veterans.[67] This is the only time in connection with a Confederate veterans' reunion that a newspaper referred to the surname "Perry" as opposed to his preferred surname, Eberhart. This distinction deserves some attention. There is no indication

Steve Perry, known as "Uncle Steve Eberhart," proved to be a popular attraction with white audiences at veterans' reunions owing to his stories of foraging during the war and his practice of carrying two chickens under each arm. (Courtesy of the Georgia Archives, Vanishing Georgia Collection, floo74)

that Perry used his former master's surname for anything other than Confederate veterans' reunions. His wife took the name Perry as did his children, and it is also listed on what is likely his death certificate.

For Perry, "Uncle Steve Eberhart" appears to have functioned as a stage name. It suggests that in later years Perry understood that he was taking on a role that was meant to entertain a predominantly white audience. Perry's public appearances and speeches were covered extensively in local and even national newspapers, and with each interview the commentary became even more comical. The stage name may also have made it easier for Perry to engage in some of these activities or been a means of maintaining his own dignity. Whatever the case, Perry carefully crafted a public persona that embraced the Lost Cause and the expectations of his white audiences.[68]

An example of this can be seen in a photograph that was taken of Perry in December 1921 at a reunion in Chattanooga and reproduced in newspapers across the country. The photograph, titled *Ex-Slave, Loyal to His Old Master*, shows Perry, dressed in his full "foraging" costume, standing next to a taller, elderly white man identified as Patrick Eberhart. The image caption, which was also reproduced in newspapers across the country, read, "Two of the most interesting figures of the reunion of Confederate veterans at Chattanooga, Tenn., recently were Patrick Eberhart, of the 'boys of '61,' and 'Uncle Steve Eberhart,' who has remained with his master ever since the war ended." It is possible, even likely, that Perry supplied the reporter with the information that ended up as the image's caption. Such photographs were not uncommon. Many appeared in the pages of *Confederate Veteran* as symbols of the continued friendship between former masters and slaves into their twilight years, but nothing about Perry's story is true.[69] Patrick Eberhart did not enlist until 1863, and Perry certainly had not remained "with his master ever since the war ended." There is no evidence that the two maintained any sort of relationship after the war. Perry briefly worked as a servant for his former master's family following the war, but by 1870 Perry was living in Athens, Georgia, where he was employed as a domestic servant. The photograph presents a heart-warming account of slave fidelity that outlasted the war and that few people would have had a reason to challenge, but it is also likely that Perry viewed it as reflecting little of his experience during the war and the broader history of slavery.

Steve Perry, Jefferson Shields, and Howard Divinity stand out among the many African Americans who participated in veterans' reunions. These men fully embraced the role of "forager," but their over-the-top and exaggerated performances bore little resemblance to the historical record of their

Three former camp slaves participate in a Confederate veterans' reunion in an unknown location in the 1930s. (Courtesy of the Alabama Department of Archives & History)

lives. The veterans themselves likely acknowledged the historic license taken by these men but had little reason to intervene, given the popularity of their performances and their positive reflection on race relations.

This does not mean that African Americans did not on occasion take their roles too far. William Mack Lee is a case in point. Following his ordination as a Baptist minister in Washington, D.C., in the 1880s, Mack Lee used reunions and other veterans' events to raise money for his church and congregation. He presented himself as a Lee family slave and as a "cook and servant" to none other than Robert E. Lee himself throughout the entire war. Mack Lee used every opportunity at reunions to raise money, including charging fifty cents for each photograph taken. He "sang his old plantation songs to appreciative audiences — so appreciative that they will stock his pantry for the coming winter."[70] Mack Lee's popularity took him to the Georgia House of Representatives, where he addressed the body "wearing a coat of Confederate gray" and "declared his perfect faith in the white man of the South doing the right thing for his race."[71]

In 1918 Mack Lee published a biographical pamphlet that once again placed himself at the center of the war with General Lee. The pamphlet includes a number of historical inaccuracies. In addition to claiming to be a former Lee family slave, Mack Lee also placed himself with Robert E. Lee at First Manassas in July 1861 and as a cook for Confederate generals "in de Wilerness" on July 3, 1863. In attendance were Stonewall Jackson and George Pickett as well as Lee. The pamphlet aligned Mack Lee with the central tenets of the "loyal slave" narrative: "The fact that the war had set him free was of small moment to him, and he stayed with his old master until his death" — again, stressing the theme that Mack Lee's devotion and service were not to the state or nation but to his owner, personally.[72]

What proved problematic for Mack Lee was not anything factual in his account; indeed, almost nothing in his pamphlet can be verified, and it is unlikely that he was anywhere near a Confederate camp during the war. Rather, it was the claim that he and Robert E. Lee were "real friends" and that the general confided in Mack Lee that attracted concern. In 1927 the editor of *Confederate Veteran* magazine, E. D. Pope, offered a direct response to the claims made by Mack Lee under the heading "More Historical 'Bunk.'" "The ridiculousness of the claim to have been a 'real friend' of General Lee," argued Pope, "is only equaled by the absurdity of the stories told by the old negro." He went on to state, "If General Lee ever made a confidant of anyone with whom he was associated it is not known, and much less he would have revealed himself to a negro servant."[73] Historical slights and exaggerations

The presence of African Americans at reunions reinforced the Lost Cause even as late as the 1940s. Dr. R. A. Gwynne (*seated, center*) attended the final Confederate veterans' reunion in Montgomery, Alabama, in 1944. He would have been roughly ten years old at the end of the war. (Courtesy of the Alabama Department of Archives & History)

could be tolerated, but the relationship depicted by Mack Lee with the great Confederate chieftain went too far and directly challenged the racial hierarchy of the postwar South.

Mack Lee's conflict with the editor of *Confederate Veteran* did not keep him from veterans' reunions. Year after year the ranks of veterans and their body servants continued to thin, but those who survived continued to attend. In 1932, the year of the last UCV reunion in the former Confederate capital of Richmond, Virginia, at least seven former body servants were present. They stayed at the Old Soldiers' Home for the duration of the reunion and could often be found sitting under a tree smoking their pipes and sharing stories with the veterans about the war. Also there was Steve "Eberhart" Perry, who now claimed to be 107 years old. In recognition of his attendance at numerous reunions, "Uncle Steve" was invited to speak at one of the formal gatherings. He did not fail to disappoint the crowd, and his brief remarks pointed to his mastery of his role as the loyal camp slave: "I have always been a white man's nigger, and the Yankees can't change me, suh!" The crowd erupted in applause.[74]

Among those at the seventy-fifth anniversary of the battle of Gettysburg was ninety-eight-year-old Abraham Mosley from New Albany, Mississippi. Verner Price, the son-in-law of Mosley, served as his escort. Both men paid their transportation costs with their own money, which reflects the importance that Mosley attached to this event and his commitment to be present. Some of the funds used likely came from a pension that he received from the state. Mosley joined approximately 500 Confederate veterans who were still able to attend. If he had known what awaited him in Gettysburg, though, Mosley and his young escort may have thought twice about going. Mosley's troubles stemmed from the fact that he took part as a former camp servant.

Once he arrived, Mosley discovered that "there was no tent for them" because he was "not recognized by the Federal department as a veteran." Authorities scrambled and managed to secure a tent for him and his son-in-law and arrange for their meals in a mess hall. Little is known about their time in camp during the reunion. Mosley's own connection to the Civil War is unclear. Though there is no reason to doubt that he served as a camp slave to a Mississippi officer, neither the unit nor his former master can be confirmed.[75] Mosley's troubles continued through the end of the reunion. After being informed that the transportation expenses that brought him to Gettysburg would not be refunded by the federal government, Mosley realized that he would not have sufficient funds for the return trip. According to a local reporter, "Mosley groped his way back to his tent, tears streaming from his eyes." The local Red Cross stepped in to help with just minutes to spare before their train departed the Gettysburg station and the Mosley and Price headed home to New Albany.[76]

Mosley was one of the few remaining camp servants alive in 1938. It is impossible to know what he thought he would experience at the seventy-fifth Gettysburg reunion or whether he believed the veterans on both sides would embrace him. Mosley likely spent those few days in Gettysburg walking the old battlefield and sharing stories with the few gray-haired Confederate veterans who remained. We cannot say for certain whether Mosley arrived in Gettysburg believing he had a claim to veteran status, but it is clear that his legal status during the war remained with him in the eyes of the few remaining Confederate veterans and the federal government seventy-five years later.

The visibility of former camp slaves in the postwar South and their close interaction with veterans at reunions at the turn of the twentieth century served as an important reminder to a younger generation of white Southerners of the "loyal slaves" who stood by their parents and grandparents before and during the Civil War. To ensure that the memory of the men who fought in Confederate ranks was not lost to future generations, white Southerners turned to constructing monuments on the grounds of their local courthouses and in prominent public spaces. Not surprisingly, the memory of camp slaves proved to be a popular motif. In 1895 the town of Fort Mill, South Carolina, dedicated a monument that was paid for by former Confederate captain Samuel Elliot White and John McKee Spratt. Both men hoped that this unveiling, as well as others dedicated to the Confederacy in Confederate Park, would promote New South values and attract business investment in the community.[77]

The Fort Mill monument was intended as a permanent reminder of the "faithful slaves" who toiled both on the home front and in the army. The thirteen-foot monument features a tapering obelisk of white marble that rests on a marble base supported by masonry steps. A slave sitting under a tree with a scythe close at hand is engraved on one side, while a loyal "Mammy" figure sits in front of a house holding a white child on another side. The engraving falls squarely within the Lost Cause narrative:

> 1860 Dedicated to the faithful slaves who, loyal to a sacred trust, toiled for the support of the Army With matchless devotion and with sterling fidelity guarded our defenseless homes, women and children during the struggle for principles of our Confederate States of America. 1865.

The ceremony highlighted the themes of racial conciliation and cooperation by giving four former slaves the honor of removing the drape covering the monument. Polk Miller, a white vocalist known for his performance of slave music, provided the entertainment. He referenced the tension between the older generation of faithful slaves who stood steadfastly by their former masters and younger, more "uppity" blacks who threatened to undercut peaceful race relations throughout the South.[78] The Fort Mill monument served as permanent reminder of the Lost Cause for white and black Southerners throughout the twentieth century and reinforced the racial status quo in the segregated New South.

Roughly twenty years later, on June 4, 1914, the United Daughters of the Confederacy dedicated a monument to the Confederate dead at Arlington

In 1914 the United Daughters of the Confederacy dedicated a monument on the grounds of Arlington National Cemetery. The design by Moses Ezekiel included the image of the loyal "Mammy" figure as well as a uniformed camp slave marching off with Confederate soldiers. This monument is often cited today as evidence of the existence of black Confederate soldiers. (Library of Congress)

National Cemetery on the grounds of the former home of Robert E. Lee. The unveiling followed a good deal of resistance to the idea of mingling Confederate dead with those who had given their lives to save the Union. The United Daughters of the Confederacy presented this project both as a gesture of sectional reconciliation as well as a vindication of the Lost Cause. The monument stood in a new section of Arlington at the center of concentric rings that contained the graves of 267 Confederate soldiers who had been relocated from the area around the nation's capital.[79] To design the monument, the United Daughters of the Confederacy commissioned Moses Ezekiel, a Confederate veteran from Richmond, who hoped to "show without any description how intensely and how seriously the men and women of every station in life had responded to the call to arms."[80] Ezekiel included thirty-two life-size reliefs that represent the Lost Cause pillars of Confederate military service, white Southern family life, and the faithful slave. One of the reliefs depicts, in the words of Colonel Hilary Herbert, who chaired the executive committee of the Arlington Confederate Monument Association, "an officer, kissing his child in the arms of an old negro 'mammy.'"[81]

Camp Slaves and the Lost Cause

To the left of this scene Ezekiel placed a black man in Confederate uniform marching alongside white soldiers and officers. Notably, and unlike the white figures surrounding him, the black man does not appear to be armed. Today, the image of this particular frieze from the Arlington monument can be found scattered on hundreds of websites and is usually interpreted as the clearest evidence that black men fought as soldiers for the Confederacy. For those who attended the dedication ceremony at Arlington, however, the presence of a uniformed black man meant something very different. Herbert described Ezekiel's scene in the official history of the monument this way:

> Then the sons and daughters of the South are seen coming from every direction. The manner in which they crowd enthusiastically upon each other is one of the most impressive features of this colossal work. There they come, representing every branch of the service, and in proper garb; soldiers, sailors, sappers and miners, all typified. On the right is a faithful negro body-servant following his young master, Mr. Thomas Nelson Page's realistic "Marse Chan" over again.[82]

In contrast to the numerous websites that celebrate this monument as an early example that honored black Confederate soldiers, no one who attended the dedication ceremony, including President Woodrow Wilson, was confused by such a description, nor would those viewing the monument have needed an explanation to understand Ezekiel's Lost Cause motifs. In fact, the monument fit neatly into the racial landscape of its immediate surroundings in 1914. Just a few years earlier, the president's home state of Virginia rewrote its constitution, resulting in the disenfranchisement of a large segment of its African American citizens. Shortly after arriving in Washington, D.C., Wilson ordered the segregation of all government offices. Jim Crow had come to the nation's capital.

The location of Moses Ezekiel's monument to the Confederate dead, located in the heart of Arlington National Cemetery, further pushed the memory of black Union soldiers into the recesses of the nation's collective memory of the war. Visitors wishing to honor the vast majority of black men who gave their "last full measure" to save the Union had to walk to the very edges of what was fast becoming the nation's military cemetery. More visitors saw Ezekiel's uniformed black man, who not only embodied the memory of the "loyal slave" and the Lost Cause's emphasis on his devotion to his master and the Confederacy but also provided a historical explanation and justification for a new racial order that by 1914 was on the march throughout the South.

Chapter Four

CAMP SLAVES AND PENSIONS

In 1926, at the age of eight-five, Weary Clyburn completed a "Soldier's Application for Pension" in Monroe County, North Carolina.[1] The elderly man filled out the same form that Confederate veterans in the state had used going back to 1889, but Clyburn's application process was anything but routine. The designation "colored" followed the applicant's name, and rather than indicate the unit in which he served during the war, Clyburn referenced that of his master: Captain Frank Clyburn, Company E., 12th South Carolina Volunteers. The section identifying the applicant as having served "in the armies of the late Confederate States" was crossed out, and in the space available it was stated that Clyburn's "services were meritorious and faithful toward his master, and the cause of the Confederacy." The application makes it clear that Clyburn's pension application was intended for a former camp slave and not a Confederate veteran.[2]

A statement from the local pension board to the state auditor, which accompanied Clyburn's application, corroborated the information provided and also went on to highlight his "meritorious" service. "While under enemy fire" at Hilton Head, South Carolina, Clyburn "carried his master out of the field of fire on his shoulder." He also, according to the statement, "performed personal services for Robert E. Lee," though the nature of those services was not specified. Finally, Clyburn's application stressed his desperate financial situation by indicating that he "has a wife and foolish boy to support; is too old to work and too proud to beg or steal." These brief statements greatly strengthened Clyburn's application by emphasizing that he had been a loyal slave during the war who was now greatly in need of financial assistance.

Weary Clyburn was one of roughly 2,800 former slaves who received pensions from former Confederate states. Although the total number was relatively small, these men remained a potent symbol within the Lost Cause narrative, shaping Southern memories of the war well into the twentieth century. Accounts of camp slaves in veterans' memoirs, popular literature, and visual culture were central to the argument that the Confederate cause united whites and blacks against an evil "Yankee" invasion that destroyed a peaceful world that the two races had built together. After the war, the presence of former slaves at Confederate veterans' reunions and other public events comforted white Southerners, who generally believed that slave loyalty to their former masters and fidelity to the memory of the Confederacy survived defeat and temporary occupation by the federal government during Reconstruction. White Southerners welcomed and celebrated former camp slaves, especially those who attended reunions, as evidence that peaceful race relations could be maintained and that the old order, built on black deference to white authority, could be maintained in the New South and during a period of continued racial tension.

Calls to pension former camp slaves were considered as early as the 1880s, but they received their most sustained support from Confederate veterans beginning in the first decade of the twentieth century as a result of their interaction during reunions and other public events. Veterans framed their support around a familiar narrative of slave loyalty to their former owners as well as the Confederate cause, but they also acknowledged a more personal shared experience: master and slave endured many of the hardships of war that included extended time away from family; periods of malnourishment; long, dusty marches; and even the dangers of the battlefield itself. Former camp slaves in their twilight years exhibited some of the same physical disabilities as the veterans and constituted a powerful argument to extend the pension program.

The pension program that emerged in the postwar South was established first to address the poverty and economic struggles of Confederate veterans with disabilities and only gradually evolved to include former camp servants. Poverty was common in the postwar years for both whites and blacks, but for any number of reasons it was a bigger and more commonplace problem within the African American community. That the veteran community came to champion expanding the program to include former camp servants attests to their memory of a shared experience during the war and even an acknowledgment of some of the same postwar struggles, but it must be remembered that the number of black men awarded pensions was exceedingly small, and the pensions were never equal to those provided to white veterans.[3]

State legislatures that extended their pension programs to include camp slaves in the 1920s reinforced the tenets of the Lost Cause narrative of the war for a new generation of white Southerners and sent a powerful political message to the black community that limited government financial assistance depended entirely on their compliance with the racial status quo and their loyalty to the Democratic Party. Pensions issued to former camp slaves provided a way for states to distinguish between the loyalty of former slaves and the defiance of a younger generation of African Americans who challenged the racial hierarchy following Reconstruction and into the twentieth century. Four former Confederate states extended their pension programs during a particularly violent decade on the racial front following the return of thousands of black veterans from the battlefields of World War I. These veterans often came home wearing their military uniforms and carrying rifles that they had wielded to make the world "safe for democracy." The experience of traveling through European towns that did not segregate emboldened many to resist or challenge the racial status quo in their own hometowns. Honoring the memory and offering financial assistance to former camp slaves who still wore Confederate gray justified the continued disenfranchisement of African Americans as well as more violent responses—often in the form of lynching—to those who challenged the racial status quo.

Former camp slaves eagerly filled out pension applications for financial gain. They provided information that reinforced well-worn Lost Cause themes of loyalty to master and the Confederacy but also embraced the process to lay claim to their own manhood in their recollections about the battlefield, which sometimes blurred the distinction between slave and soldier. In doing so, former camp slaves not only used the Lost Cause to further their own agenda but also unwittingly contributed to the eventual myth that turned them into Confederate soldiers. Today pension applications such as Clyburn's are routinely cited as evidence that African Americans served as soldiers in integrated regiments in the Confederate army before their counterparts were allowed to do so in segregated regiments in the Union army beginning in 1863. This misinterpretation of the expansion of the program—which is often belied by the detailed and sworn statements within the documents themselves—to include former slaves overlooks the divisive debate that took place in the Confederacy beginning in 1864 over the recruitment of slaves as soldiers, but more importantly it ignores why pension programs eventually came to include former slaves, how it was justified, and how it functioned to reinforce the racial hierarchy by the beginning of the twentieth century. Confederate veterans and the public officials who managed this project would be baffled, to say the least, by how these documents are often interpreted today within the neo-Confederate community.

I n 1901, readers of the *Sunny South* newspaper were introduced to "Uncle Tom" and "Aunt Jane." The elderly couple was described as "two remarkable old negroes, from a type of the race never seen or known anywhere except in the south." At the beginning of the war, Tom Jones accompanied his master into the Confederate army, tended to his every need, and, when he fell wounded in battle, "bore him in his strong arms from the lines." The loyalty that Tom displayed, according to the author, was due to the "training [he] received in industry and honesty under the system of slavery, which, maligned and reviled as it has been by those who never understood it, has and did nevertheless produce some of the finest types of the race that ever has or ever will be known." Three decades after the end of the war, the couple continued to "enjoy the confidence of the white people." Tom and Jane were viewed as model "negroes" whose lives, before and after the war, allowed white Southerners to imagine idyllic race relations that were severed only as a result of the Yankee invasion. More importantly, the couple's hard work and self-reliance late in life earned the respect of the entire community and reinforced the region's strict racial hierarchy.[4] "Old Uncle Ned" Hawkins of Culpeper County, Virginia, was also singled out for having "always been faithful and true." During the war, Hawkins, along with George Triplett and Cornelius S. Lucas, "went to war with the boys." All three men remained in the good graces of the white community, not simply because of their wartime role but because of what one writer described as "the conservatism of these colored citizens."[5] Like the Joneses, these three former camp slaves met the expectations of their white neighbors and the broader communities in which they resided.

Neither of these feature stories suggested that these former slaves were in need of financial assistance, but a number of tales of struggle and poverty became more commonplace. Newspapers and other publications increasingly placed the spotlight on financially struggling former camp slaves, active in veterans' activities and upstanding citizens, who acknowledged their place in the South's postwar racial hierarchy. These calls for monetary assistance quickly coalesced around pensions. On January 26, 1887, a brief article appeared in Georgia's *Dublin Post* calling on the state legislature "to pension the negroes who faithfully followed their southern masters through the late war as cooks, body servants, etc., and came out of the service lame and disabled." The unidentified author asked his readers to consider the former camp slave of Colonel C. S. Cayton known as "Mike," who had both feet amputated due to frostbite near Chattanooga and was now largely confined to his former master's plantation. "Though of black skin," the author concluded, "these negroes had hearts that bent warm for the confederate cause and their dearly beloved masters."[6] A pension official in Wilmington, North Carolina, shared an encounter with "an old-time darkey" by the name of Kadar Morgan, who hoped to secure a pension for his service as a camp servant. Morgan shared his adventures during the war, including his refusal to leave his master's side as a prisoner of war. His continued financial struggles left this official asking, "Isn't such a man as that entitled to a pension in his old age when he can no longer support himself?"[7] These early calls for pensions placed former camp slaves at the center of the Lost Cause narrative, relying on the readers' empathy and a recognition that the camp slaves ought to be acknowledged as casualties of war who deserved state assistance, and eventually galvanized state legislatures to action.

An increasing number of obituaries published in local newspapers at the turn of the century pointed to the limited time left to support these men in their final years. The city of New Orleans noted the passing in 1886 of Stewart Pringle, "a Confederate negro," who went through the war as Captain H. D. Brigham's camp servant. After the war Pringle worked as a public school janitor, but it was his view of the war that received the most attention. Pringle "was Southern to the core," according to the author of his obituary, "who loved to talk of Lee and Jackson." Pringle's fidelity to his master and the men in the company was highlighted by the confidence they placed in him during battle to protect their "money and watches." As in the case of other former camp slaves, local veterans took responsibility for the cost of burial.[8] Similarly, the veterans of Camp Sterling Price "supported" George E. Cooper "for a number of years" and after his passing arranged for his funeral and burial in Dallas's Oakland Cemetery. His obituary also noted that "he had no family."[9]

Veterans and others fondly recalled former camp slaves in their respective communities not only for their wartime service but also for their refusal to join the Republican Party during the Reconstruction era and beyond. Henry Brown of Darlington, South Carolina, was remembered primarily as a "'Red-shirt-'76 Democrat' of the most patriotic variety and he was a Democrat, not from hope or reward, but one from his heart."[10] The Redshirts functioned as the paramilitary arm of the Democratic Party in South Carolina and were only slightly less odious than the Ku Klux Klan itself. An African American man could not claim to be any more unreconstructed and would have satisfied even the most skeptical white supremacist. According to the local newspaper in Union City, Tennessee, "Uncle" Charley Sheppard "was known to every Confederate soldier in the country." He was laid to rest in a Confederate cemetery, "an honor which has never been before nor will likely ever again, be accorded a colored man." His loyalty during the war was noted, but the inclusion of the fact that Sheppard "never voted any other but the Democratic ticket" indicated that he fell in line with and acknowledged the old racial order.[11]

Funerals for the former camp slaves of prominent Confederate generals received special attention. "Business was suspended during the day" in Indianola, Mississippi, in 1894 for the funeral of William Gantt, which was reported to have been "the largest gathering ever witnessed" in the town. Gantt served as General Albert Sidney Johnston's "body servant" before his death at the battle of Shiloh in April 1862. The amount of attention lavished on Gantt at the end of his life, including the organization of his funeral by Confederate veterans, likely had as much to do with the identity of the man he once served as it was a recognition that he understood his place in post-Reconstruction Mississippi.[12]

Former camp slaves remained visible reminders of the war in their respective communities. Many continued to wear their old uniforms and take part in local activities organized by Confederate veterans. Local United Confederate Veterans camps often took responsibility for the welfare of these men and their families, especially during difficult times. The relationships forged between veterans and their former slaves reflected the core Lost Cause theme of loyalty and the belief that the cause of the Confederacy once united both races, but it also must be acknowledged that Confederate veterans shared many of the hardships of war with enslaved people and felt a certain obligation to assist them during hard times and even expressed anger when they were unjustly treated. Confederate veterans in Dallas were outraged by the shooting death of Henson Williams and his son while "plowing in a field." Williams had been given honorary membership in the local UCV camp as a result of his wartime service. Even though local police suspected the perpetrator to be a white man, news coverage indicated that the veterans "threaten[ed] vengeance on the assassin when captured."[13] Residents of Hattiesburg, Mississippi, rallied to help Hampton Perry after he "was struck by an automobile . . . and was badly injured, one leg being broken." "Uncle Hamp" was hit by a white man, who already had "two charges lodged against him" as a result of driving "under the influence of intoxication liquors." The white community's support for Perry was explained, in part, by his time in the army as a camp slave and the loyalty exhibited to his former master that kept them together to the very moment the latter succumbed to his wounds on the battlefield.[14]

The close interaction between former master and slave throughout the postwar period helps to explain why veterans led the effort to call on their respective states to pension former body servants by the 1890s and into the early twentieth century. "As a Confederate soldier and one who appreciates the services rendered during the four years of untold hardships," wrote one veteran, "I would request of you that you introduce a bill in the House granting a pension to the old and faithful colored man, Robert Shopshire."[15] Another veteran mailed Shopshire a small amount of money and encouraged his comrades and the rest of the community to do so as well. He also believed that his "bravery and devotion and suffering" to the cause should be "recognized by the state" in the form of a pension.[16]

No one was more important in securing formerly enslaved people pensions than Sumner Archibald Cunningham, who oversaw the publication of *Confederate Veteran* magazine starting in 1893 and continuing until his death in 1913. Cunningham served in the 41st Tennessee Infantry, which included time as a prisoner of war at Camp Morton, Indiana, before he was exchanged in Vicksburg, Mississippi, in 1862. He went on to fight in the battles of Missionary Ridge, Chickamauga, Nashville, and Franklin in 1864. After the war, Cunningham moved to Shelbyville, Tennessee, where he ran a bookstore and grew increasingly involved in the management of a number of newspapers. As opposed to other publications that commissioned feature stories from high-ranking former Confederate officers, *Confederate Veteran* welcomed submissions from the rank and file. Cunningham publicized calls to erect monuments and gave priority to submissions that highlighted the conduct of Southern armies and challenged those who placed the Confederacy in poor light, such as in its treatment of Union prisoners. Most importantly, he hoped to counter any suggestions that slavery was anything but a benign institution that benefited blacks. Accounts of camp servants were common throughout the monthly magazine's run and reinforced what had already emerged as the standard narrative about black fidelity to master and the Confederate cause. The magazine reached a broad cross-section of the Southern public and by 1897 became the official organ of the UCV, the United Daughters of the Confederacy, and the Sons of Confederate Veterans.[17]

Stories about loyal slaves with titles such as "A Notable Colored Veteran," "Fidelity of Negro Servants," and "Tributes to Faithful Slaves," as well as Cunningham's own editorial commentary, appeared almost from the beginning of the magazine's publication. The July 1894 issue, for example, included a tribute to William Rose, who served as the body servant to Confederate general Maxcy Gregg. Stories of slaves such as Rose who rushed onto the battlefield to comfort their fatally wounded masters "until the end came" was standard fare in *Confederate Veteran*, but just as much emphasis was placed on their lives after the war. Rose's presence at monument unveilings and Confederate reunions was viewed as a testament to his commitment to defend the memory of his former master and the Confederate cause.[18] The dedication on the part of Rose and others to continue to honor their masters led to calls for state support, from the establishment of "Old Slave" homes to pensions.[19]

Cunningham's desire to see former camp slaves pensioned was part of a much broader effort to bring attention to the condition of Confederate veterans throughout the former Confederacy. In contrast with Union veterans, who benefited from the federal government even before the war ended, former Confederates relied on state support. Financial resources were in short supply after the war, and veterans often went without any support for injuries sustained during the war. In 1879 North Carolina shifted from support for disabled soldiers to support for those in financial need, followed in the 1890s by eleven other states that established veterans' homes and pension programs that often included their wives. These programs were in place by the inaugural issue of *Confederate Veteran*, but Cunningham continued to remind the UCV of its responsibility to ensure that all veterans were cared for.

In 1913 Cunningham used his publication to make his own plea to expand state pension programs to include former camp slaves.

> The South loved and revered the old darkies who formerly were servants in the homes and on the plantations of the white people. They will ever occupy a sacred place in the memory of the people of the Old South and their sons. If people ever deserved to be so revered, it is the old darkies.
>
> The people of the South should do something material for the benefit of a particular class of old slaves. The servants who faithfully followed their young masters to the front during the War of the States and served as loyally as if they had been enlisted white men, doing their particular duties well and never tiring, should be allowed to draw pensions paid by the white people of the Southern states.
>
> Behold the picture: Black, ignorant, yet faithful, the servant of the sixties, at the call of his master, was quick to leave the old plantation and go to the front to bear the burdens of the master,

forage for him, and nurse him while sick or wounded, and in death lifted the body of his beloved master, bore it from the battle field, and took it back to the old plantation and family burying ground. The Negro slave delighted in serving his white folks.[20]

In characterizing their actions "as if" they had formally enlisted, Cunningham made clear that these men were not soldiers. According to Cunningham, the "old slaves" who served their masters during wartime represented a continuation of a longer history of slave fidelity that stretched back into the antebellum period and that was interrupted only as a result of defeat in 1865.

Cunningham may have been optimistic that such a proposal would be embraced given gradual moves over the years to extend benefits to former camp servants. In 1886 North Carolina's general assembly debated a "bill for the relief of disabled soldiers" that was eventually amended to include the widows of Confederate veterans as well as former "servants." The call to include these men was made loudest in the House by Hugh Cale — a free black man — from Pasquotank County. Cale argued passionately for the amendment by reminding his colleagues that he had been "one of the first to throw dirt on Roanoke Island" and had "stood by the first gun fired at Hatteras." Though it is not clear whether he volunteered for manual labor or was impressed into service, Cale now believed it was "proper to pension the colored men who had been injured" in the war. A few of Cale's fellow representatives supported this amendment by arguing that former slaves were "forced into danger" by "the command of authority" and now deserved "to receive its benefits," but it proved to be insufficient. The final version of the bill maintained the provision for widows, but financial support for former slaves was stricken from it.[21]

Two years later Mississippi became the first state to pass legislation for Confederate veterans that included former camp slaves with disabilities sustained during the war, such as the loss of a limb, that prevented them from engaging in manual labor. At first only "servants" who had received serious enough injuries were eligible for pensions, but four years later the program was expanded to include all former camp slaves. This decision cannot be understated, given the recent failures to include pensions for former slaves in other states and the limited funds available in postwar Mississippi. It is not at all clear why Mississippi chose to include former slaves. Certainly the state's racial political climate in the years following Reconstruction was a factor. The expansion of Mississippi's pension system took place on the eve of the passage of a new state constitution in 1890 that disenfranchised most of the state's African American population. Politicians may have hoped to undercut various schemes to pass an ex-slave pension bill in Congress and calls for slave reparations throughout the postwar South by activists such as Callie House.[22]

Black applicants in Mississippi filled out a form that clearly distinguished the nature of their service from that of Confederate veterans. In addition to their name and age, applicants listed the name of the individual he had served, the dates of that person's service, and the unit in which he served. This person was almost always the applicant's former master. Given the lack of contemporary records for camp slaves, the verification process relied on muster rolls to document the service of the applicant's former master. Affidavits signed by two witnesses, typically former Confederate soldiers, were required to verify the accuracy of the information provided on the application. Although the pension program was administered at the state level, all applications, including affidavits, were completed at the county level. This all but guaranteed that the applicant was known to the witnesses and was considered to be an upstanding member of the community. Applicants were not given the opportunity to discuss how they viewed the war or anything having to do with motivation. By filling out a servant's application, these men acknowledged that they were not formally enlisted in a Mississippi regiment as a soldier during the war.[23]

The steps taken by Mississippi reinforced calls in other former Confederate states to pension camp slaves. The veterans themselves continued to lead the charge. In Raleigh, North Carolina, Confederate veterans passed a resolution calling on the state legislature to pension "worthy negro servants who followed the fortunes of the southern Confederacy and rendered service to their owners and others."[24] For veterans, concerns about the maintenance of peaceful race relations were never far from view. The region's commitment to racial segregation following Reconstruction was enshrined through a wide range of state laws and legally supported by the nation's highest court, but violent riots in places like Wilmington, Atlanta, and elsewhere along with extralegal justice in the form of lynching served as a continual reminder of Jim Crow's frailty. Veterans highlighted their "faithful servants" as models of proper behavior. According to one contributor to *Confederate Veteran*, "While the race problem creates serious concern for the welfare of both races and for the country, it behooves the Southern people, who are, and ever have been, their best friends, to be on the alert for opportunities to influence all classes for the general good."[25]

For some years, Mississippi remained the only state to include former camp slaves in its pension program, but even that state's support sometimes wavered. In 1912 a proposal to remove blacks from the pension rolls was narrowly defeated. The paramount concern for Confederate veterans serving in the state legislature was directing as much of the budget to fellow soldiers in need as possible, but in doing so they occasionally denied the many tales of slaves risking their safety to come to the rescue of their masters on the battlefield or engaged in some other supportive act. In fact, a few former soldiers went as far as to testify "that they never saw during the whole war, a single negro servant on the firing line." For one representative, "as long as the state could only pay the small pittance of $35.00 to these old men, I would never vote to take one dollar of this to give to any one not a confederate soldier."[26] On the other side, supporters embraced the memory of the loyal camp slave. An editorial implored Mississippians to remember that "though freedom was often within their grasp . . . they chose rather faithfulness to their white friends and masters, coupled as it was with slavery and danger." This writer granted that denying former slaves pensions "may save a few pennies," but it would do so "at the expense of the reputation of our people for generosity and protection to an inferior race, and visited too, on the most deserving of that race."[27] Casting elderly former camp servants at the same time as both an "inferior race" and the "most deserving" acknowledged the kind of behavior that was worthy of state support even as it reinforced the racial status quo in Jim Crow Mississippi.

Four other former Confederate states — North Carolina, South Carolina, Tennessee, and Virginia — extended their pension programs to include formerly enslaved people, beginning with Tennessee in the 1920s. These political decisions were made in large part by a new generation of white Southerners who did not live through the war. The total number of blacks awarded pensions during this period remained relatively small, but the symbolic gesture may have been much more important. Concerns about maintaining racial control throughout the South was a top priority throughout this period. Highlighting the master-slave relationship during war and their continued bond long after the guns fell silent served as a model of black deference that whites demanded. It also helped to justify both legal and extralegal responses to anyone in the black community who sought to disrupt the "peaceful" racial balance that whites believed had always existed. Such concerns may have been heightened in the years immediately following World War I.

Thousands of Southern blacks who helped to "make the world safe for democracy" in Europe returned home hoping to improve their own lives and challenge racial segregation. But even before they embarked for Europe, some white Southerners expressed concern about their service following the Houston Riot of 1917 in which members of the all-black 3rd Battalion of the 24th United States Infantry were forced to defend themselves. A number of the soldiers were discharged. According to the editor of the *Charlottesville Daily Progress*, they were all "utterly unfit to serve this country in the capacity of bearing arms." He went on to suggest that "if they must be used let them be employed as they were in the Confederate Army . . . as teamsters, camp-helpers and as workmen on trench and fortification building."[28] The editor worried—just as Confederates had done toward the end of the war during the slave enlistment debate—about the implications of large numbers of black Southerners fighting overseas and then coming home to a society that still demanded a strict compliance to white rule.

After World War I, black veterans flooded major cities like Atlanta and Birmingham to look for work instead of returning to work on farms, where many whites expected them. This situation threatened to undercut labor relations and suggested that these young black men, who for the first time experienced life outside the Jim Crow South, might resist adhering to a strictly defined economic, social, and political position. A resident of New Orleans spoke for many in 1919: "Sometimes I very much fear that the return of the negro soldiers is going to be followed by trouble in the South. The negroes show a growing hostility and insolence to the whites, quite apart from their refusal to work for wages which we can afford to pay. This will probably be worse when the troops come home, flushed with praises that they have received for their work in France."[29] The problem was compounded by the return of many of these men in full military uniform.

Black veterans conjured up long-standing fears and anxieties about the sanctity of white womanhood and the danger of rape by black men. But the larger concern as they stepped off trains in towns and cities across the South in full uniform, still brandishing their weapons, was that they would try to leverage their military service to achieve the goal of full citizenship rights. For some whites the threat of a region-wide black rebellion could not be ignored. Even rumors of racial violence in places like Galveston, Texas, and Fayetteville, North Carolina, were enough to alarm the white population. The number of lynchings increased dramatically in the year following the war and continued into the 1920s. In Pensacola, Florida, a mob burned Bud Johnson to death for supposedly assaulting a white woman. Charles Kelley was murdered shortly after being discharged from Camp Gordon in Woolsey, Georgia. Even Leroy Johnston, who served as a bugler in the 369th

Infantry Regiment and bore wounds incurred at Chateau-Thierry, could not escape this racial backlash: he and his three brothers were murdered while returning from a hunting trip near Helena, Arkansas. Their crime was likely nothing more than the possession of firearms.[30]

African Americans who continued to wear their uniforms as an assertion of their manhood and patriotic service to the nation were also targeted. The young men who returned from Europe stood in sharp contrast with their elders, who once donned uniforms as slaves to serve their masters at war. The elder generation represented submission to white authority, while this new generation of black Southerners was viewed as a threat to the political, economic, and social foundation of the region. The expansion of pension programs in North Carolina, South Carolina, Tennessee, and Virginia in the 1920s helped to highlight and reinforce this crucial distinction.

On April 9, 1921, Tennessee approved an expanded "veterans pension" that included "colored men who served as servants and cooks in the Confederate army."[31] Former slaves were given ten dollars a month or thirty dollars per quarter, which was significantly less than what white veterans received. Black men filled out a form titled "Colored Man's Application for Pension" and, among other things, were required to indicate place of birth, place of enlistment, marital status, and value of their personal assets. Applicants also had to indicate whether they had an owner during the war. The overwhelming majority of the 328 black Tennesseans who applied for a pension after 1921 were formerly enslaved camp servants, regimental musicians, or cooks. Applications came from all over the state, though the largest number was sent from the counties around Memphis. The *Confederate Veteran* noted with approval the state's "new allowance for pensions to the faithful negroes who were in the war with their masters and served them to the end." The author hoped that other states would follow, applauding — with one eye on recent racial tensions — the state's decision to provide "for their old negroes, whose loyalty under the circumstances showed a fine sense of honor not apparent in later generations of the race."[32]

Two years later, on March 16, 1923, South Carolina adapted a measure to expand its state pension program to include former slaves and free blacks who had assumed various supportive roles in the Confederate army. The legislation stipulated "such Negroes as were engaged for at least six months in the service of the State . . . as servants, cooks, and attendants on the side of the Confederacy." As in the case of Tennessee, the amount of money earmarked for African Americans in South Carolina paled in comparison with that for veterans.[33] In 1924 the state appropriated $750,000 for soldiers and

$3,000 for black pensioners.[34] The efforts of local camps of the UCV, the SCV, and the United Daughters of the Confederacy to see this legislation through to its passage helped to frame it as an extension of honoring former slaves and vindicating their Lost Cause. Just prior to passage, UCV state commander for South Carolina James Fitz James Caldwell implored his state to follow the lead of Mississippi and Tennessee. "I reproach myself for my inactivity," Caldwell continued, "for I had personal knowledge of Negroes serving with the Army of Northern Virginia who not only performed their menial tasks with fidelity, but also risked their lives for their masters and employers." Caldwell relayed the story of a "free Negro" who during the battle of Gettysburg "was the first man to come to me, and that while rifle balls were still humming around."[35]

The tendency to expand state pension programs to include former camp servants was a direct result of the focus of Confederate veterans like Caldwell, who could speak directly to a personal relationship built around strong bonds of fidelity that he was convinced had survived the war. These stories fit neatly into the region's collective memory of the Lost Cause. It is no surprise that the expansion of these programs embraced specifically this community of former slaves, but unlike other states, Virginia chose to broaden its pension program even further when it passed legislation in 1924. The Commonwealth accepted applications from "any person who actually accompanied a soldier in the service, and remained faithful, and loyal as the body servant of such soldier, or who served as a cook, hostler, musician, teamster or in another supportive capacity under any command of the army, and thereby rendered service to the Confederacy." Yet even this expanded program maintained the crucial distinction between the roles that free and enslaved men assumed and those of soldiers. Those black men who satisfied this provision were awarded "an annual pension of twenty-five dollars."[36] Finally, in 1927, North Carolina became the last former Confederate state to revise its pension program to include formerly enslaved people. Pensions were issued "to such colored servants who went with their masters to the war and can prove their service to the satisfaction of the county and State pension boards." Only 193 applications were received—no doubt a reflection of how few of these men were still alive by the end of the 1920s. Of that number, roughly 20 percent of those who applied had worked on Confederate fortifications during the war. The vast majority of these men fell in line with applicants from the other states in listing "servant" or "body servant" as their primary role.[37]

The process stipulated by North Carolina, South Carolina, Tennessee, and Virginia overlapped with the framework already established by Mississippi. The application process in all five states began at the county level, though in North Carolina, Tennessee, and Virginia completed forms were submitted to state pension boards for final approval. North Carolina was the only one of these not to publish a special application form for African Americans. All states except Virginia asked the applicant to indicate his master's name, which allowed authorities to verify his presence in a specific unit by checking the Confederate muster rolls. It also serves as an important reminder that local officials and pension board members believed that they were interacting with former slaves and not soldiers. In contrast with Virginia, which accepted pension applications from African Americans in a wider range of capacities, the other states more typically allowed for short responses such as "body servant." Even though tales of bravery and sacrifice from former camp slaves were emphasized by Confederate veterans and other commentators throughout the postwar period, only Mississippi asked if the applicant had been wounded as a result of his presence in the army. As we will see, however, this and other information did make it onto forms as an explanation for why a pension should be approved.[38]

All five states required that the applicant's package include two sworn and signed affidavits by former Confederates, if possible, attesting to the truth of the information provided. In the event that this was not possible, substitutes—typically the children of Confederate soldiers—were asked to stand in for the applicant's master. The ages of the applicant and witnesses as well as the occasional use of substitutes affected the reliability of the information submitted, as did other factors. For example, applicants often did not know the year of their birth and were forced to approximate their age. Former slaves also struggled to define the exact length of their time in the Confederate army. Many simply noted that their term of service covered the duration of the conflict—a tendency that also helped to prove their loyalty to their master and the Confederacy.[39]

Despite the attempt on the part of some in the neo-Confederate community who today highlight these pensions as evidence that free and enslaved blacks fought as soldiers for the Confederacy, it is clear that the five states that instituted changes to include black men believed they were providing state aid to former body servants or camp slaves. As with any public program, mistakes were made. By the 1920s, witnesses were no longer living, memories were faulty, and bureaucratic red tape all led to applicants mistakenly being awarded pensions or rejected. But even if the program was not perfect, these documents offer insights. Each pension application approved represented part of an official state history of the relationship between the Confederacy, the army, and the enslaved population.

Financial support, however small, would have been motivation enough to apply for a pension. Many African Americans labored as sharecroppers during the 1920s and suffered economically throughout the Jim Crow era. Former slaves may have believed that they were entitled to these payments as a form of back pay. This was the only social welfare program available to African Americans before the New Deal programs of the 1930s. But the pension process also offered former camp slaves one last opportunity to tell their own stories.[40] Certainly many of these men shared stories of the war with their families to be passed down to subsequent generations, but filling out a state form may have been viewed differently. Unlike reminiscing with family members or taking part in veterans' reunions or other public events where they were expected to play a role for white audiences, this was an opportunity to have their own narrative acknowledged and archived by the state.

The conviction among former camp slaves that they were entitled to some form of compensation for their wartime efforts led many to apply even before more inclusive legislation had been passed to include African Americans. It is also likely that these men came to believe that the dangers they experienced in camp, on the march, and even on the battlefield were no different than those faced by a soldier. The vast majority of black applicants who applied for a soldiers' pension, however, received rejection letters in response. In 1920, just a year before it revised its pension program, the Tennessee state board notified F. R. Hoard that his application had been rejected. "The Board cannot pension," the letter indicated, "other than actual bona fide soldiers who stayed in the Service until the close of the war unless previously shot out." Hoard was informed that his application clearly indicated that he was not a soldier "but the servant of a soldier, and therefore you are not pensionable."[41]

Texas never instituted changes to its pension program, but that did not prevent African Americans from applying as Confederate veterans. These applications were routinely rejected with notices that indicated their names could not be located on the regimental muster rolls. That may have been irrelevant to Peter Brown, who was present with the 33rd Texas Cavalry as a slave. He still insisted on being acknowledged as a soldier: "We were mustered in as soldiers. We answered to roll call three times a day. We were ordered to fight several times and crossed Red River, but we did not get into actual engagements." Brown's witnesses testified that he "cooked, teamstered, stood guard over ammunition wagons, etc. and was a faithful servant for several years during the war." But regardless of how Brown may have understood his time in the army, according to the state of Texas he was ineligible for a pension as a Confederate veteran.[42] Multiple witnesses for B. J. Jackson testified that he claimed multiple times after the war to have served as a soldier in the Confederate army, but he, like Brown, was rejected by the pension board.[43]

Wash White's experience with the state pension system offers some insight into just how confusing and inconsistent the process could be. White, who lived in Kaufman County, Texas, after the war, applied for a pension as a Confederate veteran in 1922 and was rejected but was approved the following year after reapplying. A local law firm wrote on his behalf, "We have never found [it] possible to turn away any Ex-Confederate though he be a negro who furnishes evidence of his loyalty to the South and his 'master' during this direful conflict." In early 1932, however, White's pension was discontinued by the state comptroller's office, which informed him, "Your proof of service is not such as would entitle you to a pension . . . for the reason that proof filed shows you were a slave at the time. As I understand there was a law during the war prohibiting the conscription and arming of negroes."[44] Local attorneys attempted to once again write in support of White but to no avail. White's back-and-forth experience reflects conflict between local support for African Americans who were considered to be respected citizens during the Jim Crow era and the state, which often pushed back by clarifying the scope of the pension system.

The wives of former camp servants and impressed slaves in Texas did not fare any better when they applied for widows' pensions. Louis Estes may have shared stories with his young bride of his bravery while with the Confederate army and may have described himself as a soldier, but when Susan Estes went to apply for a widow's pension in Dallas, her application was rejected. This was not for a lack of trying. Susan applied twice, first by listing Louis's unit as the 10th Texas Cavalry and again as the 25th Battalion, Virginia Cavalry. Her witnesses' claims that Louis had "served as a Private" during the war were easily dismissed, given that his name could not be found on the muster rolls of any regiment.[45] The wife of George Hampton attempted to collect her husband's pension, which had been granted in 1923, following his death. According to his application, George "helped to herd and collect cattle and horses for the Tex. Confederate soldiers." It is unclear as to why the pension was approved, given the evidence that George was working as one of many impressed slaves. Upon review, the Comptroller of Public Accounts assessed Hampton's work as "civil and not a military service." "There were many negroes in the war doing just such service as it is claimed Hampton did," he went on to say, "but such service was being done as a slave and not as an enlisted member of any military organization."[46]

Letters of rejection for those Texans who applied in the 1930s at the height of the Great Depression must have been especially disappointing. Bud Dickson was notified that "since you have failed to make any proof of your service as a Confederate Soldier the same [pension application] is necessarily rejected."[47]

By this point, applicants certainly understood that as a condition of approval they were expected to offer testimony of their loyalty to their former masters and the Confederacy, but they also likely used the process to demonstrate their bravery and steadfastness in the midst of danger. The brief responses to specific questions and longer accounts provided by these elderly men can be seen as claims to their own martial manhood that were so often denied or dismissed every time they were referred to as "uncle" or "boy."

For former impressed slaves who constructed earthworks or worked as teamsters in Virginia, the task of adding nuance to their pension application was more challenging. Pensions for African American men who served as common laborers—as opposed to cooks or camp servants of some type—are rare. Their scarcity underscores that the vast majority of pensions were justified by direct service to a specific white soldier, not more abstractly to the military or government. Most of these men toiled in obscurity as members of large squads and rarely established the kind of visibility that body servants experienced in camp, on the march, and on the battlefield. Many of these characterized their work as "service" to the Confederacy as opposed to a laborer. This may have been done to suppress or even collapse the distinction between a slave and a soldier in their own minds. Others emphasized their commitment to remain in the army by noting specifically that they were present with the army right to the very end at Appomattox. Edward Austin of Bedford County recounted that his role as a laborer and stableman continued until 1865 when "Lee surrendered." Randol Brown went even further by stating, "I went South and was on duty when Lee surrendered." As was the case with camp servants, impressed slaves also placed themselves in close proximity to Robert E. Lee and other significant Confederate officers or at the center of the action whenever possible, another way of enhancing their war record. Impressed slaves assigned to constructing earthworks likely found it easier to color their narratives with images of war. Following the unpleasant role of burying Confederate dead in a cemetery near Richmond, Aaron Evans was reassigned to constructing "Breastworks" between Richmond and Petersburg. "Right in the midst of battle I worked on those entrenchments with my life in constant danger," he boasted.[48]

Proving a disability was certainly easier for former camp slaves who incurred wounds on the battlefield. Their vivid descriptions were intended to gain sympathy from the pension boards, but they may also have offered the applicant an opportunity to recall his own heroic acts in the face of death. Henry Neal noted that "both of my young masters were killed in the battle of Shiloh while I was shot in my left leg." Another former Tennessee camp servant came out of a battle with a "severe wound to the arm." During the Vicksburg campaign in 1863, Monroe Jones had both legs amputated at the knees. These wounds served not only as visual reminders of their "wartime loyalty" but also as claims of battlefield bravery and steadfastness in the face of shot and shell.[49]

The concern that veterans expressed for their former slaves was not limited to their affidavits. Applications often got caught up in bureaucratic red tape. Elderly black men had little power to push the process along, but they could and often did take advantage of their witnesses and others in their local veterans' camp to make inquiries and exert pressure whenever possible. Shadrack Searcy's pension in Tennessee had been approved, but he had yet to receive his first payment. W. M. Nixon, a member of a local UCV camp, informed the pension board that Searcy's "land lord has locked him out of his house, and he is in distress." Searcy was fortunate to have someone like Nixon in his corner who could speak to his "distress" and make the kinds of requests that were unavailable to African Americans at this time.[50]

Two former camp servants, Levi Miller and Richard Quarls, deserve special attention, given the continued controversy surrounding the nature of their service and their legal status during the war, and offer a window into some of the challenges involved in interpreting pension documents. Few former slaves' service has proven to be more controversial than Levi Miller's. Miller was issued a Virginia Confederate veteran's pension in 1907, seventeen years before the state expanded its program to include body servants, impressed laborers, and teamsters. Miller entered the war as the camp slave of Captain John J. MacBride of Company C, 5th Texas Infantry Regiment. His name can be found on muster sheets in the section set aside for cooks, servants, and musicians, but by 1864 he occupied a unique place in the regiment. Muster sheets dated to the bloody campaigns of the Wilderness and Spotsylvania Court House in the spring of 1864 have him listed as a private. Decades later Miller was recalled to have been "elected to the rank of private" — a ceremonial move likely made in acknowledgment of his loyalty to his master and conduct in camp.[51] According to his pension application, Miller claimed that he was "engaged in combat with the Army of Northern Virginia in their operations in Tennessee, Georgia, as well as in Virginia until surrendering with the rest of the company at Appomattox." Miller's affidavit was secured from none other than the company commander, Captain J. E. Anderson, who roughly forty years later spoke of him as if he had served as a soldier: "Levi Miller stood by my side and [no] man never fought any better than he did, and when the enemy tried to cross our little breastworks, and we clubbed and bayoneted them off, no one used his bayonet with more skill and effect than Miller."[52]

There can be little doubt that Miller occupied a unique place in his unit and that he assumed many of the roles of a soldier, most importantly as a battlefield combatant. Obituaries published after his death on February 25, 1921, followed Anderson in praising Miller's conduct on the battlefield, but they tended to frame his life as they would have for any former slave who was present with the Confederate army. The *Winchester (Va.) Evening Star*, for instance, claimed that Miller "was one of the few colored men regularly enlisted in the Confederate army," but echoes of the Lost Cause were never far removed: Miller "was affectionately known among the white as well as colored people of this section as the grand old man of his race. He always had a deep love for everything southern, and although born a slave, it was his loyalty to his state that led him to enter the southern army and fight through the four entire years of war."[53] Miller's place in the army straddled the roles of both slave and soldier, but legally he remained the property of John Mac-Bride. It is also worth noting that Miller's name does not appear on any official lists for the 5th Texas Infantry, which suggests that his status as a soldier was honorary. Miller's place within the unit by the end of the war had as much to do with the relationship he established with his master as it did with the relationship he formed with the rest of the men in the unit, but his story is unique and ought to be understood as such.

In 1915 Richard Quarls successfully applied for a South Carolina veterans' pension from his home in Pinellas County, Florida. He gave his birth date as 1833 and his place of residence in Edgefield County, South Carolina. According to his application, Quarles enlisted in 1861 in Company K of the 7th South Carolina Regiment and was "HONORABLY DISCHCHARGED" in 1865 "near Richmond . . . on account of Lee's Surrender." None of this information makes Quarls's application interesting, compared to the thousands of other veterans who took advantage of the state's pension program. What singles this particular application out from the others, however, is the fact that Richard Quarls was enslaved during the war.

Initially the state denied Quarls a pension after finding a number of discrepancies in the two witness affidavits that accompanied his pension application. One witness had been discharged in 1862 and the other was posted in Greensboro, North Carolina, in 1865 and could not possibly testify to Quarls's location at the time of Lee's surrender. Quarls was notified that his name could not be located on available muster rolls and that he would have to locate a former comrade who had "personal knowledge of the facts that you were discharged at the close of the war."[54]

Shortly thereafter Quarls secured an affidavit from Wilson Farris, who testified that he had "known Richard Quarrels all his life" and that he was "the same person whose name appears on the Muster Roll at Washington DC as J. R. Quarrels." Why this witness was accepted and Quarls's pension application approved as a result is difficult to discern, given that there is no evidence that Farris served in the 7th South Carolina. J. Richard Quarles did indeed enlist in the 7th South Carolina Volunteer Infantry on October 5, 1861, but by the end of March 1862 he was admitted to Chimboroza Hospital No. 4 in Richmond. He died of pneumonia a few weeks later. The only connection that can be established between these two men is that J. Richard Quarles was likely the older brother of H. Middleton Quarles, who claimed Richard Quarls as his property. Quarls collected his pension for ten years before his death in 1925. His widow benefited from this case of misidentification until her death in 1951.

Whether Richard Quarls understood that he was collecting the pension of a dead man cannot be known with any certainty. The more interesting question is whether Quarls saw himself as a Confederate soldier when he applied for his pension in 1915. Like countless obituaries written for former slaves, Richard Quarls was remembered as "attached to his master" and was "well known . . . among both white and colored, who thought a great deal of the old man." Confederate veterans likely knew that Quarls was not a soldier, but they welcomed him in their community and sent him to at least one national reunion in Washington, D.C. According to his obituary, "Coming back, he was the proudest man in the colored quarters of the city, as he had seen the great President Wilson."[55] Quarls continued to proudly wear his reunion pin. Unfortunately, little can be said about how he viewed his wartime experience, postwar association with Confederate veterans, or his pension application. He may have viewed the money received as payment for the work he did, but Quarls, like most veterans, probably considered the war as the defining moment in his life — a moment that forty years later had, in his own memory, transcended his legal status at the time as a slave.

In 2003, the SCV and the United Daughters of the Confederacy joined descendants of Richard Quarls at Rose Cemetery in Tarpon Springs, Florida, to dedicate a headstone for his unmarked grave. Quarls's great-granddaughter proclaimed, "He was a proud man and would have been honored to see this." After the singing of "Dixie," the new headstone was unveiled to the delight of onlookers. Both organizations ensured that their choice of inscriptions would leave little doubt that Quarls was to be remembered as a private in Company K, 7th South Carolina Infantry, CSA.[56] A small Confederate battle flag can often be found next to Quarls's headstone, but few visitors will likely question whether the "J. Richard Quarles" inscribed on it refers to the very same man buried at this site.

In 1916, just three years before his death at the age of eighty-two, Silas Chandler completed an "Application of Indigent Servants of Soldier or Sailors of the Late Confederacy." Andrew Chandler served as one of his witnesses. Silas responded in the affirmative that he was "unable to earn a support by your own labor." Shortly thereafter, the state of Mississippi approved his pension application as a former camp slave of Andrew and Benjamin S. Chandler. It is not entirely clear why Silas waited so long to apply for his pension, but his failing vision likely contributed to his financial decline late in life. One possibility, however, is that Silas did not qualify after the state expanded its pension program. Unlike the majority of freedmen in Mississippi and elsewhere, evidence suggests that Silas Chandler prospered in the years following the war.[57]

After the war, Silas returned to West Point, Mississippi, and managed to purchase land. Stories passed down among the white Chandlers maintain that Andrew donated land to Silas in nearby Palo Alto, but land records in the chancery clerk's office do not corroborate these claims. In fact, Silas and his wife, Lucy, purchased land and eventually paid off their debt. Silas remained very active in the community and managed to provide for his growing family. He and Lucy had twelve children, five of whom survived childhood. In 1868, Silas and other freedmen founded Mount Hermon Baptist Church on land adjacent to that owned by Silas's former masters. Silas may have purchased and donated the land. He became a successful businessman, building many houses in and around West Point as well as the first courthouse. Silas's business endeavors very likely benefited from his membership in the Masons. Among his children and grandchildren were a physician, an engineer, a minister, and a school administrator.

Given Silas's success after the war, it is possible that applying for state support may have been a painful process. Silas may also have been reticent about having to face his wartime experiences for the purposes of securing financial support. There is no evidence that he interacted with Confederate veterans in West Point or that he participated in reunions. He appears to have focused on providing for his family. Unlike other state pension programs, Mississippi left little room for applicants to describe their wartime experiences. Silas left blank questions that inquired into wartime wounds. Even a slight embellishment would have given him the opportunity to describe any number of moments during the war, including the bloody fight at Chickamauga, his experience escorting Andrew home following his wounding, and finally his time with Benjamin as part of Jefferson Davis's escort that resulted in his capture by Union cavalry in April 1865. Silas made no attempt to take advantage of the opportunity to recount his wartime experiences and as a result provided little that would be interpreted as an embrace of the Lost Cause. Whatever the case may be, however, by filling out the pension application, Silas ensured that for much of the twentieth century he would be remembered by the state of Mississippi as one of countless former slaves who remained faithful to his master and the Confederate cause to the very end.

Chapter Five

TURNING CAMP SLAVES INTO BLACK CONFEDERATE SOLDIERS

On September 17, 1994, the General William Barksdale Camp 1220, Sons of Confederate Veterans, and John M. Stone Chapter 380, United Daughters of the Confederacy (UDC), placed a Southern Cross of Honor on the grave of Silas Chandler in Greenwood Cemetery in West Point, Mississippi.[1] By honoring him, the SCV transformed an unknown story about an obscure slave into a full-blown legend. Films, art prints, T-shirts, and the spread of the photograph of Silas and Andrew Chandler on the Internet soon followed, all promoting Silas as a loyal son of the South who became a Confederate soldier, heroically battling Yankees alongside his white owner. The Cross of Honor, introduced in 1900 by the UDC, was intended for Confederate soldiers who performed acts of valor on the battlefield. It was about this time that Myra Chandler Sampson, the great-granddaughter of Silas, discovered the marker. For Sampson, it represented nothing less than the SCV's and UDC's goal to "perpetuate myths in attempt to rewrite and sugarcoat the shameful truth about parts of our American history for political and financial gain."[2]

The Confederate heritage community relied on a wide range of accounts of former camp slaves that became popularized by the turn of the twentieth century rather than on Lost Cause narratives from the immediate postwar period. By the 1990s, photographs of uniformed black men as well as pension applications in which the distinction between slave and soldier was sometimes clouded became evidence that the Confederacy recruited large numbers of blacks into the army as soldiers. Interpreting black men in the army as soldiers echoed the Lost Cause's insistence that African Americans were loyal but also constituted a break with the claim that they did so as slaves.

The reinterpretation of Silas Chandler and others as soldiers, serving in an equal capacity to white men, was part of a much broader counternarrative that was first introduced by the SCV in the late 1970s in response to a growing interest among academic historians and the general public in the history of slavery, the role of African Americans in the Union army during the Civil War, and the importance of emancipation. This resurgence of interest picked up speed during the civil rights era as historians and black Americans challenged the central tenets of the Lost Cause, especially the unassailable belief in the loyalty of the slave population. They emphasized the central role that slavery played in causing the war and emancipation as its most important outcome. At the center of this new narrative were stories of black Union soldiers and accounts of their role in helping to destroy the Confederacy and end slavery. Popular magazines such as *Jet* and *Ebony*, literature published by civil rights organizations, and public speeches of civil rights activists embraced the black Union soldier as a reminder of emancipation, freedom, and the "unfinished work" of achieving equal rights. New scholarship focused attention at historic sites and museums on the history of slavery, and popular television shows such as *Roots* introduced Americans to a history of slavery that did not ignore or distort its darkest aspects. This new narrative of the Civil War was later popularized in the 1989 Hollywood movie *Glory*, and aspects of it could also be found in Ken Burns's 1990 award-winning PBS documentary, *The Civil War*. Taken together, these constituted the first sustained attack against the Lost Cause and placed organizations like the SCV and the UDC on the defensive.

The SCV and others viewed this gradual shift as a direct threat to their preferred understanding of the war and the Confederacy in particular, which had remained intact throughout the first half of the twentieth century. Describing slaves like Silas Chandler as soldiers countered the increased attention now being given to the roughly 200,000 black men who served in the army and navy and helped to defeat the Confederacy, end slavery, and preserve the Union. In contrast with African Americans who served in segregated regiments, they argued, black Confederate soldiers served in integrated regiments from the very beginning of the war to its end. The numbers constantly fluctuated. Some argued that the presence of black soldiers was relatively small, numbering only a few thousand, while others insisted that it rose to the tens of thousands. For the proponents of this narrative, these black soldiers helped to defuse a growing acceptance that the goal of the

Confederacy was the protection of slavery and white supremacy. If black men served in the Confederate army as soldiers, and alongside white men, then not only was the protection of slavery not its central purpose, but its brief history could be understood as a small piece of a larger civil rights story. Heritage advocates could rightfully argue that the Confederacy was as responsible for the end of slavery as the United States was.

The scv could not have anticipated the early success of this black Confederate narrative. Stories of loyal black soldiers grew and spread, from a small number of books published by vanity presses to museum exhibits, history textbooks, and even National Park Service presentations. Silas quickly became the face of the black Confederate soldier, and with the rise of the Internet by the last decade of the twentieth century, this new narrative was soon featured on thousands of websites. Social media sites such as Facebook, Twitter, and blogs provided an ideal platform on which to introduce stories of black Confederate soldiers to the general public, which frequently uncritically accepted these accounts as historical fact. Conservatives also embraced the black Confederate narrative more openly as a way to respond to black political activism, the widening culture war, and especially the election of Barack Obama in 2008. While the black Confederate narrative has its roots in the Lost Cause memory of the war, by the beginning of the twenty-first century it had been transformed in a way that would be unidentifiable by the generation that fought the war as well as by those who commemorated the loyal camp slave through the Jim Crow era.

By the beginning of the twentieth century, former camp slaves held a central place in the Civil War memory of Confederate veterans and the broader mainstream culture. Camp servants and impressed slaves were remembered in popular works of history, advertisements, and Hollywood movies as embracing the cause of their masters and the Confederacy. No one was confused about the status of slaves in the Confederate war effort throughout much of the twentieth century. The Confederacy mobilized slaves, not soldiers, in its war for independence.

Evidence that the memory of camp servants resonated with Americans beyond the former Confederacy can be found in General Electric's use of Robert E. Lee and a camp servant in its advertisements for its new electric vacuum washing machine. In an ad that appeared in the *New York Tribune* in 1920, Lee sits in front of his tent reading over official papers while his camp servant dutifully washes his socks in a nearby stream. "Lee's body servant followed him all through the war," explains the ad. "Whenever the Southern

The use of Robert E. Lee and his camp slave to sell washing machines
in the early twentieth century points to the popularity of the Lost Cause
and the memory of the loyal body servant beyond the former Confederacy.
(Chronicling America, Library of Congress)

general set up his headquarters, there was the faithful black fellow ready to put the great leader's clothes in order." The selling point for this appliance pivoted on the reader appreciating that the machine's metal vacuum cups would "do the work by air pressure and suction more thoroughly and more delicately than the careful hands of Lee's old body servant."[3] The choice to use Lee and a camp servant to sell electrical appliances points to the popularity of the Lost Cause and, in particular, the memory of the loyal slave in popular culture by the early twentieth century.

No Hollywood film did more to shape public memory of the war and slavery in the twentieth century than the 1939 masterpiece *Gone with the Wind*. Characters such as Mammy, Prissy, and Pork typified the house slaves of the "Old South" who remained loyal through the war and Reconstruction. Although camp servants did not make an appearance in the film, it does allude to the place of African Americans in the Confederate army. During the evacuation of Atlanta, amid all the confusion of federal shells and runaway carriages, Scarlett O'Hara happens upon a long line of black men carrying shovels, including "Big Sam" and others from Tara. Scarlett learns that the Confederate government had impressed Sam and the rest of the "field hands" into service over the objections of her father "to dig ditches for white soldiers to hide in." They part company after Scarlett learns of news from Tara and Sam encourages her to not give up hope: "Don't worry, we'll stop them Yankees." Audiences in 1939 would have had little difficulty interpreting Big Sam's loyal Confederate rhetoric as that of an impressed slave and not as a soldier.

In movies set during the Civil War era, Hollywood continued well into the 1960s to present African Americans as loyal and docile slaves who were uninterested in attaining their freedom.[4] By then, however, a concerted effort was well under way to correct this narrow and misleading narrative of the role of slaves and free blacks in the Civil War. The convergence of the Civil War centennial with the civil rights movement encouraged African Americans to correct a historical record that was still influenced by the Lost Cause and the language of national reunion. Civil rights leaders such as A. Philip Randolph criticized commemoration events as a "stupendous brain-washing exercise to make the Civil War leaders of the South on par with the Civil War leaders of the North, and to strike a blow against men of color and human dignity." The authors of a pamphlet published by the Vanguard Society of America argued that centennial planners intended "to build up the Dixiecrats, to put billions of new dollars into their hands, to offset civil rights gains in the South and to destroy the broad mass movement for Negro-white unity for civil rights."[5]

As part of their critical assessment of the centennial, African Americans offered a robust counter-memory of the Civil War that highlighted the importance of slavery in bringing about secession and war, a bottom-up narrative that emphasized their own roles as full historical agents in achieving their freedom as well as the sacrifice and heroism of black soldiers on the battlefield. Popular accounts of the U.S. Colored Troops benefited from the scholarship of Benjamin Quarles, Dudley Cornish, and John Hope Franklin, all of whom published important studies in the 1950s and 1960s.[6]

This scholarly work filtered down to the black American middle class and beyond through newspapers such as the *Richmond Afro-American* and popular magazines like *Jet* and *Ebony*. These publications covered a wide range of topics related to the steps that ordinary African Americans took to win their freedom by 1865. Well-known lithographs depicting black soldiers in battle accompanied stories of Medal of Honor winners and other brave deeds on the battlefield. *Ebony* published a regular column featuring key moments in the Civil War, including battles that involved black soldiers, such as the famous charge of the 54th Massachusetts Volunteer Infantry at Battery Wagner as well as other regiments that fought at the Crater and New Market Heights.[7]

While most civil rights activists between 1961 and 1965 concentrated on the more immediate goal of political empowerment rather than on challenging popular perceptions of the Civil War, their actions, along with other factors, led to significant changes to how the war was interpreted at museums and historical sites in the decades to follow. The civil rights movement itself underscored the "unfinished work" of interpretation that was needed at historical institutions. As late as the early 1970s, no major museum had yet to move beyond the Lost Cause narrative to tackle the tough questions related to the history of slavery and its connection to the Civil War and Reconstruction. Reinterpretation came about slowly as a result of ideological resistance within institutions, the availability of artifacts necessary to interpret a more complex past, and the funds required to promote research and new exhibits. During this same time, advances in the scholarship of slavery and of the military history of the war aided the efforts of institutions, which chose to answer calls to expand and revise their site interpretations. Historians of slavery and the Civil War continued to uncover the myriad ways in which the actions of enslaved people on the plantation, in contraband camps, and eventually in the army itself contributed to Union victory, while military historians broadened their understanding of battles and campaigns to include the experiences of noncombatants and the war's impact on the home front. Such scholarship opened up opportunities for public historians to challenge many deeply ingrained institutional narratives with new exhibits and programming.[8]

This new generation of public historians and museum specialists, trained in social history, uncovered new stories that gradually moved their institutions away from outdated interpretations. By 1979 the first black reenactors, who performed roles as slaves and free blacks, could be found at Colonial Williamsburg and later at reconstructed slave quarters at nearby Carter's Grove. Efforts to broaden the interpretation at individual Civil War sites in the National Park system by including the roles of slaves and black soldiers as well as the development of new museums devoted to the civil rights movement continued the work of highlighting the nation's often contentious and dark past.[9]

It was within this environment that the first references to black Confederate soldiers emerged, not as an attempt to advance this new scholarship and public memory but to push back vigorously against it. The more immediate catalyst for this sudden shift resulted from the publication of Alex Haley's *Roots: The Saga of an American Family* in 1976 and the airing of the Emmy- and Golden Globe–award-winning television series of the same name, which aired the following year. The twelve-hour series explored the multigenerational history of author Alex Haley's family, which began with the kidnapping of Kunta Kinte in Africa and his eventual sale as a slave in Maryland in 1767. The story follows Kunta Kinte and subsequent generations through the horrors of antebellum slavery and the Civil War before finally some of the family attained property in Tennessee. The series was the third highest rated episode for any type of television series and the second most watched overall series finale in U.S. television history. The success of *Roots* demonstrated that Americans were now increasingly willing to face some of the tough questions related to the history of slavery and race. Its depiction of slavery and the Confederacy attracted the attention of the leadership in the SCV.

Since the creation of the organization in 1896, the SCV's hold on defending the legacy of the Confederacy remained unchecked throughout much of the twentieth century. In recent decades, membership has hovered around 30,000, spread out over roughly 800 local camps. Members are bound together by their shared ancestral connection to a Confederate soldier, whose legacy is their principal concern. That legacy has nearly always revolved around a defense of the Lost Cause narrative of the war, which fell under increased scrutiny by the 1970s and in response to growing calls to remove Confederate battle flags and monuments. In contrast with the UDC, which assumed a less public posture, the SCV's rhetoric took on a more defensive and political tone in its attempt to camouflage the white-supremacist history surrounding secession and Confederate policies throughout the war.[10] Its response to *Roots* was an important moment in the battle over Civil War memory.

SCV commander in chief Dean Boggs described *Roots* as the modern "'Uncle Tom's Cabin'" that did a "great disservice to our Country and the public welfare." Boggs objected to scenes that included the sale of slaves, the emotional separation of families, and the horrors associated with the rape of black women. According to Boggs, this "could only produce hatred of whites by blacks, it could only have a divisive effect." More importantly, "it slandered the South and the Southern people." In response, the SCV instituted a letter-writing campaign to the chairman of the Federal Communications Commission and the president of the American Broadcasting Company.[11]

The success of *Roots* was nothing less than a call to arms for the SCV's leadership and rank and file. In addition to concerns about *Roots*, the SCV sought to counter recent efforts by the NAACP to ban the display of the Confederate flag and the playing of "Dixie." The organization commissioned Francis W. Springer to write "a book on the contribution of Negroes in the south to the Confederate war effort"; many, it was assumed, "were under arms and in combat." The seriousness with which the SCV took the success of *Roots* proved to be prescient, given the continued calls to remove Confederate iconography from public places that only grew louder through the 1980s. By highlighting the "valuable contributions to the Confederate war effort" made by African Americans, the SCV hoped to undercut these efforts by crafting a shared narrative that united blacks and whites.[12]

The release of the movie *Glory* in 1989 constituted an even more direct challenge to the SCV's preferred narrative of a Confederate war effort that its members believed united both races. The movie introduced a wide segment of the general public to the still relatively unknown subject of the service of black Union soldiers during the Civil War. *Glory* told the story of the men who served in the 54th Massachusetts Volunteer Infantry and their commander, Colonel Robert G. Shaw, the account culminating in the failed but brave assault at Battery Wagner in July 1863. The movie, starring Denzel Washington (who won an Academy Award for Best Supporting Actor), Morgan Freeman, and Matthew Broderick, offered audiences a heroic account of

Turning Camp Slaves into Black Confederate Soldiers

the trials faced by the men in the regiment and traced the evolution of Shaw's relationship with the men under his command. In addition to the film's dramatic battle scenes, the subject of the Confederacy's disdain for black soldiers and Confederates' commitment to treating them on the battlefield as rebellious slaves was also introduced.

One year later, Ken Burns's *The Civil War* aired on PBS. Burns devoted significant time to placing slavery and emancipation at the center of the narrative as well as the service of African Americans in the U.S. military. The success of both productions and their placement of slavery and the maintenance of white supremacy as central to the Confederate experience energized those committed to telling the story of the black Confederate narrative and its implications for how the Civil War was now remembered. Throughout this period, Confederate heritage organizations like the SCV relied on the magazine *Confederate Veteran* and a small number of books to rebut an interpretation of the Civil War that now highlighted a war against the Confederacy as a fight for freedom and equality.[13]

The SCV responded directly to the success of both productions but reserved its harshest review for *The Civil War*, which it criticized for its "Northern bias, distortions, outright factual mistakes and single-cause theory for the reason for the war."[14] Pointing out Burns's many "distortions" and "bias" served as a springboard to highlight the history that the SCV believed had been intentionally overlooked, including the fact that "the great majority of Southern blacks had remained loyal to the South." In his review of the series, Joseph Mitchell offered what quickly became the standard account of the role that African Americans played in the Confederate military. Mitchell acknowledged that the Confederate Congress did not officially authorize the recruitment of slaves as soldiers until March 1865 but insisted that "from the beginning all Confederate Armies had blacks with them." Reliance on Dr. Lewis Steiner's observations of a large number of armed black men with Lee's army during the 1862 Maryland campaign, as well as an assortment of references to monuments commemorating the "loyalty" of Southern blacks and militia units, rounded out a picture of the racial profile of the army that ultimately failed to acknowledge blacks' status as slaves. According to Mitchell, "blacks were fighting for the preservation of their homes" just as their white comrades were doing.[15]

The SCV also used *Confederate Veteran* magazine to profile African Americans who it believed would help to promote "an environment in which all Southerners, whether of African or Confederate descent, can work together in harmony to build a society with a foundation planted on our common roots."[16] The November–December 1992 issue, for example, featured an article on "Ten-Cent Bill" Yopp and Amos Rucker. Both men were recognized for their roles as body servants, but the author still managed to cloud his narrative by avoiding the acknowledgment of their legal status as slaves and instead emphasizing acts that could easily be interpreted as an expression of their Confederate loyalty both during and after the war. Amos Rucker became "a brave soldier when he picked up the weapon of a dead member of his unit and charged the enemy line." Rucker "exhibited such bravery," according to the author, "that he was to perform as a combat soldier for the remainder of the war." Bill Yopp's master sent him home following the battle of Fredericksburg, but he "soon went back" and "remained with the Captain until the end of the War." Even more confusing is the author's identification of Yopp after the war as a "black veteran" who worked tirelessly to assist his former comrades in their old age by raising money for their Old Soldiers' Home. There is no attempt to understand the actions of either of the two men—during the war or after—as anything other than a reflection of their unquestioned loyalty to the men in their respective units and the Confederacy.[17]

The goal was almost always the same, regardless of the subject of the profile: counter the growing attacks on the Confederacy that "it was created" solely to protect slavery and white supremacy. Rallying Yopp, Rucker, and others once again around the colors served both as a response to Ken Burns and other perceived threats to the memory of the Confederacy and as a building block in a burgeoning interpretation that insisted that "the overwhelming majority of blacks during the War Between the States supported and defended, with armed resistance, the cause of Southern Independence." More importantly, these narratives reinforced scv members' own personal ties to their Confederate ancestors and the conviction that "our ancestors were not racist."[18]

Stories of African Americans in Confederate ranks were also utilized by the scv to counter increasing calls to remove the Confederate battle flag and monuments from public spaces. The scv mobilized a team of researchers in response to calls to take down a monument in Lake Charles, Louisiana, by a candidate for lieutenant governor who claimed it "was a symbol of racial injustice" and "an insult to Blacks." Researchers focused specifically on the history of slavery in the community in order to fend off the "inevitable charges about the Confederacy fighting to preserve slavery." In addition to pointing out the relatively low rate of slave ownership in the community, the team highlighted "three documented cases of free Black men serving

Turning Camp Slaves into Black Confederate Soldiers

in the Confederate Army" from Calcasieu Parish, including one individual who "had acquired a very distinguished combat record as an infantryman." The SCV succeeded in protecting the monument by reinterpreting it as commemorating the service and sacrifice of black and white soldiers. On Confederate Memorial Day, June 3, 1995, Lake Parish held a ceremony to rededicate its monument.[19]

Books with colorful and defiant titles such as *Southern by the Grace of God* (1988) by Michael Grissom and *The South Was Right!* (1991) by James Ronald Kennedy and Walter Donald Kennedy offered powerful defenses of the Confederacy for those people who were coming to feel increasingly under siege. The Kennedy brothers, in particular, echoed the SCV's earlier warnings by issuing a "call to action to all people who love liberty and truth . . . to take pride in their Southern heritage."[20] Members of the SCV and founding members of the League of the South, the authors argued that secession had nothing to do with slavery. They challenged the assumption that free blacks in the North were better off than slaves and denied that the Confederacy was defending slavery. Race relations in the South, according to the Kennedys, were peaceful before they were disrupted by an illegal invasion led by Lincoln, and the Southern defense united both whites and blacks. Their argument for large numbers of blacks under arms was based largely on Dr. Lewis Steiner's already discussed observations of the presence of uniformed and armed blacks with the army during the Maryland campaign of 1862. Like others, the authors accepted the account without any attempt to provide historical context. "They were there," the Kennedys concluded, "because, just like their white counterparts, they were fighting an invader." The reports alone were considered sufficient to justify their overall conclusions about the war: "With such testimony, how can anyone continue to believe the myth that Southern blacks were longing for Yankee-induced freedom? How can anyone continue to accept the Yankee abolitionist view of a hate-filled and evil South? The truth is that life in the Old South was very different from that which the 'politically correct' historians would have us believe. Yes, there were many blacks who fought for the South."[21] The authors' analysis of what it meant for blacks to fight for the Confederacy as well as their status in the army is both vague and confusing. Camp servants functioned more like "bodyguards," given the dangers they faced when present on the battlefield. According to the Kennedy brothers, any black man who risked his life, regardless of his official role, is considered to have fought for the South.

Charles Kelly Barrow, J. H. Segars, and R. B. Rosenburg's *Black Confederates*, which was published in 1995, focused more specifically on the military service of blacks in the Confederacy and remains to this day one of the most popular titles in the genre. The authors solicited documentation in the wake of *Glory* and *The Civil War* "about blacks loyal to the South" from fellow scv members and over a period of five years collected a wide range of primary sources, including pension records, memorial inscriptions, speeches, obituaries, and newspaper accounts. The book featured a uniformed camp slave from Georgia by the name of Marlboro Jones on the cover. The result is an often-confusing examination of the many roles free and enslaved blacks filled for the army as well as a consideration of individual Confederate states and the federal government in Richmond. What is lacking in analytical rigor is offset by a firm conviction that "black Confederates were not fighting for their own enslavement but sincerely believed that their ultimate freedom, prosperity, and destiny lay south of the Mason-Dixon line."[22]

None of the print sources published during this period had much of an impact beyond a small, select group of readers within the Southern heritage community. Such publications, however, did establish a foundation for the black Confederate narrative that would change very little moving forward. Barrow, Segars, and Rosenburg, the Kennedys, and other authors paid little attention to how actual Confederates understood the presence of camp servants and impressed slaves in the army both during and after the war. In stark contrast, wartime and postwar accounts of camp slaves and free blacks who served in various capacities, along with photographs, were now interpreted as indisputable evidence of loyal military service to master or the Confederacy. They all "served" or "fought" without any acknowledgment of the racial hierarchy that framed the master-slave relationship or official Confederate policy that defined and limited the roles of free and enslaved blacks during the war.

It is impossible to imagine the popularity of the black Confederate narrative today without the advent of the World Wide Web by the mid-1990s. It did not take long for stories and photographs of African Americans in Confederate uniform to populate the Internet. Many of these websites were created by members of the scv who viewed them as effective vehicles to spread their understanding of the war beyond the confines of their narrow community, but just as many have no official affiliation with any organization. Thousands of websites, created by people with little or no training in historical analysis or understanding of the history itself, now tell the story of the black Confederate soldier. Many of the primary sources that can be found are unaccompanied by any explanation or relevant historical context. An example of this approach is the scv's own website, which asserts that "over

65,000 Southern blacks were in the Confederate ranks," without any explanation of how the number was arrived at, followed by a list of fragmentary
historical references. The frequency of specific photographs and accounts
suggests that the content of many websites has been cut and pasted from
one site to another.[23] The problem is compounded by the inability on the
part of many Internet users to properly search and assess the information
produced by search engines. Consumers of the black Confederate narrative,
many of whom have no affiliation with the SCV or any other Confederate
heritage organization, also lack sufficient background knowledge with which
to evaluate these stories or the ability to effectively evaluate the reliability
of the websites themselves. Visitors to many of these websites are often un-
knowingly exposed to primary sources that have either been misinterpreted
or even manipulated.

An example of the latter involves a photograph, incorrectly referenced
as black soldiers in the Louisiana Native Guard, which can be found on hundreds of websites. In 1973 the popular magazine *Civil War Times Illustrated*
published a copy of a photograph of black Union soldiers taken at Camp
William Penn, just outside of Philadelphia, some time in 1864.[24] The original
photograph had been used during the war to create a colored lithograph for
the recruitment of African Americans into the federal army. The lithograph
was embellished by transferring the men and their white officer from a ster-
ile studio setting to a military camp surrounded by trees, tent, and flag. The
published lithograph was clearly labeled "United States soldiers at Camp
'William Penn' Philadelphia, PA," and its accompanying caption similarly
reads "United States Soldiers at Camp 'William Penn' Philadelphia" along
with the sub-caption "Rally Round the Flag, boys! Rally once again, Shout-
ing the battle cry of FREEDOM." At some point after its appearance in the
magazine, the original photograph was scanned and digitally manipulated,
most significantly by removing the white officer on the far left and door
frame on the right, which was likely intended to convince the viewer that the
image was taken in the field. Finally, a new label was added using a modern
font: "1st Louisiana Native Guard 1861." The photograph went on sale at the
now defunct online store RebelStore.com, which advertised it as "Members
of the first all Black Confederate Unit organized in New Orleans in 1861."
As we have already seen, the Louisiana Native Guard never saw service in
the Confederate army, but within a short period of time the image was featured on hundreds of websites as the clearest evidence that large numbers of
African American men fought as soldiers for the Confederacy in organized
regiments.[25]

This low-resolution image of black Union soldiers was originally published in *Civil War Times Illustrated* in 1973. A cropped and digitally manipulated version leaving out the white officer can now be found on hundreds of websites as indisputable proof of the existence of black Confederate soldiers.

The intentional manipulation of primary sources in support of the black Confederate narrative is rare. More often photographs and other representations such as monuments that depict black men in uniform are simply misinterpreted, often in ways that directly contradict how earlier generations understood their meaning. Consider recent online interpretations of the Confederate monument at Arlington National Cemetery designed by Moses Ezekiel and dedicated in 1914 by the UDC. The monument has been cited numerous times across the Internet because of its inclusion of what appears to be a black soldier marching off to battle on one of the tableaux—despite the fact that the UDC's own official history of the monument refers to the individual as a "faithful negro body-servant following his young master." According to one Internet author, Ezekiel's camp servant is a "black Confederate soldier . . . marching in rank with white Confederate soldiers," and the memorial itself is identified as "one of the first monument[s], if not the first, honoring a black American soldier."[26] Another website refers to the Ezekiel monument as evidence that black Confederates served in combat. The author assumes that because Ezekiel was Jewish, "he knew firsthand the nature of the ethnic composition of the Confederate army, observations which he recorded in the first military monument to honor a black American soldier in Washington, D.C."[27]

Arguably, the most enduring black Confederate narratives on the Internet are those centered on photographs of former camp slaves. "Black Rebels of the C.S.A.," on the Texas Confederate Veterans website, is typical, featuring a number of photographs of uniformed black men taken during and after the war. Most are unidentified and lack any reference to the date and location at which the photographs were taken. According to the author, had the Confederacy won its independence "from the tyrannical Yankee government the Southern Blacks today would be bragging on their ancestors that

Turning Camp Slaves into Black Confederate Soldiers

fought and served in Dixie's War for Independence." Just above the manipulated photograph of the Louisiana Native Guard the author goes on to suggest that the "service they rendered was made in love and devotion for their beloved Dixie and oft times with exceptional heroism."[28] Other sites simply list excerpts from wartime and postwar accounts without any attempt at providing analysis or historical context.[29] Historical analysis is almost always lacking on these websites, but they are not short on bold statements of black loyalty and condemnation of "revisionist" and "politically correct" historians who have failed to acknowledge the existence of these men or are actively trying to prevent this information from reaching the public.

On occasion the analysis provided crosses into the absurd. Consider the website created by Ann DeWitt, which now focuses on genealogical research to identify African Americans who may have been present with the Confederate army. The website's earlier iteration offered her own unique interpretation of how to understand the various roles filled by enslaved blacks. "A body servant," according to DeWitt, "is a gentleman's gentleman." "In 21st century vernacular the role is analogous to a position known as an executive assistant—a position today," continues DeWitt, "that requires a college Bachelors Degree or equivalent level experience." Needless to say, the author fails to provide any examples of executive assistants who are legally owned by their superiors.[30] Even more troubling was DeWitt's misreading of a document detailing rations for a Texas heavy regiment under the command of Colonel Joseph J. Cook as evidence that the Confederate army included an entire regiment of African American cooks. This blatant example of presentism in trying to equate chattel with executive assistants as well as the fumbling of primary sources would be worth a chuckle but for the fact that the website remains a popular destination for people interested in this subject.[31]

No photograph has proven to be more popular than that of Andrew and Silas Chandler. The photograph has been reproduced on countless websites and is an easy target for those who want to reimagine the nature of black Confederate service. At the "Black Confederate Soldiers of Petersburg" page of the *Petersburg Express* website, the image is accompanied by a caption that reads "A Picture is Worth a Thousand Words! Who is it that deny these 'Brothers' today?"[32] An scv chapter in Florida includes the image on its website with the caption "Andrew Chandler and his lifelong friend, Silas Chandler, who accompanied Andrew to war and remained true to the South his entire life." A description of the relationship between Silas and Andrew on the "Black Heroes in Gray" page of the website Bog Bit picks up on a number of themes in the black Confederate narrative. Silas, who is incorrectly referred to as a "former slave," voluntarily went to war with Andrew. The two "fought the enemy in defense of their homeland back to back." The author reaffirms Silas's loyalty to Andrew by assuming that "he could have made it to the Yankee lines if he did not want to be there or simply run off."[33]

The popularity that Andrew and Silas achieved on the Internet led them to being featured on a T-shirt from Dixie Outfitters — a company that offers a range of products for customers who are "proud" of their ancestors "who fought and died in the Southern War for Independence." Some of their more popular designs feature images of Robert E. Lee, Stonewall Jackson, and Nathan Bedford Forrest as well as the Confederate battle flag with the declaration "Fighting Terrorism Since 1861." The designers at Dixie Outfitters depict "The Chandler Boys" on a boxcar heading home following Andrew's wounding at the battle of Chickamauga. Silas wraps a fresh bandage around the leg of "his wounded boyhood friend" that he supposedly prevented doctors from amputating. The accompanying text indicates that after the war the two "remained close friends till death." Both men are in full uniform, which obscures the coercive nature of the master-slave relationship.[34]

The scv could not have anticipated the reach that the black Confederate narrative would achieve as a result of the growing pervasiveness of the Internet when it first issued its call to arms in the late 1970s. Demands to remove battle flags and monuments from public spaces grew louder during the last decade of the twentieth century. In 2001 the state of Georgia removed the Confederate battle flag from its state flag. That same year, the Confederate battle flag was lowered from atop the statehouse in Columbia, South Carolina, after having flown there continuously since 1962. As part of a compromise deal with the NAACP, the flag was transferred to a pole next to a Confederate soldier on the capitol grounds.[35] scv members and others continued to rally around stories of loyal black soldiers as a way to defend their heritage and their understanding of the history of race in the South.

Given the accessibility of the photograph of Andrew and Silas Chandler and stories of African Americans under arms for the Confederacy, it was just a matter of time before these stories moved beyond the Internet entirely. Visitors to the Old Court House Museum in Vicksburg, Mississippi, were introduced to the black Confederate narrative perhaps as early as the 1960s, but the exhibit was likely updated in the 1990s as these stories gained popularity. During a visit, which was eventually chronicled in his best-selling book *Confederates in the Attic*, author Tony Horwitz described the museum as "the most eccentric — and politically incorrect — collection I'd visited in the South." The museum contains a Ku Klux Klan hood, Confederate trousers

Turning Camp Slaves into Black Confederate Soldiers

made by a slave, as well as a minié ball that "reportedly passed through the reproductive organs of a young rebel soldier and a few seconds later penetrated a young lady who was standing on the porch of her nearby home." Nine months later, according to the exhibit, this woman gave birth.[36]

Artifacts and documents are displayed in the Old Court House Museum as part of a Lost Cause narrative that highlights the loyalty of the South's slave population throughout the war and serves as the backdrop for the *Blacks Who Wore Gray* exhibit. The exhibit features a hodgepodge of photographs, including uniformed slaves and an elderly black man waving a Confederate flag, and assorted quotes that leave the visitor with more questions than answers. "Black Confederate patriotism," the visitor learns, "took many forms." It included "slaves devoted to their masters, free blacks who donated money and labor, blacks who joined the Confederate Army, and slaves who loyally supervised plantations of absentee owners." The text accompanying the photograph of Andrew and Silas Chandler refers to both men as members of the 44th Mississippi Infantry. No information is provided about these men during or after the war. Visitors are left to fend for themselves with random quotes from Nathan Bedford Forrest and paeans "to the faithful slaves, who loyal to a sacred trust, toiled for the support of the Army, [and] with matchless devotion and sterling fidelity guarded our defenseless homes, women and children, during the struggle for the principles of our Confederate States of America." The exhibit interprets these men as soldiers, volunteering and fighting for their homes and way of life, but they are never allowed to speak for themselves — the only ones allowed to speak on their behalf are white, and even then only to praise their loyalty and fidelity to the Confederacy.

The appearance of camp servants in popular works of art also signaled their growing popularity among Civil War enthusiasts. Artist Bradley Schmehl offered two battlefield scenes in which African Americans are prominently featured. In *Grim Harvest of War*, dead and wounded soldiers on both sides litter the ground on the battlefield near Port Republic, Virginia. Stonewall Jackson looks over the scene of another in a string of victories during the Shenandoah Valley campaign of 1862. Below Jackson a uniformed camp slave rests the head of his dead master on his knee. Distraught, he looks up at the heavens, tears flowing down his face. Schmehl makes an even bolder claim in *Press Forward, Men*, which once again features the men under the command of Jackson, this time at the precise moment when they slammed into the flank of the Union Eleventh Corps at Chancellorsville in May 1863. Among those marching out of the woods and into the clearing is a uniformed and armed black man. Both paintings echo the broad trajec-

Civil War artists capitalized on the popularity of the black Confederate myth.
In *Grim Harvest of War*, Bradley Schmehl features a "black Confederate"
cradling a Confederate officer as Stonewall Jackson looks over the battlefield.
(Courtesy of Bradley Schmehl Fine Art, bradleyschmehl.com)

tory of the loyal slave narrative that stretches back to the war itself, but as examples of the new shift toward interpreting these men as soldiers in the Confederate army, they constitute a break with the Lost Cause emphasis on them as slaves.[37]

Even the National Park Service fell under the spell of the black Confederate narrative. As late as 2010, the Corinth Interpretive Center at Shiloh included a panel with the image of Andrew and Silas Chandler. Not only was Silas misidentified as Andrew's "former slave," but the description also obscured the crucial master-slave distinction: "both boys fought together at Chickamauga." The panel text also indicated that Silas later received a "Mississippi Confederate Veteran Pension," which is incorrect.[38] The National Park Service at Shiloh National Military Park eventually revised the panel text after being informed of the problems. Silas is now clearly referred to as Andrew's slave, and the pension that the former received after the war is properly identified as an "Indigent Servant's pension."

A handout made available in 2010 to visitors at Governors Island National Monument in New York indicated that "65,000 black men served as Confederate soldiers." The text included numerous factual mistakes within an overall interpretation of the Confederacy that is best described as confused, and the author speculated as to why black Southerners fought for the Confederacy: some "held strong loyalties" to their respective states, while others "desired the pay" or "were defending their homes from invading Northern troops, who would sometimes capture large groups of slaves to punish white secessionists, as well as rape black women." The author turned out to be an undergraduate from Columbia University who relied heavily on books endorsed or written by SCV members. The handout was eventually removed, though it is unclear why such "information" was shared at a historic site in New York in the first place.[39]

The presence of the black Confederate narrative in museums and NPS exhibits coincided with the continued expansion of and access to the Internet by the late 1990s and into the next century. For consumers of history incapable of properly assessing the content of individual websites, the number of search engine hits alone was viewed as sufficient proof that significant numbers of black Confederates served loyally as soldiers in Confederate armies. These easily accessible stories continued to advance the agenda of the SCV, but they also fed an increased call to uncover untapped stories from African American history, especially during Black History Month. The black Confederate was fast becoming part of the standard narrative of the Civil War.

This new focus on black soldiers led to a resurgence of interest in Major General Patrick Cleburne, whose proposal to arm slaves in early 1864 helped to push the controversial topic into the public spotlight later that same year. Cleburne quickly became a popular subject for Civil War artists. In 2009 the city of Ringgold, Georgia, dedicated a statue to Cleburne to commemorate his role at the battle of Ringgold Gap, but it was his enlistment plan that many in the SCV and beyond came to embrace as a way to recast the history of race relations in American history. Justin Murphy's *Cleburne: A Graphic Novel* begins in the middle of a dream in which the general imagines an entire regiment of black soldiers rushing onto the battlefield to save the day for the Confederacy. In Murphy's hands Cleburne is a tragic figure whose plan to enlist slaves blocked his further promotion and led to conflict with his superiors and fellow officers, who viewed him with suspicion and his actions as possibly treasonous. The author — not a member of the SCV — is on solid historical ground here, but the story enters the realm of fiction in its portrayal of Cleburne's racial attitudes. Cleburne befriends a free black man named Ned who is attached to the army as a teamster. Ned is a crack shot and manages to beat a sharpshooter in a contest but is quickly disarmed by a Confederate officer. Cleburne subsequently learns that Ned's family has been sold off to an owner in Georgia and ultimately helps to reunite them.

Ned and other African Americans want nothing more than to fight as soldiers in the Confederate army. "I'm a Southerner same as you general," explains Ned to Cleburne. In Murphy's imagination, even captured black Union soldiers are willing to shed their blue uniforms for Confederate gray with little concern for the larger consequences. For one soldier, "Freedom is freedom, blue or gray." In their final moments together before the ill-fated battle of Franklin that left Cleburne dead on the battlefield, the general hands Ned a note indicating where he can find his family in Georgia and apologizes for "failing" the army's African American laborers in their quest to fight as soldiers. According to Murphy, Cleburne's proposal went further than outlining a narrow military plan that would increase the likelihood of Confederate independence. Ultimately, Cleburne's vision of an interracial military force offered the Confederate nation the opportunity to start over in recreating the very foundation of race relations in the South.[40]

Plans to turn Murphy's *Cleburne* into a movie fell through, but by then stories of loyal African Americans had already been embraced by Hollywood. In 1999 director Ang Lee leveraged a black Confederate narrative from the periphery of the Civil War in Missouri and Kansas that pitted local Southern bushwhackers against pro-Union Jayhawkers in a violent border war. *Ride with the Devil* centers on Confederate guerrillas Jacob "Jake" or "Dutchy" Roedel (played by Toby Maguire), Jack Bull Chiles, George Clyde, and a free black man, Daniel Holt (played by Jeffrey Wright). Early on, viewers learn that George Clyde's father owned Holt before his own violent death at the hands of Jayhawkers. Audiences also learn that Holt killed three Kansas Jayhawkers who threatened Clyde and is now a target himself as a result. In one scene George Clyde leaves little doubt as to Holt's status in the film and his own feelings toward his family's former property: "He's not my nigger. He's just a nigger who I trust with my life every day and every night, that's all." Holt later reveals to Jacob Roedel that he purchased his freedom and hopes one day to search for his mother, who was sold off to a planter in Texas.

The relationship between Clyde and Holt is complex, but the latter's role within the broader unit, which at one point was led by William Clarke Quantrill in the famous raid against Lawrence, Kansas, in 1863, is not entirely clear. It is the relationship between Roedel and Holt that frames the narrative arc of the movie. Both are deemed to be outsiders whose loyalties to the

Confederacy are questioned — Roedel because of his German-born (Union-ist) family and Holt as a black man in a slave state. The two men become closer partly as a result of watching friends, including George Clyde, die vio-lent deaths and partly from their regrets at having participated in the Law-rence Raid, which left 164 civilians dead and significant personal property destroyed. Holt confesses that he did not join the unit because of his devo-tion to the Confederacy but because of his loyalty to George. With George's death Holt is able to envision a future for himself completely unshackled from slavery and the family that once claimed him as property. In the final scene, Holt leaves Jacob to search for his mother in a dramatic moment that fully embraces his emancipation from the violence of Civil War Missouri for a new life and perhaps a reunion with his mother in Texas.

Ride with the Devil offers vivid depictions of the violence that engulfed the border states in what is best characterized as a civil war within the broader Civil War. Unfortunately, the film does little to flesh out the role of African Americans (free or enslaved) in guerrilla units or explain how they understood what was transpiring around them and how it fit into the broader goal of Confederate independence. The character of Daniel Holt is based loosely on John Noland, who was present among Quantrill's band of Confederate guerrillas. There is no evidence that Noland was ever given his freedom. Contrary to the movie, Asbury Noland was not gunned down by Jayhawkers and still claimed John as his property as late as 1860. Noland revealed his legal status as a slave during the war. Finally, claims of Holt de-fending his master's family and killing three Jayhawkers, as depicted in *Ride with the Devil*, are unsupported by the available historical record.[41]

In contrast to the film, Noland did not ride off into the sunset a free man but remained in his home in Jackson County, Missouri, until his death in 1908, still constrained by the harsh realities of postwar racial violence that limited the liberty of newly freed slaves. The movie helped to blur the bound-aries between the fictional Holt and Noland, but its popularity among Con-federate heritage advocates often resulted in ascribing Noland with the mo-tivations expressed by Holt or assuming the latter's legal status as a free man. In doing so, the movie helped to undermine the importance of the master-slave relationship that evolved between Confederates and their camp slaves. Not surprisingly, Noland grew in popularity within the Confederate heritage community as a result of the movie, particularly the scv, which in the early 2000s dedicated a new headstone to him with the inscription "Black Con-federate" and "A Man Among Men."[42]

Shortly thereafter, Ron Maxwell released *Gods and Generals*, based on the novel by Jeff Shaara. The movie tells the story of the Civil War during the first three years from the perspective of key historical figures on both sides of the conflict, but it becomes clear early on that Maxwell's interests are squarely with the Confederacy and General Thomas "Stonewall" Jackson. The movie includes re-creations of the battles of First Bull Run, Fredericksburg, and Chancellorsville and offers a sympathetic portrayal of Confederate leaders like Robert E. Lee and Jackson, who are depicted as both brilliant tacticians and deeply religious. Not surprisingly, *Gods and Generals* was welcomed by the Confederate heritage community for its unapologetic embrace of central tenets of the Lost Cause, but critics skewered it. The *Washington Post* assessed the film as "clearly intended as something of a Confederate Honor Restoration Project, in which the men of the South are cut loose from the weight of slavery's evil and portrayed as God-fearing, patriotic, noble and heroic."[43] Critics may have had the depiction of Jackson and Jim Lewis in mind—a relationship that deviates significantly from the Shaara novel.

Early in the film Lewis interviews for the position as Jackson's servant and by all indications as a free man. While the film correctly notes that Lewis joined Jackson in Winchester, Virginia, in November 1861, he did so as a slave. Jackson never acknowledged Jim's legal status in his wartime letters, but he did make annual payments to one W. C. Lewis of Lexington, Virginia, for "hire of Jim."[44] Maxwell manages to collapse completely the racial hierarchy that would have defined this interview, even going so far as having Jackson refer to Jim as "Mr. Lewis." The fact that both men shared Lexington as their home offers Lewis the opportunity to explain how he views the war and his role in it: "Lexington is my home general, same as your own. If I could do my share in defending my home I would be doin' the same as you. I hear'd it was Napoleon hisself said 'An army can't march but on its stomach.'" Jackson clearly approved of what he hears and hires Jim on the spot, but not before imploring him to remember to "love your country" and "fear the Lord." The two emerge from this scene and enter the war equally committed to the Confederate cause.

Jackson's relationship with Jim and his progressive racial outlook remove any obstacle from the audience's ability to fully sympathize not only with the general but also with other Confederate leaders featured in the film as well as with the rank and file. Slavery is barely mentioned by anyone wearing a Confederate uniform. In one scene that can only be described as bizarre, Jackson and Lewis pray together just before the 1862 battle of Fredericksburg and just weeks before the Emancipation Proclamation is signed by Lincoln.

Lewis asks God how "a good Christian man like some folks I know can tolerate dey black brothers in bondage? How is it Lord, they just don't break them chains?" Jackson shares Lewis's uncertainty and desire to understand why slavery still persists. He joins Lewis in prayer as a sign of unity and asks God to "speak to us" about how to reconcile slavery with Christianity, even though Jackson himself would have been perfectly capable of offering just such a defense. Instead, in the film Jackson shares with Lewis the news that Lee and President Jefferson Davis have proposed the enlistment of slaves as soldiers in exchange for their freedom over a year before the actual plan was announced publicly.

In a scene that was deleted from the film's final cut, Maxwell blurs the distinction between slaves and soldiers even further. Camp servants can be seen placing the bodies of their masters in coffins in preparation for their final journey home following the battle of Fredericksburg. Jim Lewis engages one African American in full Confederate uniform who places his master's sword on top of his coffin and asserts, "He my boss, not my massa." His status as a free man obscures his role in the Confederate army, but there is little question as to why he remained and did not run away to join his family already in Pennsylvania. "Once I get this body to his kin in Winchester I sees the way things is," he tells Lewis. "White folks be killing one another for a while yet . . . but this here rebel give me my freedom back." Scenes like this and the relationship of Lewis and Jackson throughout the movie succeeded in detaching the Confederacy and the army from the institution of slavery. Maxwell's embrace of these stories of black loyalty and his obscuring of the master-slave relationship likely made it easier for viewers to unapologetically embrace the movie's Lost Cause–centered themes of bravery and devotion without having to worry about the lingering problems of slavery and race.[45]

The SCV's marking of John Noland's grave as a "Black Confederate" was part of its larger effort to literally inscribe its preferred interpretation of the role of African Americans in the Confederacy at their final resting places. Members of the SCV and the UDC often held elaborate ceremonies for the unveiling of new grave markers or the placement of the Southern Cross of Honor on already existing graves. They sometimes even involved their descendants, which lent credibility to a ceremony that almost always failed to acknowledge the legal status of the grave's occupant. In a ceremony that took place in 2009, members of the UDC dressed in mourning attire to decorate the graves of two former slaves who they claimed were "Confederate soldiers." One of the two was identified as "Pvt. Henry Henderson," who was reportedly eleven years old when he "entered service with the Confederate

States of America as a cook and servant to Colonel William F. Henderson, a medical doctor." Although Henderson was reportedly wounded, there is no reason to believe that he was anything more than a Confederate slave attached to his owner as a servant. For Theresa Pittman, president of the South Carolina Division of the UDC, the ceremony was a reminder that "our heritage, black and white, is intertwined."[46]

Beginning in 2003, a local chapter of the SCV commemorated Richard Poplar in Petersburg, Virginia, with an annual proclamation signed by the city's African American mayor, Annie M. Mickens. Having a black mayor sign an official city proclamation fit into the SCV's goal of appealing to an ever-wider base in its local communities, but this did not render the historical claims made any less problematic. The proclamation referred to Poplar as an "American veteran" who served in the 13th Virginia Cavalry and spent over a year as a prisoner of war in Maryland. A military-style headstone was eventually dedicated in Blandford Cemetery at a site that was believed to be the approximate location of Poplar's body. The SCV lists Poplar as a private in the Confederate army, which, among the rest of the dead, would leave little doubt to visitors that this man was indeed a Confederate soldier. But Poplar's obituary, which appeared in the *Petersburg Index-Appeal* on May 23, 1886, indicates that he "attached himself" as a "servant" and up to his capture at Gettysburg "remained faithfully attached to the regiment." Such a characterization undercuts any claim that he was formally enlisted as a soldier.[47] Local reporters covered many of these headstone ceremonies, but their lack of historical knowledge all but guaranteed that the SCV and UDC's preferred interpretation would be passed on to their readers without question.

Two high-profile stories that surfaced on the eve of the 150th anniversary of the Civil War point to the extent to which the black Confederate narrative had penetrated into the broader culture and popular memory of the war. In 2009 the original tintype of Andrew and Silas Chandler surfaced on an episode of *Antiques Roadshow*. Andrew Chandler Battaile Jr., a direct descendant of Andrew, accompanied the photograph for appraisal. Wes Cowan, who characterized the photograph as "really rare," conducted the appraisal, but the interpretation of the image was left largely to Battaile. He repeated many of the questionable claims about the relationship between the two men that by this point in time could be found on numerous websites. Andrew and Silas were close to the same age, had "worked the fields together, and continued to live closely throughout the rest of their lives." Battaile noted their having "fought in four battles together" before citing the story of Silas stepping in to save Andrew's leg from amputation. To drive home his belief that

Turning Camp Slaves into Black Confederate Soldiers

Andrew and Silas remained lifelong friends, Battaile mentioned that the two sides of the family had recently reunited, though he failed to share that at least one of Silas's descendants had already removed the Southern Cross of Honor placed on his grave by the SCV back in 1994.

Cowan confirmed that Silas had received a pension "for his service in the war" but failed to note that the pension was awarded for his presence in the army as a slave. To his credit, Cowan acknowledged that the subject of African Americans and the Confederacy is "controversial." Many black Southerners entered the army as a "manservant" or camp slave, according to Cowan, and he also correctly mentioned that the Confederate government did not authorize slave enlistment until March 1865.

Unfortunately, in Battaile's hands, Silas's legal status as a slave was not clarified, and his relationship with Andrew and place in the army were also left vague and unsupported by wartime documentation. Cowan assessed the tintype's value as between $30,000 and $40,000.[48]

The episode garnered a great deal of criticism that focused on some of the central claims made about Silas's legal status, the characterization of his place within the army, and especially the relationship between the two men that Battaile embraced and that some viewers interpreted as self-serving. In 2011 Wes Cowan returned to research the story surrounding the tintype, this time as part of PBS's *History Detectives*.[49] At the beginning of the episode Cowan is introduced to both Battaile and "friend" Bobbie Chandler, which added some suspense to the investigation. Would it confirm the stories passed down by Battaile's side of the family about the relationship between Andrew and Silas and by extension add historical weight to their own friendship? Cowan was asked by both men to find answers to a number of questions: Was Silas granted his freedom before the war? Did Silas intervene following Andrew's wounding to save his leg from amputation? Did Andrew gift Silas eighty acres of land on which to build a church? Finally, was Silas a soldier in the Confederate army?

Cowan consulted with a number of experts, each of whom undercut some aspect of the Chandler narrative. David Vaughn, an expert in Civil War–era photography, concluded that while the uniforms worn by both men in the famous photograph were authentic, the weapons displayed, especially the pepperbox in Silas's coat, were likely studio props. Vaughn also disputed that the uniform worn by Silas proved that he was a soldier and concluded that he was, in fact, Andrew's camp slave. As to Silas's free status on the eve of the war, Cowan's own research failed to uncover "a single free person of color listed in Chickasaw County" in the 1860 census. Historian Mary

Frances Berry clarified this long-disputed point by noting that the state of Mississippi prevented the manumission of slaves by the beginning of the Civil War. Berry quickly dismissed the question of whether Silas was a soldier by citing the March 1865 legislation that only then authorized slaves' enlistment with the Confederacy on the brink of collapse.

The episode did more than just challenge historical claims about the Confederacy and African Americans; it also introduced the Lost Cause myth as a way to understand how the Chandler story was manipulated decades after the war. "In the late nineteenth century and early twentieth century, there was a great tide of feeling in the South about trying to justify the war itself," said Berry, "and part of that justification was to say that slaves fought for the Confederacy, slaves were loyal to their master." As to the relationship between the two men, Berry noted "that we can never know" owing to the role of "compulsion" and "force" that defined the master-slave relationship.[50]

With so little of the story holding up under scrutiny, it should come as no surprise that the final chapter of whether Andrew's family donated land to Silas for the purposes of a church proved to be problematic as well. While Andrew's family did deed land for the construction of an African American church in Palo Alto, Silas's family attended church fifteen miles away in West Point, which to this day includes his name engraved on the cornerstone in recognition of his participation in its construction. Both men were visibly surprised by the results of the investigation. For Bobbie Chandler, the results confirmed "what some of the members of my family thought" who never accepted the narrative passed down by Andrew Chandler's side of the family. A reunion with some of these estranged family members took place in the years that followed the airing of the *History Detectives* episode. Andrew Chandler Battaile Jr. also tried to put his best face forward by acknowledging that "the story that we've shared is one that is very comfortable, and comforting to believe." At the same time he maintained that the family histories on both sides "have been, and will always be, deeply intertwined and evolving with the times." Still, the results must have been difficult to fully accept. In 2014, Battaile sold the tintype of Andrew and Silas to the Library of Congress for an undisclosed amount. It is cataloged with a description of Silas as a "family slave."[51]

A more troubling appearance of the black Confederate narrative appeared shortly after the start of the 2010 school year, when William & Mary historian Carol Sheriff came across a curious passage in her daughter's fourth-grade Virginia history textbook, *Our Virginia: Past and Present*. The book, authored by Joy Masoff, maintained that "thousands of Southern

Turning Camp Slaves into Black Confederate Soldiers

blacks fought in Confederate ranks, including two black battalions under the command of Stonewall Jackson."[52] Noted Civil War historians, including Jackson biographer James I. Robertson, James McPherson, and David Blight, were quick to correct the historical record.

For her part, Masoff stood by her research, asserting, "I am a fairly respected writer." The passage in question was an attempt on the part of Masoff to address one of the state standards, which focused on the various roles played by African Americans in the Confederacy. It was later learned that the author relied on websites that "referred to work by Sons of the Confederate Veterans or others who contend that the fight over slavery was not the main cause of the Civil War." The author's reliance on these sites reflected not only an increasing use of the Internet as a source of information but an inability to assess the reliability of its content.[53] The Virginia Department of Education responded by either replacing these books with updated versions or providing instructors with black tape or white stickers to be placed over the offending passages. State officials were confident that students would not be exposed to the black Confederate myth, given that classes would not cover the material before the spring of the following year, but problems persisted. At least one parent revealed that her daughter's study sheet for the Civil War unit included the claim that blacks fought for the Confederacy. Her teacher informed his students "that blacks fought because their masters threatened to kill them if they wouldn't."[54]

The textbook controversy in Virginia took place as the nation inaugurated its first African American president. Barack Obama had announced his candidacy for the presidency on the steps of the Old Capitol in Springfield, Illinois, where Abraham Lincoln began his political career. Obama framed his candidacy around the long march toward freedom, beginning with slavery and continuing through the dark days of Jim Crow and the promises made possible by the civil rights movement. "It is because men and women of every race . . . continued to march for freedom together after Lincoln was laid to rest," Obama told the crowd, "that today we have the chance to face the challenges of this millennium as one people — as Americans."[55] His election fit neatly into a shifting Civil War memory that acknowledged emancipation and freedom as the Civil War's most important results and created additional space to highlight the contributions of African Americans to preserving the Union and ending slavery. At times, however, the new president attempted to balance calls to reject Lost Cause commemorations with a desire to highlight emancipation. Shortly after taking office, James Loewen and Edward Sebesta petitioned the president to discontinue the practice of sending a wreath to the Confederate monument at Arlington National Cemetery. The authors pointed out that the monument continued to function as a "rally point" for the neo-Confederate movement and as "vindicating the Confederacy and the principles and ideas of the Confederacy."[56] Although not mentioned specifically in their petition, the images of the now misinterpreted uniformed black Confederate soldier and "Mammy" figure holding the son of a departing soldier were central to how the Confederate heritage community remembered and commemorated the Confederacy. Rather than discontinue the practice, though, the president chose instead to send a second wreath to the newly dedicated African American Civil War Memorial in Washington, D.C. In President Obama's understanding of the war, the right side proved victorious, but he encouraged Confederate heritage advocates to redouble their efforts with their own stories of loyal African American soldiers.

While loyal black soldiers constituted the core of the SCV's continued heritage defense, members broadened their reach to include stories that portrayed Confederate leaders as progressive in their racial outlook. In 2008 the SCV announced a campaign to finance a life-size bronze statue depicting Confederate president Jefferson Davis, his son Joseph, and Jim Limber, a young African American boy who spent one year living in the Confederate White House in Richmond, Virginia. Though the Davises cared for the boy during this time, his status within the family remains unclear. Limber was separated from the Davises as the family fled from the Confederate capital at the end of the war. The family never heard from him again. For the SCV, the story of Jim Limber was "lost in history by revisionist historians, who felt his existence would impair their contrived notions of Davis."[57] Once the statue was completed it was offered to the American Civil War Center at Tredegar (now the American Civil War Museum) in Richmond with the intention to counter the statue of Abraham Lincoln and his son Tad placed there in 2003 to commemorate their visit to the city in April 1865. The museum accepted the statue on the conditions that it alone would determine where it would be displayed and how it would be interpreted. Rather than risk seeing its statue co-opted, the SCV rescinded its offer and in 2009 donated it to the Jefferson Davis Home and Presidential Library at Beauvoir in Mississippi.[58]

In April 2010, just after the Virginia textbook scandal, Governor Robert McDonnell issued his annual proclamation commemorating Confederate History Month. The pushback was swift and directed specifically at his failure to acknowledge the evils of slavery. Governor McDonnell attempted to deflect blame by suggesting that the proclamation was "solely intended to promote the study of our history, encourage tourism in our state in advance of the 150th Anniversary of the beginning of the Civil War, and recognize Virginia's unique role in the story of America."[59] For a growing number of people throughout the state, however, that "unique role" could no longer be understood without acknowledging the cause for which the Confederacy struggled to achieve. The Virginia Division, SCV, issued a public statement in response to the governor, but that did not prevent him from delivering a new proclamation the following year recognizing April as "Civil War History in Virginia Month," which broadened the focus to include the role of African Americans and recognized the centrality of slavery and emancipation to the war.[60] The original 2010 proclamation was curious, given that Virginia had already organized a state commission to mark the 150th anniversary of the Civil War. Unlike centennial celebrations, this time around the Virginia commission refused to sponsor large battlefield reenactments and instead focused on more educational opportunities based on the latest scholarship that challenged central tenets of the Lost Cause narrative. The decision to officially begin marking events for the sesquicentennial in Virginia in 2009 with the 150th anniversary of John Brown's 1859 raid at Harpers Ferry signaled a clear shift in how the war would be commemorated.

The SCV's attempt to push back against the governor ultimately failed. It was a clear indication that while the SCV had enjoyed significant success in spreading the black Confederate narrative on the Internet and elsewhere over the past three decades, it had yet to find sustained support among the most important institutions, including schools, museums, and historic sites. And when references to black Confederate soldiers did appear in textbooks, on television, and in National Park Service exhibits, it proved to be only a temporary gain. The Virginia governor's revised proclamation was a clear sign on the eve of the 150th anniversary of the Civil War that the public memory embraced by the state and its sesquicentennial commission would directly challenge claims having to do not only with black Confederates but with any suggestion that the preservation of slavery was not central to the history of the Civil War and the Confederacy specifically.

Chapter Six

BLACK CONFEDERATES ON THE FRONT LINES OF THE CIVIL WAR SESQUICENTENNIAL

On October 14, 2002, H. K. Edgerton, dressed in a Confederate uniform, grabbed his Confederate battle flag and set out on a 1,300-mile "March across Dixie for Southern Heritage" from Asheville, North Carolina, to Austin, Texas. The march took Edgerton through South Carolina, Georgia, Alabama, Mississippi, and Louisiana and was intended to raise funds for the Southern Legal Resource Center—an organization founded by Kirk Lyons and declared a "hate group" by the Southern Poverty Law Center—and the Sons of Confederate Veterans Heritage Defense Fund. Both organizations were active at the time in defending students who were disciplined for wearing T-shirts and other clothing with the Confederate battle flag to school. Edgerton expressed concern about the growing number of cases involving students who were "either sent home or expelled, for displaying the Confederate symbol" throughout "the Southland." For Edgerton, Lyons, and the SCV, enough was enough. For many, an activist donning Confederate gray, waving the battle flag, and spreading his message of "Heritage, Not Hate" and "Southern pride" along the highways and back roads of the former Confederacy would have been a welcome sight, but nothing could prepare supporters and other observers for the realization that the man in the uniform spreading this particular message was African American.[1]

In recent years, a small number of African Americans have embraced the black Confederate narrative as a means to identify and to celebrate stories of ancestors who they believe have been long forgotten or intentionally ignored. For Edgerton it was not just his African American ancestry that cast him as an unlikely neo-Confederate warrior. Before joining Lyons and the Southern Legal Resource Center, Edgerton served as the president of the Asheville branch of the NAACP but became disillusioned with the organization as it turned more aggressive in passing resolutions against the public display of the Confederate battle flag. Edgerton's interests in the NAACP had always been about, in his words, the "fight for social and economic mobility for all people." His evolution from a local NAACP leader to defender of the Lost Cause is not entirely clear, but by the time he set off on his march, Edgerton had been fully converted to the point that he identified himself as a "Confederate-American."[2]

Edgerton was quickly embraced by Confederate heritage organizations and became a popular presence at events sponsored by the SCV, especially protests in response to growing demands for the removal of the battle flag from public spaces. White audiences viewed Edgerton as an important asset in this campaign—someone who could challenge the assumption that the battle flag divided the races and was itself a symbol of the nation's history of systemic racism. For many white Americans, Edgerton was a living reminder of the peaceful relations that existed between whites and blacks during the antebellum period that were interrupted only by Abraham Lincoln's illegal invasion. His appearance in uniform gave strength to their claims that the vast majority of free and enslaved blacks offered unquestioning loyalty to the Confederacy on the plantation and in the ranks as soldiers. Edgerton embodied a role that harked back to the presence of former camp slaves, such as Steve "Uncle Steve Eberhart" Perry, at Confederate veterans' reunions at the turn of the twentieth century who reinforced the Lost Cause for white Southerners during a period of racial uncertainty. Now at the end of the century, the SCV welcomed Edgerton as vindication of its preferred narrative that cast African Americans as loyal black Confederate soldiers. The embrace of the black Confederate myth by Edgerton and a small group of African Americans gave it a level of legitimacy that made it easier for heritage advocates to more openly defend both Confederate symbolism and an understanding of the past that was coming under increased assault.

As a result, the SCV and the rest of the Confederate heritage community moved from a defensive posture in the face of increasing attacks on Confederate iconography to a more offensive-oriented strategy that allowed African Americans themselves to speak for the organization and the Confederacy. In doing so they reinforced the myth and offered conservative black Americans an outlet to voice their political agenda within the heritage community. Pronouncements of slave loyalty to master and the Confederacy from both white and black Confederate heritage advocates were often coupled with public statements against affirmative action, the policies of the Obama administration, and the rise of the "Black Lives Matter" movement.

Yet even with the public support of African Americans from different backgrounds, the black Confederate narrative ultimately failed to achieve the goals set out by the SCV following the success of the book and TV miniseries *Roots*. The SCV's defense of the Lost Cause narrative of a war that now included real black Confederates like Edgerton as allies faced its most severe test during the Civil War sesquicentennial. Stories of free and enslaved black Southerners serving in Confederate ranks could still easily be found on thousands of websites. These stories had temporarily infiltrated National Park Service exhibits, found their way into textbooks, and even made an appearance on prime time television, but in each of these cases there was significant pushback. At the beginning of the Civil War sesquicentennial in 2011, the black Confederate narrative had yet to find a permanent home among mainstream institutions, including museums and the National Park Service, which led the effort to deepen and expand how the war was interpreted and taught to the general public. The major commemorative events that shaped the Civil War sesquicentennial point to an evolving collective memory that has largely rejected the Lost Cause and its army of black Confederates in favor of increased emphasis on the history of slavery, emancipation, and the contributions made by free and enslaved blacks in defending the Union and bringing an end to the "peculiar institution." Advocates of the black Confederate narrative were placed even more on the defensive following the murders of nine churchgoers in Charleston, South Carolina, in 2015 and the violent neo-Nazi rally that took place in Charlottesville, Virginia, on August 12, 2017. In the wake of the deadly shooting in Charleston, towns and cities, beginning with Columbia, South Carolina, lowered Confederate battle flags from prominent public spaces, and cities such as New Orleans, Baltimore, Louisville, and Dallas began removing monuments to Robert E. Lee, Stonewall Jackson, and Jefferson Davis from public spaces. The Lost Cause came under increased scrutiny within mainstream culture and even among a significant number of white Southerners that no number of mythical black Confederate soldiers could change.

The black Confederate project faced an uphill climb throughout the sesquicentennial. By 2011 a noticeable shift in public memory of the war was already clearly discernible. Decades of new scholarship influenced popular movies and documentaries as well as history textbooks, introducing a new generation of students to a narrative of the Civil War that was profoundly different from how the nation commemorated the Civil War centennial fifty years earlier. These interpretive shifts gradually took hold across the country at museums and historic sites large and small.

Changes could be seen even at the venerable Museum of the Confederacy in the former Confederate capital of Richmond, Virginia, which from its beginning had served more as a shrine to the "Old South" than anything approaching a serious museum. However, by the 1980s, major exhibits, supported in part by the National Endowment for the Humanities and informed by the latest scholarship, pushed the museum further away from its original mission. The debut of the *Victory in Defeat* exhibit in 1985 offered the first critical evaluation of the Lost Cause, but it was the groundbreaking 1991 exhibit *Before Freedom Came* that earned the museum national acclaim owing to its comprehensive examination of slavery, complete with leg irons and a photograph of a slave whose back starkly revealed the damage caused by his master's whip. Most importantly, the exhibit reinforced that slavery was central to secession, the organization of the Confederate government, and the eventual outcome of the war. Additional exhibits focusing on the Confederate home front and the role of women brought the museum more in line with other institutions, which were now finding ways to address the tough questions of race and slavery in their exhibits and other public programs.[3]

No institution proved to be more important in integrating new scholarship into its exhibits and programming than the National Park Service. Individual parks such as Petersburg National Battlefield began to institute changes by the early 1980s. The gradual shift in how the NPS approached interpretation represented a dramatic break from decades of considering Civil War sites as "quiet places of reflection and reconciliation, where veterans gathered to heal rather than cause wounds, where the nation looked for regeneration." By 2000 the NPS introduced a service-wide interpretive plan, called *Holding the High Ground*, which later served as a foundation for its sesquicentennial planning. The plan sought to "have parks challenge people with ideas, challenge them to not just understand the nature and horrid expanse of the bloodshed, but the reasons for it, and the consequences of its aftermath." The causes and consequences centered squarely on the subjects of slavery, race, and emancipation. The focus on slavery and emancipation at the Museum of the Confederacy, throughout the NPS, and elsewhere created a less than hospitable interpretive environment for the proponents of the black Confederate narrative. This did not, however, prevent the most fervent believers in this history, including a new wave of African Americans, from speaking out.[4]

By the time H. K. Edgerton set out on his first march across the Deep South, a small but vocal group of African Americans rallied around the Confederate cause and the black Confederate project. Their motivations varied widely, but some overlap can be discerned. For George Mason University's Walter Williams, who teaches economics, the black Confederate narrative fits into a broader understanding of a war between Abraham's Lincoln's introduction of an increasingly centralized and corrupt federal government and the Confederacy's commitment to political and economic principles more in line with his own libertarian outlook. Williams ignored the steps taken by the Confederate government in Richmond to centralize power through, among other things, instituting a draft, the confiscation of food and other supplies from individual states, and even the impressment of tens of thousands of slaves from owners, who often perceived their own government as having overstepped its proper bounds. According to Williams, "Patriotic black ancestors . . . marched, fought, and died to protect their homeland from what they saw as Northern aggression." They died for limited government.[5] Although Williams was not associated directly with the SCV or other Confederate heritage organizations, his writings were regularly cited by members, and his university affiliation was touted as lending credibility.

Throughout the 1990s, American University's Edward C. Smith established himself as an authority on black Confederates through appearances at SCV meetings and the publication of a small number of articles in Civil War–themed magazines. While Smith applauded the release of the movie *Glory* in 1989, he expressed concern that "no similar film is in production that examines the service of blacks in the army of the Confederacy."[6] Rather than view the Civil War as pitting white and black Southerners against one another, Smith believed the black Confederate narrative could be a panacea to heal the nation's racial divide. He characterized his own participation in a 1999 SCV celebration of a free black man who helped to construct Confederate earthworks as a fulfillment "of the dream that Martin Luther King, Jr. longed for."[7]

While some applauded Smith's goals, his grasp of the relevant history was fundamentally flawed. In defending Robert E. Lee as a model American whose legacy has the potential to bring whites and blacks closer together,

Smith claimed that Lee "never owned a single slave, because he felt that slavery was morally reprehensible."[8] In reference to African Americans in Confederate ranks, Smith estimated that somewhere around 50,000 fought as combatants, which he arrived at, in part, by citing the well-known account by Dr. Lewis Steiner during the Antietam campaign. Smith was aware that the Confederate government did not authorize the enlistment of slaves as soldiers until the very end of the war but asserted that they served unofficially at the local level. "The Confederate government was as screwed up as God knows what," according to Smith, "and so the commanders in the field did what they always do—they take advantage of the resources that are available."[9] Not surprisingly, Smith failed to provide the evidence necessary to support any of these claims.

According to Smith, the Confederate monument in Arlington National Cemetery represents the most convincing evidence of the service of a significant number of black soldiers. Despite the descriptions given by both its sculptor and the United Daughters of the Confederacy, who commissioned the monument, Smith maintained that the circular frieze depicting a black man in uniform is a soldier who offers the public another representation of "Southern patriotism." Smith either chose to overlook or was unaware of artist Moses Ezekiel's own notes as well as the UDC's official history of the monument and instead eagerly concluded that "blacks [were placed] side-by-side with the other fighters and families of the Confederacy because he [Ezekiel] wanted the memorial to be a *truthful* representation of the Southern Civil War experience."[10]

During this same time a small number of black Civil War reenactors traded in their Union blue uniforms for Confederate gray. George Hardy recalled little about the Civil War from his primary school classes that did not revolve around Lee and Jackson: "I grew up thinking that blacks didn't participate in the war at all. . . . I just thought blacks were slaves during that period." His introduction to the service of black Union soldiers was a revelation that led him to join Company B of the 54th Massachusetts Volunteer Infantry—a reenacting organization that took part in the filming of *Glory*. Hardy eventually found his way into the Southern Guard, owing to their commitment to authenticity in appearance and behavior and for the opportunity to broaden his range of roles. Hardy developed interpretations for a number of different roles, including camp servant, teamster, and soldier, but his interest in portraying black Confederates had little to do with racial politics; rather, it was about achieving a certain authenticity of experience. "There's nothing like just being out in the woods and seeing only natural things, or just hanging out with your pards," he explained. "You all have a common interest, you've all put a lot of research into what you're doing and what you're saying, and you just have that moment when everything's clicking."[11]

Shane Williams and Steffon Jones also started out reenacting as Union soldiers but soon were pulled by the novelty of wearing a gray uniform and the freedom of not having to march in step with others. Neither individual offered much in the way of a deep understanding of the roles of slaves and free blacks in the Confederate army to the reporter who featured them in an article. Jones referenced Frederick Douglass's often-quoted observation that there were "many Colored Men in the Confederate Army," including "real soldiers." "If there was just one black soldier who fired a weapon at the Union army," argued Williams, "that person needs to be portrayed."[12] On the other hand, Bobby Compton, who identifies ethnically as Hawaiian, plays the role of the black Confederate not out of any identification with the Lost Cause but simply as a Virginian who enjoys nineteenth-century fashion. Compton maintains that the Confederate cause was wrong, and he is grateful that his daughters do not have to face the same racial challenges that he experienced, but he gives little thought to lining up in the ranks next to the Confederate battle flag.[13] None of these black reenactors is at all concerned that he might be contributing to the perpetuation of a myth.

For the leaders of these modern Confederate units, their goals in recruiting new black members has often extended into the realm of racial politics and in wanting to correct the historical record. The 34th Texas Regiment, also known as Terrell's Cavalry, led the way in announcing its intentions in the popular reenacting newspaper *Camp Chase*: "'Men of Honor! Men of Color! Join the ranks of Terrell's Cavalry (Reorganized), in the fight for historical accuracy and recognition of the participation and contributions of Confederates of Color in the War for Southern Independence.'" For many black reenactors, these new roles are an opportunity to stand out from the uniform appearance of black Union reenactors. In camp they are objects of curiosity and often attract the attention of visitors. Some have suggested that it was not until the release of *Glory* that Confederate reenactors sought out black recruits, which implies that their real concerns stemmed from the growing acceptance of the centrality of slavery and white supremacy to the Confederate experience. This is borne out by the commander of the 34th Texas, Captain Michael Kelley, who confirmed that "by maintaining this false image of the Confederate army as this sea of lily-white faces, the South can be demonized" and "they can say . . . that Southerners were fighting for slavery and racism, and Yankees were fighting to free the slaves."[14] For Kelley, the presence of black men in Confederate uniform made it possible to continue to portray the Confederate soldier as honorable and fighting for a cause that had nothing to do with the preservation of slavery.[15]

During this same period, the SCV continued to welcome African Americans into their ranks to lend legitimacy to the black Confederate narrative. No one has been more vocal than Nelson W. Winbush, who joined the SCV as a full member. The decision to admit Winbush reflects the SCV's recent efforts to broaden its racial and ethnic profile and appeal across the former Confederate states, which in recent years has become increasingly ethnically diverse. Winbush was an ideal member. He joined in response to the NAACP's efforts to remove the Confederate battle flag from public spaces in the early 1990s, and from that point Winbush devoted himself to explaining to the general public what the Confederacy fought for, which he asserts was states' rights and not slavery. Winbush also denied that Lincoln played any significant role in freeing the slaves. If that was not enough to ingratiate him among his white SCV members, Winbush was known on occasion to sing a song that includes the lyrics, "Black is nothing other than a darker shade of rebel gray."[16]

All the available evidence demonstrates that Winbush's grandfather Louis Napoleon Nelson, whose owner served in Company M, 7th Tennessee Cavalry, remained a slave until the end of the war. The pension that he filled out toward the end of his life confirms this fact. His wife's own application for financial support that was filed after his death was denied owing to the fact that only the widows of Confederate veterans qualified. Even in the face of this evidence, hundreds of websites assert that Napoleon Nelson fought as a soldier in the Confederate army. In a recent interview, Winbush insisted his grandfather fought as a soldier: "My grandfather ended up fighting like everyone else. He felt the South was being invaded by the Yankees."[17] Needless to say, the Confederate heritage community embraced Winbush and presented him as an example for other African Americans to follow: "We put him forth as an example and an encouragement for other Black citizens or decedents [sic] of the South to reacquaint themselves with and proudly reclaim their Southern heritage."[18]

No one proved to be more popular during this period than H. K. Edgerton. He repeated his highly publicized march in 2007 when he walked across part of Texas in full uniform and with the battle flag to highlight the loyalty that slaves demonstrated to their masters and the Confederacy. His own website was a popular destination for people looking for information about the Confederacy and accounts of loyal slaves. According to Edgerton, some-where in the neighborhood of "50,000 African Americans served willingly and . . . almost four million stayed behind to care for the plantations and farms in the South of their own free will."[19] Edgerton set out on another march in January 2009, this time heading north to Washington, D.C., to ask newly elected president Barack Obama to embrace the Confederate battle flag as a symbol of racial "unity." "The flag represents a heritage, a way of life that my forebears had," he stated. "It represents the men and the families that lived together and fought together to preserve their country from invasion. My family volunteered for the Confederacy and fought side-by-side with white Southerners and Indian Southerners. They are all my family."[20] Edger-ton's embrace of the battle flag and the memory of the Confederacy struck many as nothing less than bizarre, but for the Confederate heritage commu-nity, especially the scv, Edgerton's emergence was perfectly timed. Edger-ton continued to profit from his association with the Confederate heritage community, which eventually included his own line of T-shirts with Dixie Outfitters that featured uniformed and armed black soldiers. He kept on entertaining audiences with colorful stories of black loyalty during the war and frequently concluded with a dramatic interpretation of "I Am Their Flag," often in the company of impersonators of Robert E. Lee, Stonewall Jackson, and other notable Confederate generals.

Edgerton's advocacy for the scv and his public appearances dressed as a Confederate soldier echoed the performances of Steve "Uncle Steve Eber-hart" Perry, Howard Divinity, and other former camp slaves who attended veterans' reunions at the turn of the twentieth century throughout the Jim Crow South. All entertained large white audiences and reassured them that the Lost Cause united both races around a shared memory of the war and the respective racial politics of the time.

African Americans aided the Confederate heritage community in pro-moting the black Confederate narrative, though their reasons for doing so varied. For Walter Williams, stories of loyal black soldiers made it easier to accept the Confederacy as a case study in the virtues of limited govern-ment for modern-day conservatives. The opportunity to highlight history that had been ignored (perhaps intentionally) appears to be what animated Edward Smith, while Nelson Winbush and H. K. Edgerton embraced mythi-cal stories of loyal slaves as the key to more peaceful race relations in the American South. Regardless of motivation, their identification with the Lost Cause and decision to ally with the scv and others took place during a period of intense political and racial unrest during the eight years of Presi-

Former NAACP chapter president H. K. Edgerton is one of the most popular supporters of the black Confederate myth and in recent years has attended numerous Confederate heritage events. (Courtesy of Samuel Febres Photography & Design)

dent Obama's presidency that witnessed high-profile shootings of black men at the hands of the police, increased scrutiny of the nation's prison system, and the eventual rise of the "Black Lives Matter" movement.

One of the most outspoken black supporters of the Lost Cause was Karen Cooper. Originally from New York and a former member of the Nation of Islam, Cooper identified closely with her new home of Richmond, Virginia, and with the Confederate heritage movement. In 2010 Cooper spoke out at Tea Party rally in Richmond in which she shared her identification as a libertarian as well as her views on such issues as taxes, "Obamacare," and legalized marijuana. She maintained that her Confederate heritage efforts were a direct extension of her modern-day political beliefs and activism. Like Williams, Cooper believed that the Confederate flag and its history "represents freedom" and limited government. Cooper's conservative outlook fit neatly into the Confederate heritage community's culture at the time. A representative of the SCV stated in April 2010 that his Confederate ancestor was "fighting for the same things that people in the Tea party are fighting for."[21]

Cooper soon found common political ground with the Virginia Flaggers, a local group that organized in 2011 to protest the removal of the Confederate flag at the "Old Soldiers' Home" in Richmond on the grounds of the Virginia Museum of Fine Arts and in other locations throughout the state and beyond. Though she once described slavery as a "choice," Cooper was quick to characterize herself as a "slave of the federal government." "I can't smoke what I want to smoke, I can't drink what I want to drink. If I want to put something into my body, it's my body—not theirs. That's tyranny!" Cooper reserves her sharpest criticism for the impact of federal welfare programs on the African American community, which she routinely describes as "lazy." "I'm just sick of liberals always babying black people," she stated in 2015. "If they act like babies, they will stay like babies until you make them grow up. Make them grow up."[22]

Cooper has never openly acknowledged the existence of black Confederate soldiers, though she has marched with H. K. Edgerton and has often been seen protesting with the Virginia Flaggers wearing one of his Dixie Outfitters T-shirts. As with the case of the SCV's embrace of African Americans, the Flaggers welcomed Cooper into their ranks, in part because doing so aided their own mission to recast the Confederate battle flag as a symbol that all Americans, regardless of race, could embrace.

Like Karen Cooper, Anthony Hervey of Oxford, Mississippi, was no stranger to the often-contentious debates surrounding the display of the Confederate battle flag. In 2000 he led protests to keep the Confederate flag flying atop the statehouse in Columbia, South Carolina, and, closer to home, challenged the University of Mississippi's attempt to replace its mascot, "Colonel Reb," and ban the singing of "Dixie" during football games. Hervey was often seen wearing a Confederate uniform and carrying a large flag in front of Oxford's soldier statue. Among his many signs could be read "White Guilt = Black Genocide," "The Welfare State Has Destroyed My People," and "Please! Do Not Hire Me Because I Am Black." According to Hervey, the policies of the federal government fueled suspicion and deepened the racial divide in the South. In his final speech in Birmingham's Linn Park as part of a protest of the city council's decision to remove a Confederate monument, Hervey announced, "I don't like black people. I don't like white people . . . but I love the hell out of me some Southerners." Shortly after leaving the rally, Hervey was involved in a car accident that took his life.[23]

This small army of modern-day black Confederates has served as a powerful promotional tool for the SCV, the UDC, and other groups, which overwhelmingly rely on stories from the Civil War and the postwar period to bolster their claims of black loyalty. The visibility of African Americans within Confederate heritage organizations has aided their efforts to appeal to a shifting demographic throughout the South, which has become much more ethnically diverse. The sight of Edgerton, Cooper, and others embracing their Confederate heritage and waving the battle flag attracted a good deal of media attention, but their activism had little impact in supplanting the Civil War sesquicentennial's dominant narrative that from the beginning placed slavery, emancipation, and the service of African Americans in the U.S. Army at its center. In contrast with the former camp slaves who preceded them at a time when the Lost Cause narrative was triumphant, this new generation of black Lost Cause advocates occupied a place outside the mainstream culture even in places with deep ties to the history and legacy of the Confederacy.

The black Confederate narrative, and the broader Lost Cause interpretation in which it was located, remained under assault throughout the entire sesquicentennial. Not surprisingly, the NPS led the way by framing its commemorative events around the broad theme of "Civil War to Civil Rights," which placed the subjects of slavery and emancipation at the center of a story that continued through the periods of Reconstruction and Jim Crow. Harpers Ferry National Historical Park opened the sesquicentennial commemoration in 2009—two years before its official start—with programs on John Brown's attempt to lead a slave insurrection at Harpers Ferry in 1859. The decision to mark the commemoration with programs and lectures about Brown signaled that slavery as a cause of the war would not be brushed under the table as it had been during the centennial.[24] Fort Sumter National Monument marked the anniversary of South Carolina's decision to secede from the Union by focusing on "the institution of slavery as the principal cause of the Civil War."[25]

The first signature event commemorating a major battle took place at Manassas National Battlefield in July 2011 and included NPS director Jon Jarvis, Virginia governor Robert McDonnell, and other dignitaries. The focus of the event differed significantly from the battle's centennial commemoration in 1961, which included a reenactment that attracted tens of thousands who applauded and cheered a Confederate victory.[26] This time around, Colonel Richard Robinson and other descendants of James Robinson—a free African American who owned much of the land on which the battle was fought—led the Pledge of Allegiance.[27] The following year the staff at Antietam stressed the importance of the battle's connection to emancipation, and on the grounds of Arlington National Cemetery the staff at Robert E. Lee's former home highlighted the lives of the family's enslaved population. Visitors to the Fredericksburg and Spotsylvania National Military Park walked the landscapes of some of the bloodiest fighting during the war, but they were also exposed to the roughly 10,000 slaves, including John Washington, who crossed the Rappahannock River to freedom upon the arrival of the Union army in 1862. Finally, at the Crater, on the grounds of the Petersburg National Battlefield, programs confronted head-on some of the most challenging questions related to participation of U.S. Colored Troops in the battle and their massacre at the hands of vengeful Confederate soldiers.[28]

The National Park Service also reached out to local African American communities, which have traditionally avoided Civil War battlefields and other sites owing to the presence of the Confederate battle flag and an interpretation that all too often avoided or distorted their stories.[29] Between April and May 2013, the staff at Vicksburg National Military Park took their sesquicentennial commemoration directly to black neighborhoods, including open-air concerts featuring the Jackson Mass Community Choir and a theater troupe from Jackson State University as well as a dramatic retelling of the black experience during the siege of the city that culminated in a decisive Union victory and the freedom of the city's enslaved population.[30] In Fredericksburg, NPS staff led tours of local African American churches that dated to the Civil War era, and in Richmond, NPS frontline interpreters confronted the black Confederate myth directly by drawing attention to the many roles performed by free and enslaved blacks in the Confederate army as well as to the vital labor they performed behind the lines at places like the Tredegar Iron Works along the James River.

The work of the NPS across the country was supported by numerous state sesquicentennial commissions, which sponsored a wide range of programs and produced a wealth of resources for public consumption. No commission was more active than the Virginia Sesquicentennial of the American Civil War Commission. Its programming included an annual Signature Conference series that featured some of the top academic historians in the field in venues that held thousands of attendees. In 2010, historian Bruce Levine addressed the black Confederate controversy as one of the most "energetically propagated" myths of the Civil War. Additional symposia during the sesquicentennial discussed the lives of enslaved people in Virginia and their role in helping to defeat the Confederacy by running off to join the Union army, as well as how African Americans remembered and commemorated the war and emancipation through Reconstruction and beyond. Partnerships with the Virginia Historical Society and other museums throughout the state supported exhibits that were informed by the latest scholarship. The commission's own traveling exhibit managed to visit every county in Virginia and delivered a wide range of "individual stories of the Civil War from the perspective of those who experienced it — young and old, enslaved and free, soldiers and civilians."[31] The effort to directly confront the black Confederate myth by academic historians and the highlighting of the account of African Americans at historic sites throughout the country left the scv and its black allies on the sidelines.

Rather than develop new technologies to engage communities during the sesquicentennial, the Georgia Historical Society chose to revise and dedicate new historical markers across the state. Many of the old markers focused on the Civil War era were inspired by the nostalgia of the Lost Cause and avoided topics related to race and slavery. The Civil War 150 Historical Marker Project added important signage that reflected the new scholarship on slavery that helped to place Sherman's March across the state in 1864 in proper historical context. Examples included the dedication of markers related to Special Field Orders No. 15 and the Crossing at Ebenezer Creek, in which hundreds of enslaved people drowned while trying to flee pursuing Confederates. Georgia's commitment to the defense of slavery was told in a marker dedicated in the state's Civil War capital of Milledgeville, where the state's Ordinance of Secession was passed. The project also addressed the subject of blacks in the Confederate army in Dalton, Georgia, with two markers. The first focused on the 44th U.S. Colored Troops, who were captured in Dalton and sent back into slavery as dictated by Confederate policy. The marker explained that the Confederate government did not view black men as soldiers but as rebellious slaves. The second even more directly challenged the narrative with a marker highlighting Confederate general Patrick Cleburne's proposal to arm slaves in early 1864. The text makes it clear that the proposal not only was rejected but directly contradicted the very reasons for secession in 1861. The marker's acknowledgment of the March 1865 legislation that authorized slave enlistment makes it clear that no widespread recruitment of black men in the Confederate army took place during the war. In contrast, the marker concludes by referencing that "nearly 200,000 free African Americans served in the U.S. armed forces."[32]

The resources available to the National Park Service, Georgia Historical Society, and other large institutions directly and indirectly challenged the black Confederate narrative or created a considerably less than hospitable environment for the Lost Cause and those people who continued to celebrate their Confederate ancestors without dealing with the tough questions surrounding race and slavery. Many in the Confederate heritage community, especially members of the SCV, dug in their heels in response and redoubled their efforts to defend their preferred narrative of the Confederacy. Allies in state government, like Republican Georgia representative and SCV member Tommy Benton, who were willing to speak out in favor of Confederate heritage were few. In April 2012 Benton offered his colleagues a "history lesson" about the service of black Confederates as part of the state's commemoration of Confederate History Month. According to Benton, somewhere around "65,000 blacks were in the Confederate ranks," and "over 13,000 of these saw the elephant, also known as seeing the enemy in combat." He also observed that while the Confederate Congress did not officially approve the enlistment of slaves until the very end of the war, officers in the field "did not obey the mandate of politicians and frequently enlisted blacks with the simple criteria, 'will you fight?'"[33] Benton's embrace of the so-called history of black Confederates was an attempt to render Confederate History Month more acceptable at a time when the state's recognition was coming under increased scrutiny by African Americans. For white conservatives, the history of black Confederates proved that their continued embrace of their ancestors and the Confederate cause generally was about "heritage, not hate."

New dedications of headstones and markers harked back to monument unveilings at Fort Mill and Arlington National Cemetery, but these new unveilings muddied the distinction between soldier and slave. In early 2012 a marker was dedicated at the final resting place of Aaron Perry; its inscription read "Served in the Confederate Army" along with a reference to the "37th NC REGT." But the available historical record demonstrates that Perry did not serve as a soldier in the Confederate army; rather, he was present as the camp servant to Lieutenant Colonel John B. Ashcraft, who served in the 37th North Carolina. Like other camp servants, Perry received a pension late in life. Later that same year a marker was unveiled in Monroe, North Carolina, commemorating ten black men, including Perry.[34]

Tony Way, a member of the SCV and local historian, organized the North Carolina marker, which was placed at the base of the local Confederate soldiers' monument that had been dedicated in 1910. Participants in the dedication acknowledged that nine of the ten men listed were enslaved during the war, but the presence of members of the SCV and other Confederate heritage organizations, along with a Confederate honor guard, gave the gathering the appearance of a military ceremony that was honoring veterans rather than slaves. The marker's inscription added to this confusion: "In Honor Of Courage & Service By All African Americans During The War Between the States (1861–1865)." Even more confusing was the decision to refer to the individuals on the marker as "Confederate Pensioners of Color." Regardless of whether it was intentional or not, the failure to acknowledge their legal status as slaves and reference to "Pensioners of Color" makes it much more likely that visitors would identify these men as Confederate veterans. At the end of the ceremony, a handbell was rung and white women in black mourning attire laid ten black roses on the marker. The honor guard concluded the service by firing off a salute and the playing of taps.[35]

The dedication of the marker in Monroe represented a step in a new direction with the inclusion of descendants in the ceremony. Greg Perry, a descendant of Aaron Perry, acknowledged the racial profile of the audience: "Some of these people would never have met under other circumstances. It's just beautiful, the humanity baby." Another descendant characterized the ceremony as a vindication of Martin Luther King's vision for white and black Southerners. Hettie Byrd Wright insisted that "I know my [great-grandfather] is in heaven smiling."[36] Descendants expressed little concern with how their ancestors were utilized by their owners and the military to advance the cause of a nation committed to the protection of slavery and white supremacy. Nor did they take issue with the word choice on the marker, which failed to acknowledge their ancestors' enslaved status during the war. History took a back seat to the sounds and sights of what was for all intents and purposes a military ceremony that acknowledged these men as loyal participants who served alongside their white comrades in a cause that united both races.

In the audience that day was Mattie Clyburn Rice, the daughter of Weary Clyburn, whose name also appeared on the marker.[37] Rice's understanding of his role in the Confederate army was largely a product of stories shared directly by her father. Early on in her quest to piece together more of her father's history, Rice turned to Earl Ijames, curator of African American History at the North Carolina Museum of History. His handling of the relevant evidence related to Clyburn has always been problematic, as is his choice to characterize men like Clyburn as "colored Confederates." The reference does little more than confuse the nature of the master-slave relationship and its reliance on coercion as a mechanism of control. At times Ijames acknowledged Clyburn's enslaved status but often contradicted it with statements that added confusion rather than clarity: "It isn't clear whether Clyburn went to war just because his friend had gone; or he thought, as some soldiers did, that no matter who won, slaves would be set free; or he believed he could raise his stature by serving; or he fought because the South was the only homeland he had ever known and he was willing to die to protect it."[38]

Ijames appeared to believe that Clyburn had a choice as to whether he would join his master. Elsewhere, Ijames had written that Clyburn "escaped slavery to serve as a body servant," though the available evidence suggests just the opposite, that it was the defeat of the Confederacy that made him free.[39]

This confusing story of a slave who appeared to willingly join the Confederate army was perfect fodder for the SCV. In 2008 the North Carolina Division, SCV, held an elaborate ceremony to dedicate a military-style headstone for Clyburn. SCV commander Tom Smith welcomed the descendants of Clyburn, whom he embraced in the name of the entire organization as "one of our own." Though Mattie Rice was unable to attend due to illness, other family members offered their appreciation to the SCV for the ceremony honoring their ancestor. "I'm happy to be here. It's a glorious day," said Mary Elizabeth Clyburn Hooks, who traveled from New Jersey for the event. "I just think it's beautiful these people chose to celebrate my grandfather's bravery and courage. It's just overwhelming." Another descendant suggested that Weary and Captain Frank Clyburn "were really good friends and that trumped everything else." In response to a reporter who inquired as to why Clyburn and other slaves joined the Confederate army, Earl Ijames explained they chose to "defend what they know versus running away and going to the unknown."[40]

Finally, the headstone itself was unveiled. It offered no indication as to the occupant's racial identity or his status as the slave of Captain Clyburn. In addition to his date of death, it reads "Member of the 12th South Carolina Infantry, CSA." The SCV ensured that future visitors to the site would conclude that Clyburn was a soldier and not a slave. In doing so, the organization succeeded in distorting not only his personal history but also the larger story of the Confederacy's commitment to keeping men like Clyburn enslaved. The SCV benefited from extensive media coverage of the event and the lack of incisive investigation by reporters, who asked few questions about the history of the Confederacy and slavery.[41]

It is unclear as to whether all or even most of Weary Clyburn's descendants subscribed to the Lost Cause narrative and the SCV's agenda. Like African Americans who took part in earlier Confederate heritage celebrations, the Clyburn family may have simply appreciated the SCV's interest in remembering their ancestor as a brave and honorable man as opposed to his enslaved status. It is also possible that the SCV cared little about the family's embrace of its preferred narrative of the war and instead focused on the visual optics of having a black family involved in the dedication of one of their own. Whatever the case may be, the involvement of Weary Clyburn's descendants demonstrates that African Americans have long played a role in legitimizing the loyal slave and black Confederate myth.

Following Mattie Rice's death in 2014, the SCV and a host of other Confederate heritage organizations held an official ceremony at her gravesite next to her father. The ceremony began with a wreath-laying and dedication for Weary Clyburn, who one speaker claimed "gave [his] all for the Confederate military." Numerous speakers, including local public officials and representatives from the Order of the Confederate Rose, Children of the Confederacy, Military Order of Stars and Bars, and the UDC, praised Mattie Rice for her commitment to uncovering and telling the true story of her father's loyalty to both his master and the Confederacy.

Former SCV commander in chief Michael Givens described Rice as a "trailblazer" who was "willing to stand up for her convictions" and "her father when people said no." According to Givens, the war was not about slavery. Instead, Southern blacks and whites stood together against an invasion of their homeland: "The same blood that coursed through Weary's veins when he stood on the front lines and he fired at an enemy that was invading his home land, the same blood that was coursing through his veins when he took his friend Frank and put him on his shoulder and carried him home, is the same blood that coursed through her veins when she stood up for her own heritage. It's the same as yours and the same as mine." According to Givens, Clyburn's legacy and the devotion of his daughter served as a reminder that "we are all the same," and in the end, confusing references such as "colored Confederates" obscured the fact that they were all "Confederate soldiers, period."[42]

The SCV also sought out public support and vindication in the form of official proclamations. The office of the mayor of High Point issued a proclamation declaring October 18, 2014, Mattie Clyburn Rice Day and described her as a "real daughter of the Confederacy" and her father as a "proud soldier of Color in the 12th South Carolina Infantry of the Confederate States of America." The city of Monroe also issued a proclamation that described Clyburn as a Confederate soldier who served "honorably" and his daughter who "searched and proved that her father wore the grey." Even Republican South Carolina governor Nikki Haley issued a tribute to Rice for her commitment to giving her father "the recognition he deserved for his service as a volunteer" in the Confederate army as well as her "invaluable contributions to our knowledge of Southern history."[43] Haley's statement was consistent with her public position in support of the continued display of the Confederate battle flag.[44] In addition to public proclamations, the SCV encouraged media coverage of Rice's funeral service and her father's unusual story, which appeared in newspapers across the country and beyond.[45]

Between the public ceremonies in 2008, 2012, and 2014, no former Confederate slave and descendant received more attention than Weary Clyburn and Mattie Rice, but ultimately it counted for little and failed to have any significant impact on the overall trajectory of the sesquicentennial and popular memory of the war. For every "black Confederate" commemoration, there were multiple observances of the service and sacrifice of U.S. Colored Troops and other African Americans who aided the Union cause. Many of these commemorations took place in former Confederate states, including Charleston, South Carolina, where the fires of secession were first kindled. In May 2012 the city marked the 150th anniversary of Robert Smalls's theft of the Confederate transport steamer *Planter*, which he used to bring his wife, children, and twelve other slaves from the city to the protection of Union warships offshore and ultimately their freedom. Smalls was eventually promoted to captain of the vessel, becoming the first African American to hold that rank in the history of the navy. After the war he was elected to the South Carolina House of Representatives. Commemorative activities included the dedication of a historical marker, and a series of lectures and tours were held in honor of Smalls.[46]

The following summer the city commemorated the 150th anniversary of the assault against Battery Wagner on Morris Island by the 54th Massachusetts Volunteer Infantry. Black reenactors from five states traveled out to Morris Island to fire a salute and lay a wreath in honor of the fallen. A concert at Fort Moultrie on Sullivan's Island was held followed by the lighting of 294 luminaries to honor the men on both sides who died in the battle. Public lectures by noted scholars, a screening of *Glory*, and the dedication of a monument to the fallen at Battery Wagner rounded out the city's commemorative events. In 2014 a monument to Denmark Vesey, whose planned slave insurrection was exposed by informants and led to his execution, was dedicated in Hampton Park in Charleston. It is difficult to imagine any of these events taking place just a few decades earlier, but they are a clear indication of how the nation's collective memory of the war had evolved even in a place like South Carolina, and they all benefited from support within local government and private organizations throughout the city. Nothing comparable took place to commemorate the black Confederate soldier during the entire sesquicentennial in a city that has long held tightly to its Lost Cause history.[47]

The dedication of new monuments to U.S. Colored Troops in the two decades leading up to the sesquicentennial in places like Lexington Park,

Maryland, provided these men with a level of exposure that Confederate heritage advocates could not replicate.[48] In addition, black reenactors were a regular presence in local parades and other ceremonies throughout the Civil War 150th.

One of the problems that plagued black Confederate advocates throughout the sesquicentennial was the almost complete absence of any support from within the academic community. Dismissals by professional historians, including the University of Virginia's Gary Gallagher, who characterized the entire black Confederate movement as "demented," spoke for the vast majority within academia. Two notable exceptions, however, include Harvard scholars Henry Louis Gates and John Stauffer. Gates, who is currently the director of Harvard's Hutchins Center for African and African American Research and host of the popular PBS series *The African Americans: Many Rivers to Cross* and *Finding Your Roots*, apparently first came across stories of black Confederates during the filming of the documentary *Looking for Lincoln*, which aired in 2009. Gates and his film crew attended the 2008 ceremony in Raleigh, North Carolina, for Weary Clyburn that featured Earl Ijames as one of the speakers. Gates would later cite Ijames in the preface of his book *Lincoln on Race and Slavery* and praised him for his "pioneering research" on African Americans who "fought in the Confederate Army," though Ijames had yet to publish anything on the subject in a reputable scholarly journal.[49]

There is also no evidence that Gates has conducted any serious research on this subject, but that has not prevented him from making any number of unsubstantiated claims about the existence of loyal black soldiers. According to Gates, the failure among African Americans to acknowledge these men reflects an unwillingness to admit that some blacks may have been complicit with the Confederacy. "There were enough free negroes who supported the Confederacy," Gates stated in one interview, "that they voluntarily formed a regiment in North Carolina." Unfortunately, Gates failed to cite any supporting evidence for the claim.[50]

Gates has also leveled accusations at his fellow academic historians who he believes have intentionally ignored evidence of blacks fighting in the ranks of the Confederate army. Following the staging of *Father Comes Home from the Wars (Parts 1, 2 & 3)* in 2015, Gates joined historian Eric Foner and director Suzan-Lori Parks for a discussion about the history explored in the play. The play tells the story of Hero, a slave who is offered his freedom if he joins his master as his camp servant. Hero must choose whether to leave the woman and friends he loves for what may be yet another empty promise. With Hero now facing the challenges of life in the army, friends and family left behind debate whether to wait for his return or abandon the plantation. Parks complicates the story by outfitting Hero in a Confederate uniform, but there is never any indication that he is a soldier; the distinction between master and slave is maintained throughout the story. This fact, however, did not prevent Gates from suggesting that academic historians of a "left-of-center bent" often "censor" themselves rather than acknowledge the "complexity of the African American community" for fear of being called a "racist." One of the ways they have done this, according to Gates, is by ignoring the roughly 3,000 black men who voluntarily fought for the Confederacy. Once again, Gates offered no evidence to support these claims, which echo similar attacks from members of the neo-Confederate community who also believe that the political preferences of historians have steered them away from acknowledging the presence of black Confederate soldiers.[51]

More recently, Gates used his popular PBS show *Finding Your Roots* to introduce the black Confederate narrative with guest Bryant Gumbel. Gumbel learned during the course of the episode that his great-great-grandfather on his maternal side Martin Lamotte had been freed before 1860 and that he briefly served in the Louisiana Native Guard early in the war. Gates also correctly shared with Gumbel that this unit pledged its loyalty to the Confederacy early on and that members' motivation for doing so was likely one of self-preservation or an attempt to protect their wealth and status in New Orleans. Where Gates deviated from the historical record, however, was in concluding that the Louisiana Native Guard functioned as part of the Confederate army. As has already been shown, this unit was never accepted into Confederate service, but that did not stop Gates from asking Gumbel, "Did you know that any black men served the Confederacy?" According to Gates, "the evidence was undeniable." Gumbel learned that Lamotte eventually joined the Union army after the fall of New Orleans in April 1862. It is not clear how such a mistake could be made given the availability of numerous scholarly books and articles about this unit, but what can be said is that finding a black Confederate in the family tree of a prominent African American made for entertaining and provocative television.[52]

When questioned about his belief that the Confederate army included roughly 3,000 black volunteers, Gates regularly referenced an essay published in *The Root* by Harvard colleague John Stauffer in January 2015. Stauffer, who teaches in the English, American studies, and African American studies departments, first spoke publicly on the subject of black Confederates at Harvard in 2011.[53] At that lecture Stauffer was introduced by Gates, which may help to explain Gates's exposure to the subject, though it remains unclear as to why he took any interest at all. Stauffer is the author of books on, among other things, the abolitionist movement and Jones County, Mississippi, during the Civil War, as well as a dual biography of Abraham Lincoln and Frederick Douglass. In his essay "Yes, There Were Black Confederates. Here's Why," Stauffer makes the stunning claim "that between 3,000 and 6,000 served as Confederate soldiers." While Stauffer correctly noted that large numbers of slaves were impressed and worked as laborers, teamsters, and servants, he fails to offer a single shred of evidence supporting his claim that thousands of these men served specifically as soldiers. While the numbers may have been "statistically insignificant," they still, according to Stauffer, "carry immense symbolic weight, for they explode the myth that a slave wouldn't fight on behalf of masters."[54]

Stauffer's handling of key pieces of evidence is even more troubling. He accepted reports without question, such as that of a fugitive slave who observed 2,700 black men on the march toward Manassas before the battle and that of Henry Johnson, a free black man who managed to enlist in the 8th Connecticut Volunteer Infantry who attributed Confederate victory at Manassas to "three regiments of blacks." In neither case did Stauffer make an attempt to identify these units. Needless to say, one will not find any evidence of an entire regiment of black Confederate soldiers in any of the many military studies published about this battle. Testimony about the presence of "real [black] soldiers" in the Confederate army attributed to Frederick Douglass in July 1861 was, in fact, not shared with the public until the following February. Stauffer correctly noted that many of these reports were used to convince the Lincoln administration to begin recruiting black soldiers into the United States army, and he would have been on solid ground if he had stopped there.[55]

Neither Gates nor Stauffer appears to have had any interest in understanding how the Confederate military, the government in Richmond, and white Southerners generally understood the crucial distinction between a slave and a soldier over the course of the war. Stauffer's conclusion that "the majority of blacks who became Confederate soldiers did so not at the end of the war . . . but at the beginning of the war" would have been news to anyone who lived through the war in the Confederacy and who followed the debate over whether to recruit slaves as soldiers that culminated in legislation in March 1865. Yet even with all the essay's shortcomings, it continues to be regularly cited by the neo-Confederate community, which is more than happy to embrace its conclusions and the gravitas that a Harvard scholar brings to the debate.

By the time Stauffer published his essay, the sesquicentennial was winding down in early 2015. It concluded with commemorative events in Virginia focused on the challenges that the end of slavery posed to the nation moving forward and the role of U.S. Colored Troops in bringing about Confederate defeat. Once again the former capital of the Confederacy, Richmond, proved to be a bellwether of Civil War memory. The Future of Richmond's Past coalition facilitated community discussions throughout the Civil War 150th that attracted thousands of residents to discuss some of the toughest questions surrounding the continued legacy of the war for the city. Working with smaller institutions, the Future of Richmond's Past hosted the city's first Civil War and Emancipation Day Weekend, which drew more than 4,000 residents and visitors. The city even embraced the opportunity to serve as the backdrop for the filming of Steven Spielberg's movie *Lincoln*, but it was the commemoration of the fall of Richmond in early April 2015 that highlighted just how far the Lost Cause had been marginalized. Simulated flames were projected on buildings that had been set afire by fleeing Confederates. Thousands gathered on the Capitol Square Grounds to watch black and white reenactors of Union soldiers, along with Abraham Lincoln, march through the city to mark its capture and the liberation of its enslaved population.[56]

A week later the nation turned its attention to the final commemoration of the sesquicentennial of Robert E. Lee's surrender at Appomattox Court House on April 9, 1865. The event had been ignored entirely during the centennial celebrations, but this time around the reenactment of Lee's formal surrender in Wilmer McLean's parlor room, organized by the NPS, was complemented by public addresses and a ceremony that placed the causes and consequences of the war on full display. The highlight of the event was a ceremony that honored Hannah Reynolds, the only known black civilian casualty of the battles around Appomattox Court House, and the roughly 4,600 African Americans who emerged from Lee's surrender as free people. Luminaries representing the passage to freedom of each enslaved person were spread out over the landscape as speakers eulogized Reynolds.[57] Nearby, a reenactment marking the Appomattox anniversary took place that struck a decidedly different tone from the one organized by the NPS. Men dressed in blue and gray uniforms maneuvered onto a field, as they had done throughout the sesquicentennial, to shoot at one another before embracing one another again as fellow Americans. There was little talk of slavery or the consequences for the nation now that four million people were free among the soldiers, except for Leslie, a first-generation American from Guyana, who portrayed one of Lee's camp servants. "We need to realize it's nothing to be ashamed of. We have to learn from it," she said. Leslie offered a blunt assessment for onlookers that linked her role as a camp servant with the broader history of slavery. "As you learn from reading, they stripped slaves of everything. They stripped them of their name and reduced them to an animal. And even an animal has self-determination. They took that from human beings." Meanwhile, in the town of Appomattox, H. K. Edgerton defended a corner along what is now called Confederate Avenue. Dressed in his Confederate uniform and holding tightly to his battle flag, Edgerton seemed out of place, but that did not prevent him from reflecting on the meaning of Appomattox: "For me, [Lee's surrender] was the worst day in [the] history for Southern black folks, and Northern black folks as well. The Christian white folks in the South were the only ones who ever cared about the African, period."[58]

Edgerton's isolation on a street corner in a small south-central Virginia town was a fitting metaphor for the trajectory of the black Confederate narrative that emerged from the sesquicentennial in 2015. Die-hard believers in black Confederates were further isolated as a result of a division within the neo-Confederate community, which now referred to people like Edgerton as "Rainbow Confederates" for their failure to embrace the Confederacy's commitment to white supremacy. According to the League of the South's president, Michael Hill, the belief in black Confederates is the result of a failure to acknowledge that "Confederate armies were led and staffed overwhelmingly by white men" and that "they were fighting for the particular interests of their own Folk." Hill and others criticized the SCV's embrace of black Confederates as part of an attempt to appeal to a more diverse and multi-ethnic populace.[59] Billboards placed along highways outside of Kansas City and St. Louis, Missouri, by the SCV depicting three black men in uniform with the accompanying text "75,000 Confederates of Color?," as well as its campaign to highlight the service and bravery of Hispanic, Chinese, and Native Americans, had come to be viewed as a betrayal of the principles outlined by Confederate vice president Alexander Stephens in his "Cornerstone Speech" in March 1861.[60]

Members of the SCV, the UDC, and other Confederate heritage organizations continue to promote the black Confederate narrative, as they have done since the late 1970s. For the true believers not directly associated with these organizations, there remain plenty of opportunities to rally around the Confederate cause and the loyalty of African Americans in virtual communities located on social media platforms such as Facebook. Groups with names like Black Confederate Historical Resources, Black Confederates and

Other Minorities in the War of Northern Aggression, and Black Confederates in the Civil War offer members the opportunity to interact with other like-minded people without having to acknowledge any detractors. Popular photographs of Silas Chandler and the manipulated photograph depicting the Louisiana Native Guard, along with accounts that have long been debunked, continue to be posted as direct evidence of loyal black soldiers.

It is much too early to be able to assess the place of the black Confederate narrative in Civil War memory. A study conducted in 2012 and 2013 among undergraduate and graduate students at Virginia Commonwealth University in Richmond found that 16 percent of respondents affirmed that "blacks fought for the Confederacy alone or for the Confederacy and Union both, with no attempt to contrast the scale of their participation on the Union side with their Confederate role or to indicate that fighting for the Confederate cause was a rare exception rather than the rule." The responses of another 4 percent made a similar but more qualified statement about the presence and role of these men in the Confederate army and on the battlefield. Interestingly, the study found no statistically significant association between the belief in black Confederate soldiers and the race or place of origin of the respondent, which suggests that the belief had been acquired at some point but was not part of a larger identification with the Lost Cause or personal association with the neo-Confederate community.[61]

Even with the black Confederate myth gaining popularity among such groups as the SCV and the UDC between 1977 and 2015, along with a small but vocal group of African Americans, mainstream culture, including white Southerners, has largely rejected it. The poll also suggests that the purpose of the black Confederate narrative as a desperate attempt to defend the Lost Cause on various fronts has also failed. This would become even more apparent just a few short months following the official end of the Civil War sesquicentennial.

Conclusion

Civil War memory has always been a contested landscape. Adherence to the Lost Cause and the embrace of the loyal slave and later black Confederate narratives were never primarily about the past but rather about trying to make sense of the present. In the period immediately after the Civil War, white Southerners adopted the Lost Cause as a way to explain defeat and to justify their failed cause — which they believed remained a righteous one — to the rest of the world. By the turn of the twentieth century, former camp servants were a popular presence at veterans' reunions and other public events that celebrated the legacy of the Confederacy and the men who fought for its independence. The attendance of former camp servants followed the well-worn loyal slave narrative, but these individuals were also celebrated as representatives of a race that knew their place in the racial hierarchy of the Jim Crow South at a time of increased racial tension. Decades later, these men morphed into black Confederate soldiers to defend against a concerted challenge to the memory of the Lost Cause by a new generation of historians who placed slavery and emancipation at the center of the Civil War, black political activists who called for the removal of Confederate battle flags from public spaces, and a changing demographic throughout the Southern states that appeared to many to undercut the region's commitment to "traditional conservative values."

By the close of the Civil War sesquicentennial, the Confederate heritage community was clearly on the defensive in the face of louder cries calling for the removal of Confederate symbolism from public spaces throughout the country. Few people, however, could have anticipated the outcry against symbols of the Confederacy that followed the brutal murders that took place at the Emanuel African Methodist Episcopal Church in Charleston, South Carolina, on June 17, 2015. Dylann Roof, a twenty-one-year-old white supremacist, entered the church, where a Bible study was underway, and violently murdered nine people, including State Senator and Reverend Clementa Pinckney. In the days that followed, it was revealed that Roof had visited a number of local sites in and around Charleston connected to the history of the Civil War and slavery in preparation for his murderous spree. Roof posed for pictures at Magnolia Plantation, Boone Hall, and McLeod Plantation as well as next to a historical marker on Sullivan's Island, which served as an entry point for African slaves. Roof hoped to incite a race war with his deadly act and framed it as following in a long line of proud white supremacists.[1]

But it was the photographs of Roof posing with Confederate flags that led to demanding the removal of the battle flag on the statehouse grounds, where it had flown since 1962, first on top of the dome and since 1991 next to a Confederate monument. Calls for removal united Democrats and Republicans, including President Barack Obama, former South Carolina legislator Glenn McConnell, and presidential hopefuls Mitt Romney, Jeb Bush, and Ted Cruz. Confederate heritage advocates once again found themselves on the defensive in the face of what quickly became a national discussion encouraged by local, national, and even international coverage. Sons of Confederate Veterans leadership and even H. K. Edgerton appeared on CNN and other media outlets to distance themselves and their cherished Confederate symbols from Roof.

The South Carolina Division, SCV, quickly issued a statement in an attempt to reclaim the battle flag from its association with Roof and his heinous act. In front of the flag and Confederate soldier monument on the capitol grounds, the SCV reminded the media and onlookers of the presence of courageous black men who took up arms for the Confederacy. It was the same argument that the SCV had embraced since the late 1970s: "Historical fact shows there were Black Confederate soldiers. These brave men fought in the trenches beside their White brothers, all under the Confederate Battle Flag. This same Flag stands as a memorial to these soldiers on the grounds of the SC Statehouse today. The Sons of Confederate Veterans, a historical honor society, does not delineate which Confederate soldier we will remember or honor. We cherish and revere the memory of all Confederate veterans. None of them, Black or White, shall be forgotten." The SCV offered this argument not only to stem the tide of calls to lower the Confederate flag in Columbia but as a desperate attempt to suggest that the flag had nothing at all to do with racial divisions in South Carolina in the present or the past. The Confederate flag — properly understood — they argued, ought to unite black and white South Carolinians. According to the SCV's spokesman, Roof's violent act and close identification with the Confederate flag was the product of the "deranged mind of a horrendous individual."[2]

The scv's argument fell on deaf ears. Sustained national media coverage that focused on Roof's identification with Confederate iconography, especially the battle flag, placed Confederate heritage defenders in an even more isolated position. Nine days after the murders, President Obama, along with First Lady Michelle Obama, Vice President Joe Biden, House Speaker John Boehner, Republican governor Nikki Haley, and former secretary of state Hillary Clinton, took part in a memorial ceremony for the slain state senator and pastor. In his eulogy, the president included a passionate appeal to finally remove the battle flag from the grounds of the state capitol. Removal of the flag, according to the president, "would not be an act of political correctness; it would not be an insult to the valor of Confederate soldiers. It would simply be an acknowledgment that the cause for which they fought—the cause of slavery—was wrong—the imposition of Jim Crow after the Civil War, the resistance to civil rights for all people was wrong." Taking down the flag, continued the president, "would be one step in an honest accounting of America's history; a modest but meaningful balm for so many unhealed wounds."[3] The president's words were a direct rebuke of the Lost Cause that helped to galvanize additional support for the removal of Confederate symbols in South Carolina and elsewhere.

Haley quickly emerged in favor of removing the Confederate battle flag on the capitol grounds in Columbia. On July 6, the South Carolina State Senate took up the debate and eventually passed a bill for removal by a vote of 37–3. The House debate proved to be more divisive but eventually passed the bill as well, though by a slimmer margin. Within hours of the passage of the bill authorizing removal of the battle flag in the state assembly, Haley signed it into law. The next day hundreds of people gathered at the Confederate Soldiers Monument to watch a detachment from the South Carolina Highway Patrol lower the flag for the final time to the jeers of some and the cheers of others.[4] Even before it was lowered in Columbia, the governor of Alabama ordered the removal of the battle flag on the capitol grounds in Montgomery.[5] The events in South Carolina led quickly to public debates in Southern cities and towns over the appropriateness of the battle flag on public grounds, but the discussion soon broadened to include memorials, monuments, and markers as well.

Over the next two years, cities such as Louisville, Orlando, Baltimore, and Dallas and the campus of the University of Texas at Austin removed or relocated Confederate monuments, but it was the city of New Orleans that received the most media attention.[6] Between April and May 2017, after a year of public debate, the city removed three monuments honoring Generals Robert E. Lee, Pierre G. T. Beauregard, and President Jefferson Davis, as well as a monument commemorating the opponents of a biracial Reconstruction government. In a powerful public address to his community, the city's white mayor, Mitch Landrieu, challenged the tenets of the Lost Cause as workers removed Robert E. Lee from atop his pedestal. He cited Alexander Stephen's justification for the Confederacy but also asked his audience to think about the sight of the city's monuments from the perspective of African American parents who have to explain to their young daughter why such an individual has been given such a prominent and lauded place in their own community: "Can you look into that young girl's eyes and convince her that Robert E. Lee is there to encourage her?" Landrieu undercut the Lost Cause and the black Confederate myth directly by stating in no uncertain terms that "the Confederacy was on the wrong side of history and humanity. It sought to tear apart our nation and subjugate our fellow Americans to slavery."[7] The removal of the city's four monuments represented the most significant alteration to a public commemorative landscape devoted to the Civil War and Reconstruction to date.

Demands for removing Confederate monuments placed elected leaders on the front lines of this highly toxic and divisive debate. In 2016 Richmond mayoral candidate Joseph D. Morrissey initially called for the removal of the Jefferson Davis monument on the city's famed Monument Avenue but soon backtracked in response to public criticism. He eventually announced a revised position that involved altering instead of removing the monument. "What I would like to do," explained Morrissey, "is have a statue including Jefferson Davis and Union black soldiers and Confederate black soldiers showing unification."[8] His proposal to construct a monument that would satisfy competing Civil War memories never materialized. During his race for a senate seat in Louisiana, candidate Arden Wells took a similar position in his attempt to defuse calls by New Orleans's black community to remove the Confederate monuments by reminding them of the presence of black soldiers in the army.[9] Both candidates tried to rally the support of conservative constituents in their defense of Confederate symbols and stave off demands for their removal by liberals by reminding them that the Confederacy embraced African Americans as soldiers.

The public display of the Confederate battle flag in Lexington, Virginia, the home of Washington & Lee University, where Robert E. Lee served as president after the war and where both he and Stonewall Jackson are buried, remained controversial throughout this period. Even before the Charleston murders, the city banned the display of the battle flag on city lampposts during annual scv reunions and parades commemorating Lee-Jackson Day. In 2014 a group of African American law students at the university demanded, among other things, that Confederate flags be removed from inside Lee Chapel and that the scv and other neo-Confederate groups be banned from gathering inside the building. The increasingly hostile reception to a group that considered Lexington sacred ground led the scv to issue a statement in 2016 that by this time had become all too common. In addition to pointing out that "membership is open to all races and creeds," the scv argued that Lee had always expressed disapproval of slavery and reminded the public that Jackson had once led a Sunday school class for Lexington's enslaved community. Finally, members referenced the local gravesite of Levi Miller, who they claimed was "a free black Confederate soldier."[10] As with previous statements, this appeal to black Confederates made no noticeable impact on how the public perceived the scv or the history it purportedly claimed to honor.

The removal of Confederate iconography even extended to the markers of honor placed at the graves of "black Confederate" soldiers. Just a few months after the Charleston murders, the descendants of Creed Holland, a slave who worked as a teamster in the Confederate army, removed the Southern Cross of Honor that was placed on his grave in 2002 by the scv. Holland's great-grandson William Holland came to reject the scv's continued insistence that slavery was not the cause of the war and that it played only a minor role in shaping its outcome. He also maintained that the scv's embrace of his ancestor was part of a public relations push to make the organization more appealing. "They were happy to get African American members in their group," he said. "They were just using it as a publicity stunt." This is the only known example of a black family returning a memorial marker to the scv or the United Daughters of the Confederacy, but it reflects a more aggressive push on the part of African Americans demanding the removal of vestiges of the Confederacy from prominent places.[11]

The Holland family's choice to remove the memorial marker from their ancestor's grave has not prevented the scv from dedicating new headstones to fictitious black soldiers. In 2016 the Norfolk Country Grays Camp No. 1549, scv, honored William Mack Lee—who claimed to be none other than Robert E. Lee's personal camp servant—for his service. Organizers of the event were confident that Mack Lee's story had been reviewed and that all of the information inscribed on the headstone had been confirmed. No indication of his racial identity was included, but that was irrelevant to Frank Earnest, a member of the local scv: "What color he was or wasn't is of no concern to the Sons of Confederate Veterans. The only color of concern to us is Confederate gray."[12] Unfortunately, in its claims to have scoured the historical record, the SCV overlooked published articles from its members' own ancestors who had—as we have already seen—all but declared Mack Lee to be a fraud in the very pages of *Confederate Veteran* magazine. The decision to honor Mack Lee as a soldier underscores the flimsy research process that informs these dedications and the flawed understanding of the history of the Confederacy. It also helps to explain why these accounts are so easily challenged along with the broader Lost Cause narrative in which they rest.

Any lingering belief that using the Confederacy's mythical black soldiers in defense of Confederate iconography and the Lost Cause might prove successful was settled by a white-nationalist rally that took place in Charlottesville, Virginia, on August 12, 2017, just three months after monuments had been removed in New Orleans. Violent clashes between white nationalists led by Richard Spencer and a larger crowd of counterprotesters in the vicinity of the Robert E. Lee monument left nineteen people injured and a thirty-two-year-old woman by the name of Heather Heyer dead. Spencer's group had traveled to Charlottesville to defend the Lee monument, which the city council had recently voted to remove, but national coverage of the event and President Donald Trump's own public statements defending Confederate monuments guaranteed that the discussion would remain highly politicized and divisive. While Charlottesville is still waiting for a state court to rule on whether its monuments can be removed, other states chose to forge ahead. Shortly thereafter, in the dark of night, the city of Baltimore removed a large monument commemorating Lee and Jackson. Kansas City, West Palm Beach, Orlando, Austin, Dallas, and a host of smaller communities soon followed by removing monuments, markers, and battle flags from popular public spaces.

Even monuments dedicated at the turn of the twentieth century honoring the Confederacy's loyal black slaves came under increased scrutiny as well. The monument in Fort Mills, South Carolina, "dedicated to the faithful slaves who, loyal to a sacred trust, toiled for the support of the Army," came to divide the African American and broader community over whether it should remain in the wake of Charlottesville. While some have had trouble with its Lost Cause message, others prefer to keep standing one of the only signs that their ancestors existed at all in their community. In addition, the large Confederate monument nestled among the graves of Arlington National Cemetery, with its motifs of the "Mammy" figure and a uniformed black man who continues to be mistaken for a soldier, has also come under scrutiny, by the very descendants of the monument's sculptor, Moses Eze-kiel. "All of us agree that monuments to the Confederacy are racist justi-fications of slavery, of owning people," explained Judith Ezekiel, a visiting professor of women's studies and African American studies at Wright State University in Ohio. "We wanted to say that although Ezekiel is a relative of ours, we still believe it's a relic of a racist past."[13]

Almost on cue, in October 2017 two Republican legislators in South Carolina called for a monument honoring African Americans who fought for the Confederacy to be erected at the statehouse in Columbia—the site where the most recent wave of Confederate flag and monument removals began in the summer of 2015. Mike Burns hoped the monument would "help educate current and future generations of a little known" chapter of South Carolina history. According to Burns, black and white South Caro-linians both "stepped up to defend their home state," though he never ac-knowledged that more than 50 percent of the state's population in 1860 was enslaved. For Bill Chumley, the dedication of this monument would fulfill what he believes to be a biblical obligation "to honor our fathers and mothers . . . who showed more than 150 years ago that they loved their state."[14] Both Burns and Chumley voted against the removal of the Confederate battle flag in 2015, and they remain outspoken defenders of Confederate monuments. Their proposal was both an attempt to right the wrong that they failed to prevent in July 2015 and to forestall the removal of future monuments with one that imagines a shared legacy of defense of home that united both black and white South Carolinians. Burns and Chumley are the most recent in a long line of Americans who have never been able to acknowledge what Confederates so clearly expressed throughout the war with their own words and deeds. Those who led the Confederacy in the halls of Richmond's capi-tol building and who fought for it on countless battlefields (past the point where many believed that independence was still possible) were willing to sacrifice everything, including their lives, in the defense of slavery and white supremacy.

The proposal by Burns and Chumley suggests that the mythical black Confederate narrative will continue to be embraced by those who believe it will serve their agenda. No amount of contrary evidence or careful his-torical interpretation will likely persuade them otherwise. Ultimately, the battle over the memory of the black Confederate soldier is one small part of a much larger conversation about the meaning and legacy of our civil war that Americans will continue to debate. Disagreements over the place of Afri-can Americans within the Confederate war effort and the larger Civil War are about more than how we understand history. These disagreements point to the extent to which we are willing to face some of the toughest questions about what was at stake for four million enslaved people as well as the nation between 1861 and 1865. In the end, an army of black Confederate soldiers never came to the aid of the Confederacy, but free and formerly enslaved African Americans did join the United States Army and ultimately helped to destroy the slaveholders' rebellion. These men played a key role in ending slavery and set the United States on a profoundly different course as a free nation, one that we are still struggling to come to terms with 150 years later.

Acknowledgments

Over the past decade, I have amassed numerous debts throughout the researching and writing of this book. Thanking the many people who have assisted me is a fitting way to finally bring this project to a close. I benefited immensely from conversations at different stages with David Blight, Keith Bohannon, Glenn David Brasher, Peter Carmichael, John Coski, Gary Gallagher, Barbara Gannon, M. Keith Harris, John Hennessy, Caroline Janney, Bruce Levine, and Brooks Simpson. Numerous people shared sources that in many cases I would have overlooked. They include Robert Baker, Christopher Barr, Vicki Betts, Margaret Blough, Yulanda Burgess, David Dixon, Greg Downs, Mark Dunkelman, Lisa Foster, Donald Frazier, W. Todd Groce, John Heiser, John Hennessy, Eric Jacobson, Ethan J. Kytle, Chris Lese, Chris Meekins, Mike Musick, Wayne Motts, Barton Myers, Ken Noe, Nancy Noe, Jason Phillips, Patricia Poland, John Sampson, Stuart Sanders, Katharina Schlichtherle, Timothy Smith, Tim Talbott, Paul Taylor, Bruce Vail, and Daniel Weinfeld.

I am grateful to a number of editors at various publications online and in print for providing me the opportunity to test ideas about this subject with their readers. Thanks go to Terry Johnston at the *Civil War Monitor*, Malcolm Jones at the *Daily Beast*, Clay Risen at the *New York Times*, Aaron Sheehan-Dean at the *Journal of the Civil War Era*, Dana Shoaf at *Civil War Times*, Rick Shenkman at *History News Network*, and Brian Wolly at *Smithsonian*. I also appreciate invitations from the National Civil War Center, the Medford Historical Society, the Civil War Institute at Gettysburg College, Longwood University, and Genesee Community College to speak on this subject as part of their workshops and speaker series.

I wrote my first blog post on the subject of the myth of the black Confederate soldier on December 11, 2005. Little did I know that the subject would consume so much attention at *Civil War Memory* over the course of the next thirteen years and eventually result in this book. Hundreds of blog posts have been written that now contain thousands of reader comments.

Civil War Memory has placed me in touch with an incredible community of fellow Civil War enthusiasts and students of history. Many of the ideas contained in this book were first shared on the blog. Perusing the archive of posts and comments is a road map of how my own thinking has evolved on this subject over the years. My readers have been indispensable in correcting mistakes, providing additional sources, and forcing me to rethink certain assumptions. My thanks go to Bob Beatty, Shoshana Bee, Margaret Blough, Bryan Cheesboro, Emmanuel Dabney, Jimmy Dick, Jonathan Dresner, James Epperson, Christopher Graham, Neil Hamilton, Boyd Harris, Thomas Heaney, Patrick Jennings, William Kerrigan, Scott Mackenzie, Al Mackey, A. D. Powell, James Simcoe, Mark Snell, John Stoudt, David Woodbury, and Patrick Young. I hope that the entire Civil War Memory community will embrace this book as a token of my gratitude.

Meeting Myra Chandler Sampson, great-granddaughter of Silas Chandler, was one of the highlights on this journey of researching and writing about black Confederates. I stand in awe of her efforts over the years to defend the memory of her famous ancestor through careful research in local and state archives, and I especially appreciate her willingness to entrust what she discovered with me. Myra was never far from my mind during those moments when I put this project aside or thought about abandoning it altogether. It was an honor to have the opportunity to coauthor a magazine article with Myra about Silas Chandler for the fiftieth anniversary issue of Civil War Times in 2012.

Thanks go to Andy Hall, who took the time to read and comment on the first four chapters of the manuscript. Readers of Andy's blog, Dead Confederates, have benefited greatly from his insights and original research into this subject. I also want to thank Colin Woodward for reviewing and commenting on part of this manuscript. His 2014 book, Marching Masters, was essential in helping me organize the first two chapters.

Closer to home, I benefited from the wise counsel and friendship of my fellow Book Squad members, Liz Covart, Sara Georgini, Megan Kate Nelson, Heather Cox Richardson, Nina Silber, and Thomas Thurston. Their thorough critiques of early chapter drafts as well as of the book proposal were not always pleasant to read, but they proved to be essential in pointing out interpretive problems and highlighting questions and perspectives that I had not considered. Our time together reminds me of just how important community was to me in maintaining the level of focus and commitment necessary to complete this project.

At the University of North Carolina Press, I want to thank Mark

Simpson-Vos for his encouragement and support throughout the process, as well as Jessica Newman and Jay Mazzocchi. Thanks go as well to the two anonymous reviewers who provided feedback on the first draft of the manuscript. Aaron Sheehan-Dean, Peter Carmichael, and Caroline Janney have long supported my research efforts. It is an honor to have this book included in UNC Press's Civil War America series, which they now oversee.

My wife, Michaela, has been with this project from the beginning. Her love and support have meant the world to me. I can't imagine completing this or any other project without her by my side. Finally, this book is lovingly dedicated to my parents, Alan and Judy Levin, whom I owe more than they will ever know.

Notes

CV   *Confederate Veteran*
CWM   *Civil War Memory* (blog)

INTRODUCTION

1. For further analysis of Ruffin's *Anticipations*, see Binnington, *Confederate Visions*, 44–69; and Jason Phillips, "The Prophecy of Edmund Ruffin: Anticipating the Future of Civil War History," in Wright and Dresser, *Apocalypse and the Millennium*, 13–30.

2. Ruffin, *Anticipations*, 264–65.

3. Ruffin, 304–5.

4. See Genovese and Fox-Genovese, *Fatal Self-Deception*, 143.

5. While I prefer to refer to these men as camp slaves, as a clear acknowledgment of their legal status and racial hierarchy, I also utilize references to "camp servants" and "body servants" as an acknowledgment of the language employed by Confederates and postwar commentators and to improve the narrative flow. In all cases their legal status remains the same unless noted otherwise.

6. A number of historians maintain that the number of camp slaves dropped dramatically after 1863. These historians have tended to rely on Bell I. Wiley's *Southern Negroes, 1861–1865*, which in turn relied on Walter L. Fleming's 1905 book *Civil War and Reconstruction in Alabama*, which finally can be traced back to former Virginia governor and Confederate John S. Wise's *The End of An Era* (1899). See Hollandsworth, "Looking for Bob," 299–300.

7. "What Caused the Civil War?," Pew Research Center, May 11, 2018, http://www.pew research.org/fact-tank/2011/05/18/what-caused-the-civil-war/ (accessed April 2, 2018).

8. Emma Brown and Scott Clement, "Poll: Americans Divided over Whether Slavery Was the Civil War's Main Cause," *Washington Post*, August 6, 2015, https://www .washingtonpost.com/news/education/wp/2015/08/06/poll-americans-divided-over -whether-slavery-was-the-civil-wars-main-cause/?utm_term=.27403d1c3cb0 (accessed July 30, 2018).

9. "SPLC Report: U.S. Education on American Slavery Sorely Lacking," Southern Poverty Law Center, January 31, 2018, https://www.splcenter.org/news/2018/01/31/splc -report-us-education-american-slavery-sorely-lacking (accessed April 2, 2018).

10. Interview with Gary W. Gallagher, American Forum, May 13, 2014, https://www .youtube.com/watch?v=fYFIWlGJhjM&t=6s (accessed April 1, 2018).

11. Recent scholarship includes Jordan, *Black Confederates and Afro-Yankees*; Mohr, *On the Threshold of Freedom*; Levine, *Confederate Emancipation*; Glatthaar, *General Lee's Army*; McCurry, *Confederate Reckoning*; Brasher, *Peninsula Campaign*; Woodward, *Marching Masters*; and Dillard, *Jefferson Davis's Final Campaign*.

12. Kevin M. Levin, "The Myth of the Black Confederate Soldier," *Daily Beast*, August 8, 2015, https://www.thedailybeast.com/the-myth-of-the-black-confederate-soldier (accessed April 3, 2018).

CHAPTER 1

1. "Glimpses of Soldiers' Lives: A. M. Chandler and Silas Chandler, Family Slave," Prints and Photographs Division, Library of Congress, http://www.loc.gov/rr/print/coll /SoldierbiosChandler.html/.

2. A consultant for the *History Detectives* episode about this photograph concluded that the weapons were likely studio props. "Chandler Tintype," *History Detectives* (season 9, episode 12), http://www.pbs.org/opb/historydetectives/investigation/chandler-tintype/ (accessed April 15, 2017).

3. 1850 U.S. Census and 1860 U.S. Census; 1860 Slave Schedule. On slaveholders who moved west, see Cashin, *Family Venture*.

4. On the place of slavery in the formation of Confederate identity, see Rubin, *Shattered Nation*, 101–2.

5. A. Robinson, *Bitter Fruits of Bondage*, 106–9.

6. On the use of slave labor at Tredegar Iron Works, see Dew, *Ironmaker to the Confederacy*; on slave impressment, see Brewer, *Confederate Negro*; McCurry, *Confederate Reckoning*, 263–309; and Martinez, *Confederate Slave Impressment*.

7. K. Brown, *Retreat from Gettysburg*, 49.

8. Ford and Ford, *Life in the Confederate Army*, 75.

9. John Rees, "War as Waiter: Soldier Servants," *Journal of the American Revolution*, April 28, 2015, https://allthingsliberty.com/2015/04/war-as-a-waiter-soldier-servants/ (accessed April 4, 2018); Greenberg, *Wicked War*, 162–63.

10. A collection of state secession statements can be found in Loewen and Sebesta, *Confederate and Neo-Confederate Reader*.

11. Quoted in Rubin, *Shattered Nation*, 101.

12. T. Moore, *God Our Refuge*, 19.

13. Smith, *Palmetto Boy*, 26.

14. Bledsoe, *Citizen-Officers*, 62–101.

15. Charles S. Lieberman to Miss Lenora, August 23, 1861, typescript copy of original provided to the author.

16. Glatthaar, *General Lee's Army*, 309.

17. Woodward, *Marching Masters*, 82–83, quoted in Fleming, *Civil War and Reconstruction in Alabama*, 207.

18. Allen and Bohannon, *Campaigning with "Old Stonewall,"* 132.

19. John Christopher Winsmith to Kate, October 3, 1861, John Christopher Winsmith Papers, Eleanor S. Brockenbrough Library, Museum of the Confederacy, Richmond, Va.

20. Gallagher, *Fighting for the Confederacy*, 76; legal ownership of Charley did not transfer to Alexander. An account was open in a Richmond bank from which his owner could withdraw payment for his services for the duration of the war.

21. Ford, *Hour of Our Nation's Agony*, 50.

22. Eggleston, *Rebel's Recollection*, 36.

23. Hubard, *Civil War Memoirs* , 21.

24. Quoted in Emerson, *Sons of Privilege*, 27.

25. Stone, *Wandering to Glory*, 12.

26. Quoted in Jordan, *Black Confederates and Afro-Yankees*, 185.

27. "DONELSON: Recollections of a Private Who Participated in That Able and Bloody Fight," *Pulaski (Tenn.) Citizen*, October 15, 1887.

28. Owen, *In Camp and Battle*, 21–22.

29. Quoted in Aubrecht, *Civil War in Spotsylvania County*, 63.

30. Quoted in Jordan, *Black Confederates and Afro-Yankees*, 185. For a postwar description of the importance of camp cooks, see Allen C. Redwood, "The Cook of the Confederate Army," *Scribner's Monthly*, August 1879, 560–68.

31. R. Moore, *Life for the Confederacy*, 67.

32. Yetman, *When I Was a Slave*, 131–33.

33. Quoted in A. Robinson, *Bitter Fruits of Bondage*, 92.

34. Smith, *Palmetto Boy*, 51, 57.

35. Dozier, *Gunner in Lee's Army*; Andrew Chandler to his mother, August 31, 1862, typescript photocopy in possession of the author.

36. Quoted in Glatthaar, *General Lee's Army*, 310.

37. Dozier, *Gunner in Lee's Army*, 44.

38. The first two accounts can be found in Litwack, *Been in the Storm So Long*, 40; McCarthy, *Detailed Minutiae of Soldier Life*, 19.

39. Pearson, *Lee and Jackson's Bloody Twelfth*, 127.

40. Smith, *Palmetto Boy*, 79; Pearson, *Lee and Jackson's Bloody Twelfth*, 137.

41. Wiley, *Southern Negroes*, 137.

42. John Christopher Winsmith to Kate, April 26, 1861, Winsmith Papers.

43. Pearson, *Lee and Jackson's Bloody Twelfth*, 108, 121.

44. Quoted in Noe, *Reluctant Rebels*, 41–42.

45. Quoted in Aubrecht, *Civil War in Spotsylvania County*, 60.

46. Gallagher, *Fighting for the Confederacy*, 76–77.

47. Blomquist and Taylor, *This Cruel War*, 133.

48. Hassler, *One of Lee's Best Men*, 177, 186. In December 1861, Pender attempted to "Christianize" Joe. "He seems to be a good boy and desirous of doing right and says he likes for me to read and talk to him, but he is rather unlearned as a darky would say. If I could bring him to a true Christian condition I should feel that I had done some good in this world" (108–9).

49. John B. Evans, Richmond, to wife, December 2, 1864, John B. Evans Papers, 1862–1865, Perkins Library, Special Collections Library, Duke University, Durham, N.C.

50. See Power, *Lee's Miserables*, 221–25.

51. Allen and Bohannon, *Campaigning with "Old Stonewall,"* 86–87.

52. Louisa Chandler to Andrew M. Chandler, March 26, 1863, copy in possession of the author.

53. Typescript copies of letters of General James Cantey, November 19, 1861, in possession of the author.

54. Smith, *Palmetto Boy*, 64, 110.

55. Smith, 74, 80, 84.

56. Emerson, *Sons of Privilege*, 27.

57. *Regulations for the Army of the Confederate States*, 77.

58. Hackethan, "Reading Marlboro Jones."

59. Robertson, *Soldiers Blue and Gray*, 31.

60. Jordan, *Black Confederates and Afro-Yankees*, 189; Caffey, *Battle-fields of the South*, 158.

61. Fremantle, *Three Months in the Southern States*, 281.

62. Caffey, *Battle-fields of the South*, 65.

63. Avary, *Virginia Girl in the Civil War*, 292–93.

64. A servant's influence among slaves may have depended in part on the military rank of his owner. Jordan, *Black Confederates and Afro-Yankees*, 186.

65. "Black Confederates," Sons of Confederate Veterans, http://www.scv.org/new /contributed-works/black-confederates/ (accessed April 3, 2018).

66. Steiner, *Report of Lewis H. Steiner*, 19.

67. Wilkinson and Woodworth, *Scythe of Fire*, 224.

68. Wiley, *Southern Negroes*, 143.

69. Craig, *Upcountry South Carolina*, 109.

70. Quoted in Wiley, *Southern Negroes*, 143.

71. *Petersburg (Va.) Daily Express*, May 30, 1862.

72. John Claiborne to his wife, May 22, 1864, Letters of John Herbert Claiborne, 1864–1865, Accession #3633, Albert and Shirley Small Special Collections Library, University of Virginia, Charlottesville.

73. John Christopher Winsmith to J. N. Moore, July 28, 1862, Winsmith Papers.

74. Ford, *Hour of Our Nation's Agony*, 102.

75. Quoted in Woodward, *Marching Masters*, 125.

76. Sampson and Levin, "Loyalty of Silas Chandler."

77. For more on some of the dangers of emancipation, see Downs, *Sick from Freedom*; and Manning, *Troubled Refuge*.

CHAPTER 2

1. A.M. Chandler obituary, *CV*, July 1920, 270.

2. A. M. Chandler obituary, 270.

3. Quoted in Sampson and Levin, "Loyalty of Silas Chandler," 33.

4. Quoted in Genovese and Fox-Genovese, *Fatal Self-Deception*, 145.

5. Foner, *Fiery Trial*, 166–69; Gallagher, *Union War*, 33–35.

6. U.S. War Department, *War of the Rebellion* (hereafter *Official Records*), series 3, vol. 4, 1009.

7. "Henry Hill Scenes," *Chelsea (Mass.) Telegraph and Pioneer*, August 3, 1861, 3.

8. Quoted in Ash, *Black Experience*, 42.

9. Last three quotes from Covey and Eisnach, *How the Slaves Saw the Civil War*, 151.

10. Segars and Barrow, *Black Southerners in Confederate Armies*, 133. Originally published in *Macon (Ga.) Telegraph*, October 4, 1862.

11. Richard Rollins, "Servants and Soldiers: Tennessee's Black Southerners in Gray," in Rollins, *Black Southerners in Gray*, 180.

12. Segars and Barrow, *Black Southerners in Confederate Armies*, 139. Originally published in the *Columbus (Ga.) Daily Sun*, November 26, 1861.

13. Stephen Moore to his wife Rachel, July 8, 1862, in Tom Moore Craig, ed., *Upcountry South Carolina*, 97–98.

14. Jacob Stroyer quoted in Litwack, *Been in the Storm So Long*, 39.

15. *Charleston Daily Courier*, May 29, 1863, quoted in Wiley, *Southern Negroes*, 141–42.

16. Quoted in Brasher, *Peninsula Campaign*, 113, 115.

17. *Douglass Monthly*, September 4, 1861, 516.

18. Brasher, *Peninsula Campaign*, 178–80.

19. Quoted in Kate Masur, "Slavery and Freedom at Bull Run," *Disunion (blog)*, July 27, 2011, http://opinionator.blogs.nytimes.com/2011/07/27/slavery-and-freedom-at-bull-run/ (accessed April 26, 2017).

20. Andy Hall, "Frederick Douglass' Black Confederate," *Dead Confederates: A Civil War Era Blog*, February 20, 2015, http://deadconfederates.com/2015/02/20/frederick-douglass-black-confederate/ (accessed March 5, 2017); Brasher, *Peninsula Campaign*, 76–77.

21. Brasher, *Peninsula Campaign*, 95.

22. Hollandsworth, *Louisiana Native Guards*, 1–10.

23. Members of the Creole community in Mobile, Alabama, offered their military service for the first time in April 1862. In November 1863 General Dabney Maury, who commanded Mobile's defenses, received a response from Secretary of War James Seddon, who reminded him that "our position with the North and before the world will not allow the employment as armed soldiers of negroes." See Bergeron, *Confederate Mobile*, 105–6; Levine, *Confederate Emancipation*, 19.

24. Deserino, *Wearing the Gray Suit*, 19; *Journal of the Congress of the Confederate States of America*, 1st Cong., 2nd sess., vol. 2, 113, 118, 145, 152, 174; vol. 5, 54, 79, 141–59, 199, 250, 262.

25. Jones, *Rebel War Clerk's Diary*, 278.

26. K. Brown, *Retreat from Gettysburg*, 49–50.

27. Fremantle, *Three Months in the Southern States*, 234.

28. Wilkinson and Woodworth, *Scythe of Fire*, 224.

29. Hassler, *One of Lee's Best Men*, 254.

30. Creighton, *Colors of Courage*, 131–33.

31. Tom Elmore, "Southern Slaves at Gettysburg," Civil War Talk, April 19, 2016, https://civilwartalk.com/threads/southern-slaves-at-gettysburg.123686/ (accessed April 4, 2017).

32. Quoted in Guelzo, *Gettysburg*, 188.

33. Quoted in Richard Rollins, "Black Confederates at Gettysburg," in Rollins, *Black Southerners in Gray*, 132–33.

34. Gallagher, *Fighting for the Confederacy*, 243–44; Edward Porter Alexander, "Artillery Fighting at Gettysburg," in *Battles and Leaders of the Civil War*, vol. 3, 360.

35. Lee's retreat is covered extensively in K. Brown, *Retreat from Gettysburg*.

36. K. Brown, 53, 142, 180.

37. Paradis, *African Americans and the Gettysburg Campaign*, 59–61.

38. K. Brown, *Retreat from Gettysburg*, 300.

39. Quoted in Dreese, *Torn Families*, 150–51.

40. Faust, *This Republic of Suffering*, 3–32.

41. Barefoot, *Let Us Die Like Brave Men*, 135–38.

42. A. Davis, *Boy Colonel of the Confederacy*, 336–37.

43. Rollins, "Black Confederates at Gettysburg," 137–38; Michael W. Hofe, *That There Be No Stain upon My Stones*.

44. Glatthaar, *General Lee's Army*, 313–14.

45. Glatthaar, 313; Emerson, *Sons of Privilege*, 64–65; Krick, "Repairing an Army," 38.

46. Quoted in Mohr, *On the Threshold of Freedom*, 288–89.

47. On Confederate surrender at Vicksburg, see Ballard, *Vicksburg*, 398–404.

48. Quoted in Glatthaar, *General Lee's Army*, 90.

49. Quoted in Wiley, *Southern Negroes*, 139.

50. Owen, *In Camp and Battle*, 22.

51. Gallagher, *Fighting for the Confederacy*.

52. S. C. Mitchell, "Recollections of a Private," typescript, copy in possession of Timothy B. Smith.

53. Thompson, *Civil War in the Southwest*, 40.

54. Quoted in Wiley, 139.

55. Peter S. Carmichael, "We Were 'Men,'" 1–2.

56. Parkinson, *Common Cause*, 172–76.

57. On July 20, 1862, Ewell wrote to his niece Lizzie, "It is astonishing to me that our people do not pass laws to form Regiments of blacks. The Yankees are fighting low foreinors against the best of our people, whereas were we to fight our negroes they would be a fair offset & we would not be as now fighting kings against men to use a comparison from chequers." Quoted in Pfanz, *Richard S. Ewell*, 139.

58. Levine, *Confederate Emancipation*, 18.

59. R. Robinson, *General Orders*, General Orders No. 138, October 24, 1863, 190–92.

60. See Gallagher, *Lee and His Army*, 151–90.

61. *Montgomery Monthly Advertiser*, January 6, 1864; President Jefferson Davis, state of the country speech delivered to the Confederate Congress, December 7, 1863, for the First Congress, Fourth Session, December 7, 1863, to February 17, 1864, in Richardson, *Messages and Papers of the Confederacy*, 1:345–82.

62. *Official Records*, series 4, vol. 3, 208; *Public Laws of the Confederate States of America*, 235–36. On social unrest in the Confederacy, see Levine, *Confederate Emancipation*, 22–24.

63. Quoted in Durden, *Gray and the Black*, 54.

64. Quoted in Durden, 59.

65. On Cleburne's slave enlistment plan, see Symonds, *Stonewall of the West*, 181–201.

66. Jefferson Davis to General William H. Walker, 13 January 1864, *Official Records*, series 1, vol. 52, pt. 2, 596.

67. Quoted in Durden, *Gray and the Black*, 58.

68. See Levine, *Confederate Emancipation*, 32–34.

69. Even British observer Arthur Fremantle was not confused about the status of enslaved people attached to the Confederate army. During the retreat following the battle of Gettysburg, Fremantle observed a slave wearing a Union uniform escorting prisoners:

> From what I have seen of the Southern negroes, I am of the opinion that the Confederates could, if they chose, convert a great number into soldiers; and from the affection which undoubtedly exists as a general rule between the slaves and their masters, I think that they would prove more efficient than black troops under any other circumstances. But I do not imagine that such an experiment will be tried, except as a very last resort, partly on account of the great value of the negroes, and partly because the Southerners consider it improper to introduce such an element on a large scale into civilized warfare. Any person who has seen negro

features convulsed with rage, may form a slight estimate of what the result would
be of arming a vast number of blacks, rousing their passions, and then allowing
them free scope. (*Three Months in the Southern States*, 282)

70. Howell Cobb to James A. Seddon, January 8, 1865, in *Official Records*, series 4, vol. 3,
1009–10.

71. Credit goes to Andy Hall for this last point, "Real Confederates Didn't Know about
Black Confederates," *Dead Confederates: A Civil War Era Blog*, January 8, 2015, https://
deadconfederates.com/tag/howell-cobb/ (accessed June 2, 2017).

72. See Dillard, *Jefferson Davis's Final Campaign*.

73. Quoted in Durden, *Gray and the Black*, 108; on the debate to arm slaves, see Bruce
Levine, *Confederate Emancipation*.

74. *Richmond Whig*, November 8, 1864.

75. *Richmond Sentinel*, November 8, 1864.

76. Quoted in Durden, *Gray and the Black*, 180.

77. Quoted in Allen and Bohannon, *Campaigning with "Old Stonewall,"* 137.

78. Hubbs, *Voices from Company D*, 355; Durden, *Gray and the Black*, 223.

79. *Richmond Whig*, February 18, 1865.

80. Quoted in Dillard, *Jefferson Davis's Final Campaign*, 147.

81. Quoted in Manning, *What This Cruel War Was Over*, 208–9.

82. Quoted in Manning, 209.

83. See Levine, *Confederate Emancipation*, 115–16.

84. *Richmond Daily Dispatch*, December 28, 1864.

85. Robert E. Lee to Senator Andrew Hunter, January 18, 1865, in *Official Records*,
series 4, vol. 3, 1012–13.

86. *Richmond Sentinel*, March 21, 1865.

87. See Levine, *Confederate Emancipation*, 125–28.

88. "The Cause Progressing," *Richmond Daily Dispatch*, March 25, 1865; *Richmond
Examiner*, March 27, 1865; Hughes, *Boy's Experience in the Civil War*, 13.

89. Gallagher, *Fighting for the Confederacy*, 545.

90. Gallagher, *Fighting for the Confederacy*, 545.

91. Quoted in Ward, *Slaves' War*, 93.

CHAPTER 3

1. "Many Speeches Are Delivered," *Charlotte Observer*, June 5, 1929, 10.

2. "Reunion All Set Now; Uncle Steve Eberhart Is in Town," *Charlotte Observer*, June 5,
1929, 1.

3. Steve Perry claimed to be over 100 years old in Charlotte, but that may have been
another way of solidifying his connection to an idealized antebellum past for the benefit of
his audiences as well as an acknowledgment that he did not know his age. As is the case for
the vast majority of slaves, it is impossible to pin down a birth date, but it is likely that he
was born sometime between 1845 and 1850 in Oglethorpe County, Georgia. Six male slaves
between the ages of fourteen and seventeen are listed among the 14 total slaves owned
by the Eberharts in 1860. He was one of 6,589 slaves in Oglethorpe County, constituting
roughly two-thirds of the population on the eve of the Civil War.

4. Quoted in Hardy, *Civil War Charlotte*, 154.

5. "Reunion All Set Now; Uncle Steve Eberhart Is in Town," 1.

6. "Forrest's Valet Admits Lee and Jackson Were Good Too," and "'COMRADES,'" *Charlotte Observer*, June 5, 1929, 10.

7. Pollard, *Lost Cause*, 660.

8. Levin, "'When Johnny Comes Marching Home,'" 96.

9. On Klan violence, see Parsons, *Ku-Klux*.

10. See Blair, *Contesting the Memory*; and Neff, *Honoring the Civil War Dead*.

11. On the Lost Cause, see Janney, *Remembering the Civil War*, 133–59; and Foster, *Ghosts of the Confederacy*, 11–47.

12. Eggleston, *Rebel's Recollection*, 185.

13. McCarthy, *Detailed Minutiae of Soldier Life*, 19; Humphries, *Journal of Archibald C. McKinley*, 36.

14. "A.B. Carter Searching for Benjamin Harris," Last Seen: Finding Family after Slavery, http://informationwanted.org/items/show/2186 (accessed April 3, 2018).

15. Quoted in Taylor, *Destruction and Reconstruction*, 63.

16. Barrow, Segars, and Rosenburg, *Black Confederates*, 137.

17. Curran, *John Dooley's Civil War*, 59.

18. Quoted in Eanes, *Virginia's Black Confederates*, 12–13.

19. See Rubin, *Through the Heart of Dixie*, 57–61.

20. "Faithful Slave and Friend," *CV*, March 1904, 123.

21. "'Uncle' Charles Perkins," *CV*, September 1903, 422.

22. Quoted in Angelika Krüger-Kahloula, "History, Memory, and Politics Written in Stone: Early African American Grave Inscriptions," The Middle Passage Project, https://www.wm.edu/sites/middlepassage/documents/MBA_Kruger.pdf (accessed November 5, 2017).

23. "Survivors in Council. Oration of General Hood and Address of Bishop Quintard," *Charleston Daily*, December 13, 1872.

24. Goodloe, *Confederate Echoes*, 195.

25. Stiles, *Four Years under Marse Robert*, 136.

26. Sorrel, *Recollections of a Confederate Staff Officer*, 64–65.

27. Neely, Holzer, and Boritt, *Confederate Image*, 120–23; Wilson, *Baptized in Blood*, 69–70.

28. Harvey, *Civil War and American Art*, 130–31.

29. Page, *Marse Chan*, 39.

30. See McElya, *Clinging to Mammy*.

31. John B. Evans, Richmond, to wife, December 2, 1864, John B. Evans Papers.

32. On the New South, see Ayers, *Promise of the New South*.

33. Quoted in Link, *Atlanta*, 151.

34. "Grady in Boston," *Atlanta Constitution*, December 15, 1889.

35. Levin, *Remembering the Battle of the Crater*, 25–32.

36. *Proceedings of the Conference for Education in the South* (New York: Committee on Publication, 1903), 207–8.

37. McElya, *Clinging to Mammy*, 27–32.

38. See Silber, *Romance of Reunion*, 66–92.

39. "Negro Plays Santa to Old Confederates," *New York Times*, December 25, 1919, 11.

40. "Billy Rose's Unique Life," *New York Times*, August 8, 1897, 7; T. Brown, *Civil War Canon*, 104.

41. Booker T. Washington, "Atlanta Exposition Address," Digital History, http://www
.digitalhistory.uh.edu/disp_textbook.cfm?smtID=3&psid=3613 (accessed March 15, 2017).

42. Washington, *Frederick Douglass*, 235.

43. "White People and Negroes," *CV*, September 1905, 421.

44. Stevens, *Reminiscences of the Civil War*, 205, 207–12.

45. On reunions, see Foster, *Ghosts of the Confederacy*, 168–71; and Keith S. Bohannon,
"'These Few Gray-Haired, Battle-Scarred Veterans,'" 89–110.

46. Reported in the *Pascagoula (Miss.) Democrat-Star*, June 28, 1901.

47. "Score of Negro War Veterans at Reunion," unidentified newspaper clipping in
personal collection.

48. *Richmond Times*, July 25, 1902.

49. "A White Man's Love for a Negro," *Indianapolis Journal*, October 1903.

50. "90-Year-Old Negro Solicits Funds to Go to Big Reunion," *Memphis News Scimitar*,
1919, 10; *Wautaga Democrat* (Boone, N.C.), March 9, 1911.

51. "Old Negro Goes to Reunion," *The State* (Columbia), April 26, 1910.

52. Quoted in Segars and Barrow, *Black Southerners in Confederate Armies*, 152.

53. "Old Time Negro Attracts Much Attention," *The Gazette* (Lexington, Va.),
November 4, 1903.

54. Quoted in Battey, *History of Rome and Floyd County*, 302.

55. *The Standard* (Ga.), September 6, 1889.

56. "Slave Reunions Should Be Held throughout South," *Monroe (N.C.) Journal*,
September 23, 1912, 3.

57. *Pickens (S.C.) Sentinel*, August 14, 1913.

58. *Minutes of the Seventeenth Annual Meeting*, 10–14. The minutes also claim that a few
of the attendees "were enlisted soldiers who bore their muskets beside their masters." This
is a confusing reference to the possibility of actual black Confederate soldiers who were
still legally owned (14).

59. *Minutes of the Seventeenth Annual Meeting*, 43.

60. Quoted in Goldfield, "Segregation and Racism," 30.

61. Quoted in Goldfield, *Still Fighting the Civil War*, 196.

62. "'Stonewall' Jackson's Cook Still Loyal to Lost Cause," *Richmond Times*,
November 3, 1901, 18. Jefferson Shields does not appear in James I. Robertson Jr.'s
biography of Jackson.

63. *Fort Worth Morning Register*, May 18, 1902.

64. *New Orleans Times-Picayune*, April 29, 1910.

65. *San Diego Union*, April 14, 1923.

66. Battey, *History of Rome and Floyd County*, v.

67. *Rome Tribune-Herald*, September 23, 1911.

68. During this period Eberhart claimed to have worked as Henry Grady's personal
valet during his college years, but there is no evidence to support this claim. This may have
been another way for Eberhart to situate himself in the good graces of his white audiences.

69. "Steve Perry and 'Uncle Steve Eberhart,'" *Dead Confederates: A Civil War Era Blog*,
November 11, 2011, https://deadconfederates.com/2011/11/11/everyone-laughs-both-at
-and-with-steve/ (accessed April 7, 2017).

70. "Lee's Cook Wore Genuine Rebel Uniform in Parade," *Monroe Journal*, November
12, 1920, 8.

71. *Kansas City Sun*, August 21, 1920, 7.

72. Lee, *History of the Life of Rev. Wm. Mack Lee*, 4.

73. E. D. Pope, "More Historical 'Bunk,'" *CV*, September 1927, 324.

74. Quoted in Dabney, *Last Review*, 39.

75. Mosley may have been the camp slave for Dr. Samuel Walker of the 2nd Mississippi Cavalry, a militia unit that never left the state.

76. "Here and There with the Vets," *Gettysburg Times*, July 6, 1938.

77. Poole, *Never Surrender*, 188.

78. Kytle and Roberts, *Denmark Vesey's Garden*, 147–50.

79. Cox, *Dixie's Daughters*, 68–72; McElya, *Politics of Mourning*, 151–69.

80. Ezekiel, *Memoirs from the Baths of Diocletian*, 441.

81. Herbert, *History of the Arlington Confederate Monument*, 77.

82. Herbert, 77.

CHAPTER 4

1. Clyburn applied for his pension in 1926, though the state of North Carolina did not authorize pensions for former slaves until the following year. In this case, as in others, the State Board of Pensions utilized its "discretionary powers" in approving Clyburn's pension application. North Carolina State Archives, State Auditor, Pension Office, Confederate Pension Records, Applications for Pensions, Act of 1901, Box 6.259, "Weary D. Clyburn."

2. North Carolina was the only state that did not create a separate form for former camp slaves.

3. On the Confederate pension system, see Marten, *Sing Not War*, 16–17, 203–4.

4. K. A. Nisbett, "A Rapidly Dying Type of Negro Is This," *Sunny South* (Atlanta), August 31, 1901, 3.

5. "Old Uncle Ned," *CV*, January 1916, 422.

6. "A Chance for Some Politician," *Dublin (Ga.) Post*, January 26, 1887.

7. "A Confederate Negro," *Raleigh News and Observer*, August 9, 1901.

8. "A Confederate Negro's Death," *Anderson (S.C.) Intelligencer*, March 18, 1886.

9. "George E. 'Old Confed' Cooper," *Dallas News*, June 13, 1915.

10. *The State*, November 2, 1907.

11. "'Old Negro Confederate' Uncle Charley Sheppard," *St. Louis Republic*, August 11, 1900.

12. "Johnston's Body Servant," *Bolivar (Tenn.) Bulletin*, September 21, 1894, 1.

13. "Negro Confederate Veteran Shot," *New York Times*, June 15, 1900. Though the report describes the victim as a "soldier," it is likely that he was present in the army as a body servant.

14. "Negro Confederate 'Vet' 100 Years Old, Hit by Auto," *New Orleans Times-Picayune*, December 28, 1919.

15. Quoted in Segars and Barrow, *Black Southerners in Confederate Armies*, 92.

16. Quoted in Segars and Barrow, 92. Robert Shopshire attended numerous veterans' reunions and when he died in 1907 was buried in a Confederate uniform. "Confederate Negro Will Be Buried in Gray Uniform He Loved," *New Orleans Times-Picayune*, December 18, 1907.

17. Cunningham, *S. A. Cunningham*.

18. "A Notable Colored Veteran," *CV*, August 1884, 233; "Fidelity of Negro Servants," *CV*, March 1897, 119; "Tributes to Faithful Slaves," *CV*, September 1900, 399.

19. "Give the Old Slave a Home," *CV*, March 1893, 80; "Pensioning Old Slaves," *CV*, March 1903, 108–10; "Payment for Negroes Suggested," *CV*, March 1910, 120.

20. "Pension Slaves Who Served in the Civil War," *CV*, October 1913, 481.

21. "The General Assembly," *Raleigh News and Observer*, February 4, 1885.

22. Kendi, *Stamped from the Beginning*, 270–71; Berry, *My Face Is Black Is True*.

23. James G. Hollandsworth Jr., "Black Pensioners after the Civil War," *Mississippi History Now*, http://www.mshistorynow.mdah.ms.gov/articles/289/black-confederate-pensioners-after-the-civil-war (accessed June 1, 2017).

24. "Pension for Negro Servants," *Wilmington (N.C.) Semi-weekly Messenger*, January 8, 1907.

25. "Tributes to Faithful Servants," *CV*, December 1900, 399.

26. "Letter from Big Bud," *Macon (Ga.) Beacon*, March 1, 1912.

27. "Colored Confederates," *Macon Beacon*, February 23, 1912.

28. *Charlottesville Daily Progress*, June 27, 1917.

29. Quoted in Williams, *Torchbearers of Democracy*, 227–28.

30. Williams, 228–37.

31. *Public Acts of the State of Tennessee*, "Chapter No. 129, An Act to be entitled an Act to provide pensions for those colored men who served as servants and cooks in the Confederate Army in the war between the States: 1861–1865," approved April 9, 1921, 351.

32. "Pensions for Faithful Slaves," *CV*, August 1921, 284.

33. *Journal of the Senate of the General Assembly*, 204, 212, 219, 241, 735, 912; *Journal of the House of Representatives*, 338, 421, 459, 916, 917, 996.

34. Helsley, "Notes and News from the Archives," 184–85.

35. "Pensions for Faithful Negroes," *CV*, February 1922, 77.

36. *Acts and Joint Resolutions*, 294–303.

37. Quoted in Martinez, *Confederate Slave Impressment*, 161.

38. I relied heavily on Hollandsworth, "Looking for Bob."

39. Hollandsworth, 310.

40. Those few who lived into the 1930s would have one last opportunity to share their stories with a representative from the state through the New Deal's WPA program.

41. The Tennessee Colored Pension Applications, microfilm roll #1, 1–111, and roll #2, 112–385, Tennessee State Library and Archives, Nashville, copies of F. R. Hoard pension (1920) provided to author.

42. Peter Brown, #41122, Confederate Pension Applications, Texas State Library and Archives Commission, Austin, Archives and Information Services Division, Texas Comptroller's Office.

43. B. J. Jackson, #25233, Confederate Pension Applications.

44. Wash White, #39363, Confederate Pension Applications.

45. Susan Estes, #45486, Confederate Pension Applications.

46. George Hampton, #39149, Confederate Pension Applications.

47. Bud Dickson, #Rejected, Confederate Pension Applications.

48. Eanes, *Virginia's Black Confederates*, 134.

49. Quoted in Deserino "Wearing the Gray Suit," 261.

50. The Tennessee Colored Pension Applications, Shadrack Searcy pension, microfilm roll #235.

51. "Levi Miller, Confederate Veteran," *CV*, September 1921, 358.

52. Accession no. 27684, Levi Miller, application number 26, Index to Confederate

Pension Applications Filed by Virginia Confederate Veterans and Widows, State of Virginia Government Records Collection, Library of Virginia, Richmond.

53. "Confederate Pension for a Colored Man," *Winchester (Va.) Evening Star*, February 25, 1921; "Levi Miller Has a Good War Record," *Winchester Evening Star*, February 26, 1921.

54. Andy Hall, "Richard Quarls and the Dead Man's Pension," Dead Confederates, A Civil War Era Blog, February 12, 2011, https://deadconfederates.com/2011/02/12/richard-quarls-more-questions-than-answers/ (accessed September 21, 2017).

55. Hall, "Richard Quarls and the Dead Man's Pension."

56. Terri D. Reeves, "For Former Slave, Soldier, a Chance to Rest in Peace," *St. Petersburg Times*, February 23, 2003, http://www.sptimes.com/2003/02/23/NorthPinellas/For_former_slave__sol.shtml (accessed June 15, 2017).

57. Sampson and Levin, "Loyalty of Silas Chandler," 34; Silas Chandler pension record, Mississippi Department of Archives and History, Mississippi Office of the State Auditor, Series 1201: Confederate Pension Applications, 1889–1932.

CHAPTER 5

1. "Dedication of Grave of Silas Chandler Held in West Point," *Jackson (Miss.) Advocate*, September 22–28, 1994, 3A.

2. Myra Chandler Sampson, research packet on Silas Chandler, copy in possession of the author.

3. "General Lee's Socks and the 'Easy' Electric Vacuum Washing Machine," *New York Tribune*, November 21, 1920.

4. There are a few exceptions, most notably with the release of *Shenandoah* in 1965. See Gallagher, *Causes Won*, 41–56.

5. Quoted in Levin, *Remembering the Battle of the Crater*, 116.

6. See Franklin, *From Slavery to Freedom*; Quarles, *Negro in the Civil War*; and Cornish, *Sable Arm*.

7. See Levin, *Remembering the Battle of the Crater*, 117–18.

8. On recent developments within the field of Civil War military history, see Gallagher, "Blueprint for Victory"; and Gallagher and Meier, "Coming to Terms with Civil War Military History."

9. Brundage, *Southern Past*, 293–303; Greenspan *Creating Colonial Williamsburg*.

10. Katy Waldman, "Guardians of White Innocence," *Slate*, September 25, 2017, https://slate.com/news-and-politics/2017/09/the-sons-of-confederate-veterans-are-the-guardians-of-white-innocence.html (accessed April 3, 2018).

11. Report of the Adjutant-in-Chief, January 31, 1977, General Headquarters, Sons of Confederate Veterans, Jackson, Miss. I am indebted to Asa Gordon for uncovering these reports.

12. Report of the Adjutant-in-Chief, February 28, 1977, General Headquarters, Sons of Confederate Veterans.

13. Historians have offered a wide range of responses to Burns's documentary. See Robert Brent Toplin, *Ken Burns's "The Civil War."*

14. Dr. John McGlone, "Attacks on the Colors," *CV*, January–February 1992, 4.

15. Joseph B. Mitchell, "Attacks on the Colors," *CV*, March–April 1992, 7–8.

16. "Attacks on the Colors," *CV*, July–August 1992, 6.

17. P. Charles Lunsford, "The Forgotten Confederates," *CV*, November–December 1992, 12–15.

18. Lunsford, 12, 15.

19. Michael Dan Jones, "The Battle of Lake Charles: A Case Study for Saving a Confederate Monument," *CV*, January–February 1996, 21–24.

20. Kennedy and Kennedy, *South Was Right!*, 9.

21. Kennedy and Kennedy, 91.

22. Barrow, Segars, and Rosenburg, *Black Confederates*, 4.

23. "Black Confederates," Sons of Confederate Veterans, http://www.scv.org/new /contributed-works/black-confederates/ (accessed July 7, 2017).

24. It is worth pointing out that *Civil War Times Illustrated* never published an article during this period that in any way supported the black Confederate narrative. In 1977 the magazine published an article about Patrick Cleburne's proposal to enlist slaves as soldiers, but at no point did its author assume that blacks were already serving in that capacity. The absence of any reference to black Confederates in such a popular publication during this period remains consistent with the conclusion that the first references were made from within the SCV. S. Davis, "'That Extraordinary Document.'"

25. Jerome S. Handler and Michael L. Tuite Jr., Retouching History: The Modern Falsification of a Civil War Photograph, http://people.virginia.edu/~jh3v/retouching history/essay.html (accessed July 9, 2017).

26. Scott K. Williams, *Black Confederates in the Civil War*, http://www.pricecamp.org /blackcs.htm (accessed July 15, 2017).

27. Vernon R. Padgett, "Did Blacks Serve in Combat?," CaliforniaSCV.org, http:// californiascv.org/Did%20Black%20Confederates%20Serve%20in%20Combat%20PDF .pdf (accessed December 9, 2018); A recent Google search for "Black Confederate" and "Arlington Monument" yielded 242 results.

28. "Black Rebels in the C.S.A.," Texas Confederate Veterans, http://www. texasconfederateveterans.com/Black%20Confederates.htm (accessed August 9, 2016).

29. Kelly, "Black Confederate Combat Soldiers," Latin American Studies, http://www .latinamericanstudies.org/slavery/black-confederates.htm (accessed August 9, 2017); "Black Confederates," http://www.florida-scv.org/Camp1316/Black%20Confederates .htm, accessed August 9, 2017.

30. Kevin M. Levin, "Ann DeWitt Is at It Again," *CWM*, September 20, 2010, http:// cwmemory.com/2010/09/20/ann-dewitt-is-at-it-again/ (accessed August 1, 2017).

31. Andy Hall, "Famous 'Negro Cooks Regiment' Found — in My Own Backyard!," *Dead Confederates: A Civil War Era Blog*, August 8, 2011, https://deadconfederates.com /2011/08/08/famous-negro-cooks-regiment-found-in-my-own-backyard/ (accessed August 10, 2017).

32. "Black Confederate Soldiers of Petersburg," *Petersburg Express*, http://www .petersburgexpress.com/Petersburg_Black-CSA.html (accessed August 9, 2017).

33. Gainesville Volunteers, SCV Camp 373, "Confederate and Confederate-related links," http://www.gainesville-vols.org/links.html (accessed August 10, 2017); "Black Heroes in Gray: The Forgotten Heroes of the Confederate States of America," https:// bogbit.com/black-heroes-in-gray-the-forgotten-heroes-of-the-confederate-states-of -america/ (accessed August 9, 2017).

34. Dixie Outfitters, https://dixieoutfitters.com/ (accessed June 10, 2017).

35. See Emerson, "Commemoration, Conflict, and Constraints."

36. Horwitz, *Confederates in the Attic*, 199–200.

37. Artwork can be found on the website of Bradley Schmehl, http://bradleyschmehl .com/index.php/gallery/ (accessed October 2, 2017). For more on how Schmehl's work fits into the broader subject of popular Civil War art, see Gallagher, *Causes Won*, 135–208.

38. Kevin M. Levin, "The National Park Service's Black Confederates (Part 2)," *CWM*, December 28, 2010, http://cwmemory.com/2010/12/28/the-national-park-services -black-confederates-part-2/ (accessed August 15, 2017); Kevin M. Levin, "Stacy D. Allen Responds," *CWM*, December 29, 2010, http://cwmemory.com/2010/12/29/stacy-d-allen -responds/ (accessed August 15, 2017). Updates on the panel were provided in an email, Ashley Berry to Kevin M. Levin, September 29, 2017.

39. Kevin M. Levin, "The National Park Service's Black Confederates," *CWM*, August 26, 2010, http://cwmemory.com/2010/08/26/the-national-park-services-black -confederates/ (accessed September 25, 2017).

40. Murphy, *Cleburne*.

41. Hulbert, *Ghosts of Guerrilla Memory*, 102–3. Email correspondence with Matthew Hulbert has also informed my understanding of the history and historical memory surrounding Holt.

42. On the neo-Confederate interpretation of Noland, see "Black Confederates," Dixie Outfitters, June 7, 2012, https://dixieoutfitters.com/2015/04/04/black-confederates -collier-noland-etc/ (accessed September 25, 2017).

43. Quoted in Gallagher, *Causes Won*, 73.

44. The 1860 census reveals that W. C. Lewis owned seven slaves, one of whom fits the description of Jim Lewis.

45. For another interpretation of the movie, see Hettle, *Inventing Stonewall Jackson*, 138–45.

46. Kevin M. Levin, "Mourning Black Confederates," *CWM*, April 14, 2009, http:// cwmemory.com/2009/04/14/mourning-black-confederates/ (accessed May 3, 2017); Kevin M. Levin, "The UDC Uses and Abuses the History of Slavery," *CWM*, April 18 2009, http://cwmemory.com/2009/04/18/udc-uses-and-abuses-the-history-of-slavery/ (accessed May 3, 2017).

47. Kevin M. Levin, "Happy Richard Poplar Day," *CWM*, September 18, 2010, http:// cwmemory.com/2010/09/18/happy-richard-poplar-day/, (accessed May 8, 2017).

48. "Confederate Master and Slave Tintype," ca. 1861, *Antiques Roadshow*, http://www .pbs.org/wgbh/roadshow/season/14/raleigh-nc/appraisals/confederate-master-slave -tintype--200902A33/ (accessed June 4, 2017).

49. "Chandler Tintype," *History Detectives: Special Investigations*, http://www.pbs.org /opb/historydetectives/investigation/chandler-tintype/ (accessed September 22, 2017).

50. "Chandler Tintype."

51. The available evidence does not support the claim that Silas and Andrew and subsequent generations on both side of the family maintained friendly relations. In 1959 George Chandler, son of Silas, was listed twice in a report from the Mississippi State Sovereignty Commission as one of the individuals they "thought might possibly belong to the NAACP and who might possibly be a trouble maker in the event of a racial crisis." One of Andrew M. Chandler's descendants was listed as a member of the Clay County Citizens' Council who reported to the Sovereignty Commission. Myra Chandler Sampson, research packet on Silas Chandler, copy in possession of the author.

52. Kevin Seiff, "Virginia 4th-Grade Textbook Criticized over Claims on Black Confederate Soldiers," *Washington Post*, October 20, 2010.

53. Seiff, "Virginia 4th-Grade Textbook."

54. Kevin M. Levin, "Are Virginia Schools Still Teaching the Black Confederate Myth?," *CWM*, April 11, 2011, http://cwmemory.com/2011/04/18/are-virginia-schools-still-teaching-the-black-confederate-myth/ (accessed September 2, 2017).

55. Barack Obama, "Senator Obama's Announcement," *New York Times*, February 10, 2007, http://nytimes.com/2007/02/10/us/politics/10obama-text.html?pagewanted=print&_r=0 (accessed June 9, 2017).

56. James Loewen and Edward Sebesta, "Dear President Obama: Please Don't Honor the Arlington Confederate Monument," History News Network, May 20, 2009, http://historynewsnetwork.org/article/85884 (accessed June 2, 2017).

57. J. M. Coski, "Jim Limber," *Encyclopedia Virginia*, April 21, 2009, https://www.encyclopediavirginia.org/Limber_Jim (accessed August 13, 2017).

58. Kevin M. Levin, "Jim Limber Kidnapped and Brought to Beauvoir," *CWM*, October 30, 2009, http://cwmemory.com/2009/10/30/jim-limber-kidnapped-and-brought-to-beauvoir/ (accessed September 13, 2017).

59. Kevin M. Levin, "Governor McDonnell Apologizes," *CWM*, April 7, 2010, http://cwmemory.com/2010/04/07/governor-mcdonnell-apologizes/ (accessed May 15, 2017).

60. Kevin M. Levin, "Sons of Confederate Veterans Respond to Governor McDonnell," *CWM*, April 13, 2010, http://cwmemory.com/2010/04/13/sons-of-confederate-veterans-respond-to-governor-mcdonnell/ (accessed May 17, 2017); Kevin M. Levin, "Civil War History in Virginia Month," *CWM*, April 6, 2011, http://cwmemory.com/2011/04/06/civil-war-history-in-virginia-month/ (accessed May 17, 2017).

CHAPTER 6

1. "Southern Pride Fuels 1,300 Mile March," *Washington Times*, October 13, 2002, https://www.washingtontimes.com/news/2002/oct/13/20021013-092356-3553r/ (accessed October 5, 2017).

2. "Southern Pride Fuels 1,300 Mile March."

3. On the history of the Museum of the Confederacy, see Coleman, "Among the Ruins," 1–12.

4. See Sutton, *Rally on the High Ground*; and Dwight T. Pitcaithley, "'A Cosmic Threat': The National Park Service Addresses the Causes of the American Civil War," in Horton and Horton, *Slavery and Public History*, 169–86.

5. Walter E. Williams, "Black Confederates Served Patriotically in War between States," *Human Events*, February 11, 2000, 18.

6. Edward C. Smith, "Blacks in Blue and Gray: The African-American Contribution to the Waging of the Civil War," 5th Annual Gettysburg Seminar, National Park Service: History eLibrary, http://npshistory.com/series/symposia/gettysburg_seminars/5/essay3.htm (accessed December 5, 2017).

7. Bruce Levine, "In Search of a Usable Past," in Horton and Horton, *Slavery and Public History*, 191.

8. Levine, 195.

9. Quoted in Eddie Dean, "The Black and the Gray," *Washington City Paper*, July 17, 1998,

https://www.washingtoncitypaper.com/news/article/13015799/the-black-and-the-gray (accessed September 10, 2017).

10. Edward C. Smith, "Calico, Black and Gray: Women and Blacks in the Confederacy," *Civil War*, issue 23, 16.

11. Dean, "Black and the Gray."

12. Brian Albrecht, "Re-enactors Portray Unusual Roles of Civil War," Cleveland.com, http://www.cleveland.com/metro/index.ssf/2013/05/black_re-enactors_portray_unus.html (accessed September 5, 2017).

13. Jesse Dukes and Jonno Rattman, "Lost Causes," 102–3.

14. Dean, "Black and the Gray."

15. On the debate within the reenacting community over the presence of black Confederates, see Kevin M. Levin, "When Civil War Reenactors Legitimize Racism," *CWM*, http://cwmemory.com/2016/08/15/when-civil-war-reenactors-legitimize-racism/ (accessed September 4, 2017).

16. Stephanie Garry, "In Defense of His Confederate Pride," *Tampa Bay Times*, October 7, 2007, http://spofga.org/flag/2007/oct/images/State%20In%20defense%20of%20his%20Confederate%20pride.htm (accessed September 5, 2017).

17. Kimberly Kindy and Julie Tate, "Tributes to Confederate and Union Troops in the Same Florida Park Reflect an Ongoing War over the Monuments," *Washington Post*, September 21, 2017, https://www.washingtonpost.com/politics/tributes-to-confederate-and-union-troops-in-the-same-florida-park-reflect-an-ongoing-war-over-the-monuments/2017/09/22/e2a81802-98d3-11e7-b569-3360011663b4_story.html?utm_term=.9a9b76388986 (accessed September 25, 2017).

18. "Black Is Gray: Nelson W. Winbush," *Confederate American*, February 22, 2011, http://confederateblog.com/2011/02/black-is-gray-nelson-w-winbush/ (accessed August 5, 2017).

19. Kevin M. Levin, "H. K. Edgerton Marches through Texas," *CWM*, December 13, 2017, http://cwmemory.com/2007/12/13/hk-edgerton-marches-through-texas/ (accessed August 16, 2017).

20. Kevin M. Levin, "H. K. Edgerton Goes to Washington," *CWM*, January 17, 2009, http://cwmemory.com/2009/01/17/hk-edgerton-goes-to-washington/ (accessed August 18, 2017).

21. Quoted in Frank Rich, "Welcome to Confederate History Month," *New York Times*, April 18, 2010.

22. Kevin M. Levin, "What Does This Have to Do with Confederate Heritage?," *CWM*, February 3, 2015, http://cwmemory.com/2015/02/03/what-does-this-have-to-do-with-confederate-heritage/ (accessed August 18, 2017).

23. Kevin M. Levin, "The Myth of the Black Confederate Soldier," *Daily Beast*, July 8, 2015, https://www.thedailybeast.com/the-myth-of-the-black-confederate-soldier (accessed October 4, 2017).

24. On the centennial, see Cook, *Troubled Commemoration*.

25. *Civil War Sesquicentennial, 2011–2015, Southeast Region: A Strategic Plan for Commemorating the Civil War's Important Places and Compelling Stories within the National Park Service's Southeast Region*, National Park Service pamphlet, https://www.nps.gov/ande/learn/management/upload/SERO_CW150_action_plan.pdf (accessed March 5, 2018).

26. Cook, *Troubled Commemoration*, 126–31.

27. Rudy, "From Tokenism to True Partnership," 70.

28. Dabney, Parnicza, and Levin, "Interpreting Race."

29. On why African Americans avoid Civil War–related sites, see Coates, *We Were Eight Years in Power*, 71–84. On Coates's observations about why some African Americans embrace the black Confederate narrative, see Coates, "Blacks Who Support Black Confederate Mythology," *The Atlantic*, November 1, 2010, https://www.theatlantic.com /national/archive/2010/11/blacks-who-support-black-confederate-mythology/65499/ (accessed October 1, 2017).

30. Rudy, "From Tokenism to True Partnership," 66.

31. Virginia Reports to the General Assembly, *RD520-Virginia Sesquicentennial of the American Civil War Commission 2015 Annual Report— The Civil War Sesquicentennial in Virginia: Final Impact and Lasting Legacies*, https://rga.lis.virginia.gov/Published/2015 /RD520 (accessed October 1, 2017).

32. Groce, "New Wine in Old Bottles," 45–60.

33. Kevin M. Levin, "Why We Need History Education: Black Confederate Edition," *CWM*, February 7, 2012, http://cwmemory.com/2012/02/07/why-we-need-history -education-black-confederate-edition/ (accessed August 12, 2017). In 2014 Georgia governor Sonny Perdue signed a proclamation in honor of William "Ten-Cent Bill" Yopp as part of Confederate heritage month. See "Honoring William 'Ten Cent Bill' Yopp," Laurens County African American History, February 2, 2014, http:// laurenscountyafricanamericanhistory.blogspot.com/2014/02/honoring-ten-cent-bill -there-was.html?m=1 (accessed August 12, 2017).

34. Perry's pension can be found at North Carolina Digital Collections, 1901 Confederate Pension Applications, http://digital.ncdcr.gov/cdm/compoundobject /collection/p16062coll21/id/113361/rec/19 (accessed March 18, 2018).

35. Memorial for Confederate pensioners of color, "Commemorative Landscapes," Documenting the American South, http://docsouth.unc.edu/commland/monument /353/ (accessed September 5, 2017).

36. Adam Bell, "Monroe Ceremony Honors Slaves Who Served in Confederate Army," *Charlotte Observer*, December 8, 2012, http://www.charlotteobserver.com/news/local /article9085517.html (accessed October 1, 2017).

37. No one has questioned Mattie Clyburn Rice's claim to be the daughter of Weary Clyburn, but it should be pointed out that the latter was born in 1841 and died in 1930. His daughter was born in 1922, which would mean Clyburn was in his seventies when she was conceived.

38. Kevin M. Levin, "Earl Ijames's 'Colored Confederates,'" *CWM*, May 11, 2009, http:// cwmemory.com/2009/05/11/earl-ijamess-colored-confederates/ (accessed August 14, 2017).

39. Earl L. Ijames, "Black Soldiers, North and South, 1861–1865," *Abbeville Institute: The Abbeville Blog*, January 8, 2016, https://www.abbevilleinstitute.org/blog/black-soldiers -north-and-south-1861–1865/ (accessed August 14, 2017).

40. Kimberly Harrington, "Duty. Honor. Confederacy," *Charlotte Post*, July 24, 2008, http://www.thecharlottepost.com/index.php?src=news&refno=1005&category=News (accessed August 15, 2017).

41. National coverage of this ceremony included NPR. Kevin M. Levin, "National

Public Radio Falls for the Black Confederate Myth," *CWM*, August 7, 2011, http://cwmemory.com/2011/08/07/national-public-radio-falls-for-the-black-confederate-myth/ (accessed August 16, 2017).

42. "Mattie Rice Clyburn Memorial Dedication," YouTube, October 22, 2014, https://www.youtube.com/watch?v=hqJU9Gtmcas&t=5s (accessed August 16, 2017).

43. Copies of proclamations in possession of the author.

44. "Nikki Haley Defends Confederate Flag: CEOs Haven't Complained," Talking Points Memo, October 15, 2014, http://talkingpointsmemo.com/livewire/nikki-haley-confederate-flag-ceos (accessed August 16, 2017).

45. Kieran Corcoran, "Buried under the Fluttering Confederate Flag: Daughter of Black Slave Who Fought FOR Southern Forces in Civil War Is Buried, More Than 150 Years after Her Father Went to War," *Daily Mail*, October 18, 2014, http://www.dailymail.co.uk/news/article-2798741/buried-fluttering-confederate-flag-daughter-black-slave-fought-southern-forces-civil-war-buried-150-years-father-went-war.html (accessed August 17, 2017).

46. "The Robert Small Commemorative Weekend, May 12–13, 2012," Robert Smalls.com, http://robertsmalls.com/schedule.html (accessed August 16, 2017).

47. Stratton Lawrence, "Local Group Reenacts the Glory of the Black Union Soldiers of the 54th Massachusetts," *Charleston City Paper*, July 10, 2013, https://www.charlestoncitypaper.com/charleston/local-group-reenacts-the-glory-of-the-black-union-soldiers-of-the-54th-massachusetts/Content?oid=4664070 (accessed August 17, 2017); Brian Hicks, "The Battle That Changed Charleston: Morris Island Feud Began City's Fall during Civil War," *Charleston Post and Courier*, July 12, 2013, http://www.postandcourier.com/news/the-battle-that-changed-charleston-morris-island-feud-began-city/article_57f9d7d1-55c6-5306-998e-ea0b6a41fbcd.html (accessed August 16, 2017); Adam Parker, "Denmark Vesey Monument Unveiled before Hundreds," *Charleston Post and Courier*, February 14, 2014, http://www.postandcourier.com/features/arts_and_travel/denmark-vesey-monument-unveiled-before-hundreds/article_35622532-8a45-5060-a819-0e33a47c8a20.html (accessed August 18, 2017).

48. "Monuments to the United States Colored Troops (USCT [African American Civil War Soldiers]): The List," *Jubilo! The Emancipation Century*, May 30, 2011, https://jubiloemancipationcentury.wordpress.com/2011/05/30/monuments-to-the-united-states-colored-troops-usct-the-list/ (accessed August 17, 2017); John Bohanan, "U.S. Colored Troops Civil War Memorial Monument Dedicated," *Lexington Park (Md.) Leader*, June 17, 2012, https://lexleader.net/colored-troops-civil-war-memorial-monument-dedicated/ (accessed August 18, 2017).

49. Kevin M. Levin, "Earl Ijames, Henry Louis Gates, and 'Colored Confederates,'" *CWM*, August 15, 2010, http://cwmemory.com/2010/08/15/earl-ijames-henry-louis-gates-and-colored-confederates/ (accessed August 19, 2017).

50. "Henry Louis Gates on Abraham Lincoln," C-SPAN, July 1, 2009, https://www.c-span.org/video/?287410-1/henry-louis-gates-abraham-lincoln (accessed August 19, 2017).

51. "Fighting for Freedom: The Civil War and Its Legacies—The A.R.T. of Human Rights—Harvard University," YouTube, February 12, 2015, https://www.youtube.com/watch?time_continue=1121&v=d7RwskI-2g4 (accessed September 2, 2017).

52. "Black Like Me," *Finding Your Roots* (season 4, episode 6), http://www.pbs.org/weta/finding-your-roots/home/ (accessed November 10, 2017).

53. The author attended this talk.

54. John Stauffer, "Yes, There Were Black Confederates. Here's Why," *The Root*, January

20, 2015, http://www.theroot.com/yes-there-were-black-confederates-here-s-why
-1790858546 (accessed July 20, 2017).

55. Stauffer, "Yes, There Were Black Confederates"; Andy Hall, "Frederick Douglass, Time Traveler?," *Dead Confederates: A Civil War Era Blog*, January 20, 2015, https://deadconfederates.com/2015/01/20/frederick-douglass-time-traveler/ (accessed September 20, 2017).

56. Coleman, "Among the Ruins," 9, 11.

57. Cook, *Troubled Commemoration*, 206–7; Rudy, "From Tokenism to True Partnership," 71–72.

58. Jamelle Bouie, "Remembering History as Fable," *Slate*, April 14, 2015, http://www.slate.com/articles/news_and_politics/history/2015/04/appomattox_150th_anniversary_neglects_emancipation_our_commemoration_of.html (accessed October 20, 2017).

59. "Racial Division along the Neo-Confederate Spectrum," Southern Poverty Law Center, March 2, 2017, https://www.splcenter.org/hatewatch/2017/03/02/racial-division-along-neo-confederate-spectrum (accessed August 25, 2017).

60. Kevin M. Levin, "'75,000 Confederates of Color?' on a Billboard," *CWM*, August 13, 2016, http://cwmemory.com/2016/08/13/75000-confederates-of-color-on-a-billboard/ (accessed August 25, 2017).

61. Gabriel A. Reich and Amy Corning, "Anatomy of a Belief: The Collective Memory of African American Confederate Soldiers," *Historical Encounters: A Journal of Historical Consciousness, Historical Cultures, and History Education* 4, no. 4 (2017): 11–22, http://hej.hermes-history.net/index.php/HEJ/article/view/72 (accessed January 5, 2018).

CONCLUSION

1. On Dylann Roof, see Ethan J. Kytle and Blain Roberts, *Denmark Vesey's Garden*, 337–40.

2. Kevin M. Levin, "The Myth of the Black Confederate Soldier," *Daily Beast*, July 8, 2015, https://www.thedailybeast.com/the-myth-of-the-black-confederate-soldier (accessed October 4, 2017).

3. Barack Obama, "Remarks by the President in Eulogy for the Honorable Reverend Clementa Pinckney," The White House, June 26, 2015, https://obamawhitehouse.archives.gov/the-press-office/2015/06/26/remarks-president-eulogy-honorable-reverend-clementa-pinckney, accessed August 25, 2017.

4. On the history of the Confederate battle flag debate in South Carolina, see Emerson, "Commemoration, Conflict, and Constraints," 83–84.

5. Emerson, 83–84; Mark Berman, "Alabama Governor Has Confederate Flag Removed from State Capitol Grounds," *Washington Post*, June 24, 2015, https://www.washingtonpost.com/news/post-nation/wp/2015/06/24/alabama-governor-has-confederate-flag-removed-from-state-capitol-grounds/?utm_term=.f758ada95675 (accessed August 26, 2017).

6. Adam K. Raymond, "A Running List of Confederate Monuments Removed across the Country," *New York Daily Intelligencer*, August 25, 2017, http://nymag.com/daily/intelligencer/2017/08/running-list-of-confederate-monuments-that-have-been-removed.html (accessed August 28, 2017).

7. "Mitch Landrieu's Speech on the Removal of Confederate Monuments in New

Orleans," *New York Times*, May 23, 2017, https://www.nytimes.com/2017/05/23/opinion/mitch-landrieus-speech-transcript.html (accessed August 28, 2017).

8. Kevin M. Levin, "Step Away from the Monument, Mr. Morrissey," *CWM*, October 11, 2016, http://cwmemory.com/2016/10/11/step-away-from-the-monument-mr-morrissey/ (accessed September 2, 2017).

9. Kevin M. Levin, "Arden Wells Falls for Black Confederate Myth," *CWM*, August 3, 2016, http://cwmemory.com/2016/08/03/arden-wells-falls-for-black-confederate-myth/ (accessed September 2, 2017).

10. Kevin M. Levin, "Black Confederates to the Rescue in Lexington, Virginia," *CWM*, October 28, 2016, http://cwmemory.com/2016/10/28/black-confederates-to-the-rescue-in-lexington-virginia/ (accessed September 2, 2017).

11. Casey Fabris, "Family Removes Confederate Memorial Marker from Ex-slave's Grave," *Roanoke (Va.) Times*, October 16, 2015, http://www.roanoke.com/news/local/franklin_county/family-removes-confederate-memorial-marker-from-ex-slave-s-grave/article_8b42614a-ddae-5c8f-9e6d-3bd8d252006e.htm (accessed September 3, 2017).

12. Bob Ruegsegger, "Norfolk Grave of Gen. Lee's Servant Finally Gets Marker," *Virginia Pilot*, May 23, 2016, https://pilotonline.com/news/local/norfolk-grave-of-gen-lee-s-servant-finally-gets-marker/article_4387b5b8-7c6b-5dbc-9b36-51806e0fb8c2.html (accessed September 3, 2017); Kevin M. Levin, "The Making of a Black Confederate Soldier," *CWM*, May 24, 2016, http://cwmemory.com/2016/05/24/the-making-of-a-black-confederate-soldier/ (accessed September 4, 2017).

13. T. Rees Shapiro, "Descendants of Rebel Sculptor: Remove Confederate Memorial from Arlington National Cemetery," *Washington Post*, August 18, 2017, https://www.washingtonpost.com/local/virginia-politics/descendants-of-rebel-sculptor-remove-confederate-memorial-from-arlington-national-cemetery/2017/08/18/d4da6a3e-842b-11e7-ab27-1a21a8e006ab_story.html?utm_term=.fe306d4f73cd (accessed October 15, 2017).

14. Andy Shain, "Confederate Monument Honoring African Americans Who Fought for the Confederacy Proposed," *Charleston Post and Courier*, October 9, 2017, http://www.postandcourier.com/politics/monument-honoring-african-americans-who-fought-for-the-confederacy-proposed/article_defd66dc-acf9-11e7-ab99-3354d981ab03.html (accessed October 12, 2017).

Bibliography

PRIMARY SOURCES

Manuscripts

Albert and Shirley Small Special Collections Library, University of Virginia, Charlottesville
    John H. Claiborne Letters
Eleanor S. Brockenbrough Library, Museum of the Confederacy, Richmond, Va.
    John Christopher Winsmith Papers
Library of Virginia, State of Virginia Government Records Collection, Richmond
    Index to Confederate Pension Applications Filed by
        Virginia Confederate Veterans and Widows
Mississippi Department of Archives and History, Jackson
    Confederate Pension Applications, 1889–1932
North Carolina State Archives, Raleigh
    Confederate Pension Records
Perkins Library, Special Collections Library, Duke University, Durham, N.C.
    John B. Evans Papers, 1862–1865
Tennessee State Library and Archives, Nashville
    Tennessee Colored Pension Applications
Texas Comptroller's Office, Archives and Information Services Division, Texas State
    Library and Archives Commission, Austin
    Confederate Pension Applications

Online Databases

Ancestry, https://www.ancestry.com/
Library of Congress, Prints and Photographs Division, http://www.loc.gov/rr/print
    /coll/SoldierbiosChandler.html/
Andrew and Silas Chandler Photograph
North Carolina Digital Collections, http://digital.ncdcr.gov/cdm/compoundobject
    /collection/p16062coll21/id/113361/rec/19
Aaron Perry Pension

Published Primary Sources

Acts and Joint Resolutions (Amending the Constitution) of the General Assembly of the State of Virginia, Session Which Commenced at the State Capitol on Wednesday, 9 January 1924. Richmond: Davis Bottom, Superintendent of Public Printing, 1924.

Allen, Randall, and Keith S. Bohannon, eds. *Campaigning with "Old Stonewall": Confederate Captain Ujanirtus Allen's Letters to His Wife.* Baton Rouge: Louisiana State University Press, 1998.

Avary, Myrta Lockett, ed. *A Virginia Girl in the Civil War, 1861–1865.* New York: D. Appleton, 1903.

Battey, George Magruder. *A History of Rome and Floyd County, State of Georgia, United States of America: Including Numerous Incidents of More Than Local Interest, 1540–1922.* Atlanta: Webb and Vary, 1922.

Battles and Leaders of the Civil War: Being for the Most Part Contributions by Union and Confederate Officers. 4 vols. Introduction by Roy F. Nichols. 1884–88. Reprint, New York: T. Yoseloff, 1956.

Blomquist, Ann K., and Robert A. Taylor, eds. *This Cruel War: The Civil War Letters of Grant and Malinda Taylor.* Macon: Mercer University Press, 2000.

Caffey, Thomas. *Battle-fields of the South, from Bull Run to Fredericksburg.* New York: John Bradburn, 1864.

Covey, Herbert C., and Dwight Eisnach, eds. *How the Slaves Saw the Civil War: Recollections of the War through the WPA Slave Narratives.* Santa Barbara: Praeger, 2014.

Craig, Tom Moore, ed. *Upcountry South Carolina Goes to War: Letters of the Anderson, Brockman, and Moore Families, 1853–1865.* Columbia: University of South Carolina Press, 2009.

Curran, Robert E., ed. *John Dooley's Civil War: An Irish American's Journey in the First Virginia Infantry Regiment.* Knoxville: University of Tennessee Press, 2012.

Dozier, Graham T., ed. *A Gunner in Lee's Army: The Civil War Letters of Thomas Henry Carter.* Chapel Hill: University of North Carolina Press, 2015.

Eggleston, George Cary. *A Rebel's Recollection.* 1875. Reprint, Baton Rouge: Louisiana State University Press, 1996.

Ezekiel, Moses Jacob. *Memoirs from the Baths of Diocletian.* Edited by Joseph Guttman and Stanley F. Chyet. Detroit: Wayne State University Press, 1975.

Ford, Arthur P., and Marion J. Ford. *Life in the Confederate Army and Some Experiences and Sketches of Southern Life.* New York: Neale, 1905.

Ford, Jennifer W., ed. *The Hour of Our Nation's Agony: The Civil War Letters of Lt. William Cowper Nelson of Mississippi.* Knoxville: University of Tennessee Press, 2007.

Fremantle, Arthur J. L. *Three Months in the Southern States: April–June 1863.* 1864. Reprint, Lincoln, Neb.: Bison Books, 1991.

Gallagher, Gary W., ed. *Fighting for the Confederacy: The Personal Recollections of General Edward Porter Alexander.* Chapel Hill: University of North Carolina Press, 1989.

Goodloe, A. T. *Confederate Echoes: A Voice from the South in the Days of Secession and the Southern Confederacy.* Nashville: Smith and Lamar, 1907.

Hassler, William W., ed. *One of Lee's Best Men: The Civil War Letters of General William Dorsey Pender.* Chapel Hill: University of North Carolina Press, 1965.

Herbert, Hillary A. *History of the Arlington Confederate Monument.* Washington, D.C.: B. S. Adams, 1914.

Hubard, Robert T. *The Civil War Memoirs of a Virginia Cavalryman*. Edited by Thomas P. Nanzig. Tuscaloosa: University of Alabama Press, 2007.

Hubbs, G. Ward, ed. *Voices from Company D: Diaries by the Greensboro Guards, Fifth Alabama Infantry Regiment, Army of Northern Virginia*. Athens: University of Georgia Press, 2003.

Hughes, Thomas. *A Boy's Experience in the Civil War, 1860–1865*. Baltimore: Daily Record, 1904.

Humphries, Robert L., ed. *The Journal of Archibald C. McKinley*. Athens: University of Georgia Press, 1991.

Jones, John Beauchamp. *A Rebel War Clerk's Diary at the Confederate States Capital*. Philadelphia: J. B. Lippincott, 1866.

Journal of the Congress of the Confederate States of America, 1861–1865. 7 vols. Washington, D.C.: Government Printing Office, 1904.

Journal of the House of Representatives of the First Session of the 75th General Assembly of the State of South Carolina, Being the Regular Session Beginning Tuesday, 9 January 1923. Columbia: Gonzalez and Bryan, State Printer, 1923.

Journal of the Senate of the General Assembly of the State of South Carolina, Being the Regular Session Beginning Tuesday, 9 January 1923. Columbia: Gonzales and Bryan, State Printer, 1923.

Lee, William Mack. *History of the Life of Rev. Wm. Mack Lee, Body Servant of General Robert E. Lee through the Civil War: Cook from 1861 to 1865*. Self-published, 1918.

McCarthy, Carlton. *Detailed Minutiae of Soldier Life in the Army of Northern Virginia, 1861–1865, 1882*. Reprint, Lincoln: University of Nebraska Press, 1993.

Minutes of the Seventeenth Annual Meeting and Re-union of the United Confederate Veterans. New Orleans: Press of Schumert and Warfield, 1907.

Minutes of the Sixteenth Annual Convention of the United Daughters of the Confederacy. Opelika, Ala.: Post, 1909.

Moore, T. V. *God Our Refuge and Strength in This War*. Richmond: W. Hargrave White, 1861.

Owen, William Miller. *In Camp and Battle with the Washington Artillery of New Orleans*. Reprint, Baton Rouge: Louisiana University Press, 1999.

Page, Thomas Nelson. *Marse Chan*. New York: Charles Scribner's Sons, 1892.

Pearson, Johnnie Perry, ed. *Lee and Jackson's Bloody Twelfth: The Letters of Irby Goodwin Scott, First Lieutenant, Company G, Putnam Light Infantry, Twelfth Georgia Volunteer Infantry*. Knoxville: University of Tennessee Press, 2010.

Pollard, Edward A. *The Lost Cause*. New York: E. B. Treat, 1867.

Proceedings of the Conference for Education in the South. New York: Committee on Publications, 1903.

Public Acts of the State of Tennessee Passed by the Forty Third General Assembly, 1921. Jackson, Tenn.: McCowat-Mercer, 1921.

Public Laws of the Confederate States of America Passed by the Fourth Session of the First Congress, 1863–1864. Richmond: R. M. Smith, Printer to the Congress, 1864.

Regulations for the Army of the Confederate States, 1863. Richmond: West and Johnston, 1862.

Rhodes, James F. *History of the Civil War, 1861–1865*. New York: Macmillan, 1917.

Richardson, James D., ed. *A Compilation of the Messages and Papers of the Confederacy*. 2 vols. Nashville: United States Publishing Company, 1906.

Robinson, R. H. P. *General Orders from the Adjutant and Inspector General's Office, Confederate States Army, for the Year 1863*. Richmond: A. Morris, 1864.

Ruffin, Edmund. *Anticipations of the Future, to Serve as Lessons for the Present Time*. Richmond: J. W. Randolph, 1860.

Smith, Bobbie Swearingen, ed. *A Palmetto Boy: Civil War–Era Diaries and Letters of James Adam Tillman*. Columbia: University of South Carolina Press, 2010.

Sorrel, G. Moxley. *Recollections of a Confederate Staff Officer*. New York: Neale, 1905.

Steiner, Lewis H. *Report of Lewis H. Steiner, M.D., Inspector of the Sanitary Commission Containing a Diary Kept during the Rebel Occupation of Frederick and an Account of Operations of the U.S. Sanitary Commission during the Campaign in Maryland, September, 1862*. New York: Anson D. F. Randolph, 1862.

Stevens, John W. *Reminiscences of the Civil War*. Hillsboro, Tex.: Hillsboro Mirror Print, 1902.

Stiles, Robert. *Four Years under Marse Robert*. New York: Neale, 1904.

Taylor, Richard. *Destruction and Reconstruction: Personal Experiences of the Civil War*. New York: D. Appleton, 1883.

U.S. War Department. *The War of the Rebellion: A Compilation of the Official Records of the Union and Confederate Armies*. 128 vols. Washington, D.C.: Government Printing Office, 1880–1901.

Virginia Reports to the General Assembly. *RD520-Virginia Sesquicentennial of the American Civil War Commission 2015 Annual Report — The Civil War Sesquicentennial in Virginia: Final Impact and Lasting Legacies*.

Washington, Booker T. *Frederick Douglass*. Philadelphia: George W. Jacobs, 1907.

Yetman, Norman, ed. *When I Was a Slave: Memoirs from the Slave Narrative Collection*. New York: Dover, 2002.

Periodicals

Anderson (S.C.) Intelligencer

Atlanta Constitution

Bolivar (Tenn.) Bulletin

Charleston City Paper

Charleston Daily

Charleston Daily Courier

Charleston Post and Courier

Charlotte Observer

Charlotte Post

Charlottesville Daily Progress

Chelsea (Mass.) Telegraph and Pioneer

Civil War

Civil War Times Illustrated

Columbus (Ga.) Daily Sun

Confederate Veteran

Daily Mail (UK)

Dallas News

Douglass Monthly

Dublin (Ga.) Post

Alexandria (Va.) Gazette

Gettysburg Times

Human Events

Indianapolis Journal

Jackson (Miss.) Advocate

Kansas City Sun

Lexington Park (Md.) Leader

Macon (Ga.) Beacon

Macon (Ga.) Telegraph

Memphis News Scimitar

Monroe (N.C.) Journal

Montgomery Monthly Advertiser

New Orleans Times-Picayune

New York Daily Intelligencer

New York Times

New York Tribune

Pascagoula (Miss.) Democrat-Star

Petersburg (Va.) Daily Express
Pickens (S.C.) Sentinel
Pulaski (Tenn.) Citizen
Raleigh News and Observer
Richmond Daily Dispatch
Richmond Sentinel
Richmond Times
Richmond Whig
Roanoke (Va.) Times
Rome (Ga.) Tribune-Herald
San Diego Union
Scribner's Monthly
The Standard (Ga.)

The State (Columbia)
St. Louis Republic
St. Petersburg Times
Sunny South (Atlanta)
Tampa Bay Times
Virginia Pilot
Washington City Paper
Washington Post
Washington Times
Wautaga (N.C.) Democrat
Wilmington (N.C.) Semi-weekly Messenger
Winchester (Va.) Evening Star

SECONDARY SOURCES

Books

Ash, Stephen V. *The Black Experience in the Civil War*. Dulles, Va.: Potomac Books, 2012.

Aubrecht, Michael. *The Civil War in Spotsylvania County: Confederate Campfires at the Crossroads*. Stroud, UK: History Press, 2009.

Ayers, Edward L. *The Promise of the New South: Life after Reconstruction*. New York: Oxford University Press, 1992.

Ballard, Michael B. *Vicksburg: The Campaign That Opened the Mississippi*. Chapel Hill: University of North Carolina Press, 2004.

Barefoot, Daniel W. *Let Us Die Like Brave Men: Behind the Dying Words of Confederate Warriors*. Winston Salem: John F. Blair, 2005.

Barrow, Charles Kelly, J. H. Segars, and R. B. Rosenburg, eds. *Black Confederates*. Gretna, La.: Pelican Publishing, 2004.

Bergeron, Arthur, Jr. *Confederate Mobile*. Jackson: University Press of Mississippi, 1991.

Berry, Mary Frances. *My Face Is Black Is True: Callie House and the Struggle for Ex-slave Reparations*. New York: Knopf, 2005.

Binnington, Ian. *Confederate Visions: Nationalism, Symbolism, and the Imagined South in the Civil War*. Charlottesville: University Press of Virginia, 2013.

Blair, William. *Contesting the Memory of the Civil War in the South, 1864–1914*. Chapel Hill: University of North Carolina Press, 2004.

Bledsoe, Andrew S. *Citizen-Officers: The Union and Confederate Volunteer Junior Officer Corps in the American Civil War*. Baton Rouge: Louisiana State University Press, 2015.

Blight, David W. *Race and Reunion: The Civil War in American Memory*. Cambridge, Mass.: Harvard University Press, 2001.

Brasher, Glenn David. *The Peninsula Campaign and the Necessity of Emancipation: African Americans and the Fight for Freedom*. Chapel Hill: University of North Carolina Press, 2012.

Brewer, James H. *The Confederate Negro: Virginia's Craftsmen and Military Laborers, 1861–1865*. Tuscaloosa: University of Alabama Press, 1969.

Brown, Kent Masterson. *Retreat from Gettysburg: Lee, Logistics, and the Pennsylvania Campaign*. Chapel Hill: University of North Carolina Press, 2005.

Brown, Thomas J. *Civil War Canon: Sites of Confederate Memory in South Carolina*. Chapel Hill: University of North Carolina Press, 2015.

Brundage, W. Fitzhugh. *The Southern Past: A Clash of Race and Memory*. Cambridge, Mass.: Harvard University Press, 2005.

Cashin, Joan E. *A Family Venture: Men and Women on the Southern Frontier*. Baltimore: Johns Hopkins University Press, 1991.

Coates, Ta-Nehisi. *We Were Eight Years in Power: An American Tragedy*. New York: One World, 2017.

Coddington, Ronald S. *African American Faces of the Civil War: An Album*. Baltimore: Johns Hopkins University Press, 2012.

Cook, Robert J. *Troubled Commemoration: The American Civil War Centennial, 1961–1965*. Baton Rouge: Louisiana State University Press, 2007.

Cornish, Dudley. *The Sable Arm: Negro Troops in the Union Army, 1861–1865*. New York: 1966.

Cox, Karen L. *Dixie's Daughters: The United Daughters of the Confederacy and the Preservation of Confederate Culture*. Gainesville: University Press of Florida, 2003.

Creighton, Margaret. *The Colors of Courage: Gettysburg's Forgotten History*. New York: Basic Books, 2005.

Cunningham, John A. *S. A. Cunningham and the Confederate Heritage*. Athens: University of Georgia Press, 1994.

Dabney, Virginius. *The Last Review: The Confederate Reunion, Richmond 1932*. Chapel Hill: Algonquin Books, 1984.

Davis, Archie K. *Boy Colonel of the Confederacy: The Life and Times of Henry King Burgwyn, Jr.* Chapel Hill: University of North Carolina Press, 1985.

Davis, William C., and James I. Robertson Jr., eds. *Virginia at War, 1865*. Lexington: University Press of Kentucky, 2012.

Dew, Charles B. *Ironmaker to the Confederacy: Joseph R. Anderson and the Tredegar Iron Works*. Richmond: Library of Virginia, 1999.

Dillard, Philip D. *Jefferson Davis's Final Campaign: Confederate Nationalism and the Fight to Arm Slaves*. Macon: Mercer University Press, 2017.

Downs, Jim. *Sick from Freedom: African-American Illness and Suffering during the Civil War and Reconstruction*. New York: Oxford University Press, 2012.

Dreese, Michael A. *Torn Families: Death and Kinship at the Battle of Gettysburg*. Jefferson, N.C.: McFarland, 2007.

Durden, Robert F. *The Gray and the Black: The Confederate Debate on Emancipation*. Baton Rouge: Louisiana State University Press, 1971.

Eanes, Greg. *Virginia's Black Confederates: Essays and Rosters*. Crewe, Va.: Eanes Group, 2014.

Emerson, W. Eric. *Sons of Privilege: The Charleston Light Dragoons in the Civil War*. Columbia: University of South Carolina Press, 2005.

Faust, Drew G. *This Republic of Suffering: Death and the American Civil War*. New York: Knopf, 2008.

Fleming, Walter L. *Civil War and Reconstruction in Alabama*. New York: Columbia University Press, 1905.

Foner, Eric. *The Fiery Trial: Abraham Lincoln and American Slavery*. New York: W. W. Norton, 2010.

Foster, Gaines M. *Ghosts of the Confederacy: Defeat, the Lost Cause, and the Emergence of the New South*. New York: Oxford University Press, 1987.

Franklin, John Hope. *From Slavery to Freedom: A History of Negro Americans*. New York: Knopf, 1947.

Gallagher, Gary W. *Causes Won, Lost, and Forgotten: How Hollywood and Popular Art Shape What We Know about the Civil War*. Chapel Hill: University of North Carolina Press, 2008.

———. *Lee and His Army in Confederate History*. Chapel Hill: University of North Carolina Press, 2011.

———. *The Union War*. Cambridge, Mass.: Harvard University Press, 2011.

Gallagher, Gary W., and Caroline E. Janney, eds. *Cold Harbor to the Crater: The End of the Overland Campaign*. Chapel Hill: University of North Carolina Press, 2015.

Gallagher, Gary W., and Alan T. Nolan, eds. *The Myth of the Lost Cause and Civil War History*. Bloomington: Indiana University Press, 2000.

Genovese, Eugene D., and Elizabeth Fox-Genovese. *Fatal Self-Deception: Slaveholding Paternalism in the Old South*. Cambridge: Cambridge University Press, 2011.

Glatthaar, Joseph T. *General Lee's Army: From Victory to Collapse*. New York: Free Press, 2008.

Goldfield, David R. *Still Fighting the Civil War: The American South and Southern History*. Baton Rouge: Louisiana State University Press, 2002.

Greenberg, Amy S. *A Wicked War: Polk, Clay, Lincoln, and the 1846 U.S. Invasion of Mexico*. New York: Knopf, 2012.

Greene, A. Wilson. *Civil War Petersburg: Confederate City in the Crucible of War*. Charlottesville: University Press of Virginia, 2006.

Greenspan, Anders. *Creating Colonial Williamsburg*. Washington, D.C.: Smithsonian Institution Press, 1998.

Guelzo, Allen C. *Gettysburg: The Last Invasion*. New York: Knopf, 2013.

Hardy, Michael C. *Civil War Charlotte: The Last Capital of the Confederacy*. Charleston: History Press, 2012.

Harvey, Eleanor Jones. *The Civil War and American Art*. Washington, D.C.: Smithsonian American Art Museum, 2012.

Hettle, Wallace. *Inventing Stonewall Jackson: A Civil War Hero in History and Memory*. Baton Rouge: Louisiana State University Press, 2011.

Hofe, Michael W. *That There Be No Stain upon My Stones: Colonel William L. McLeod, 38th Georgia Regiment, 1842–1863*. Gettysburg: Thomas Publications, 1996.

Hollandsworth, James G., Jr. *The Louisiana Native Guards: The Black Military Experience during the War*. Baton Rouge: Louisiana State University Press, 1995.

Horton, James O., and Louis E. Horton, eds. *Slavery and Public History: The Tough Stuff of American History*. New York: The New Press, 2006.

Horwitz, Tony. *Confederates in the Attic: Dispatches from the Unfinished War*. New York: Vintage Books, 1998.

Hulbert, Matthew C. *The Ghosts of Guerrilla Memory: How Civil War Bushwhackers Became Gunslingers in the American West*. Athens: University of Georgia Press, 2016.

Jacoway, Elizabeth, and C. Fred Williams, eds. *Understanding the Little Rock Crisis: An Exercise in Remembrance and Reconciliation*. Fayetteville: University of Arkansas Press, 1999.

Janney, Caroline E. *Remembering the Civil War: Reunion and the Limits of Reconciliation.* Chapel Hill: University of North Carolina Press, 2013.

Jordan, Ervin L., Jr. *Black Confederates and Afro-Yankees in Civil War Virginia.* Charlottesville: University Press of Virginia, 1995.

Kendi, Ibram X. *Stamped from the Beginning: The Definitive History of Racist Ideas in America.* New York: Nation Books, 2016.

Kennedy, James Ronald, and Walter Donald Kennedy. *The South Was Right!* Gretna, La.: Pelican Publishing, 1991.

Kytle, Ethan J., and Blain Roberts. *Denmark Vesey's Garden: Slavery and Memory in the Cradle of the Confederacy.* New York: New Press, 2018.

Levin, Kevin M. *Remembering the Battle of the Crater: War as Murder.* Lexington: University Press of Kentucky, 2012.

———, ed. *Interpreting the Civil War at Museums and Historic Sites.* Lanham, Md.: Rowman and Littlefield, 2017.

Levine, Bruce. *Confederate Emancipation: Southern Plans to Free and Arm Slaves during the Civil War.* New York: Oxford University Press, 2007.

Link, William A. *Atlanta, Cradle of the New South: Race and Remembrance in the Civil War's Aftermath.* Chapel Hill: University of North Carolina Press, 2013.

Litwack, Leon. *Been in the Storm So Long: The Aftermath of Slavery.* New York: Vintage, 1979.

Loewen, James, and Edward H. Sebesta, eds. *The Confederate and Neo-Confederate Reader: The "Great Truth" about the "Lost Cause."* Jackson: University Press of Mississippi, 2010.

Manning, Chandra. *Troubled Refuge: Struggling for Freedom in the Civil War.* New York: Knopf, 2016.

———. *What This Cruel War Was Over: Soldiers, Slavery, and the Civil War.* New York: New York, Knopf, 2007.

Marten, James. *Sing Not War: The Lives of Union and Confederate Veterans in Gilded Age America.* Chapel Hill: University of North Carolina Press, 2011.

Martinez, Jaime A. *Confederate Slave Impressment in the Upper South.* Chapel Hill: University of North Carolina Press, 2013.

McCurry, Stephanie. *Confederate Reckoning: Power and Politics in the Civil War South.* Cambridge, Mass.: Harvard University Press, 2010.

McElya, Micki. *Clinging to Mammy: The Faithful Slave in Twentieth-Century America.* Cambridge, Mass.: Harvard University Press, 2007.

———. *The Politics of Mourning: Death and Honor in Arlington National Cemetery.* Cambridge, Mass.: Harvard University Press, 2016.

McPherson, James M., and William J. Cooper Jr., eds. *Writing the Civil War: The Quest to Understand.* Columbia: University of South Carolina Press, 1998.

Mohr, Clarence. *On the Threshold of Freedom: Masters and Slaves in Civil War Georgia.* Baton Rouge: Louisiana State University Press, 2001.

Moore, Robert A. *A Life for the Confederacy.* Wilmington, N.C.: Broadfoot, 1987.

Murphy, Justin. *Cleburne: A Graphic Novel.* Jacksonville, Fla.: Rampart Press, 2008.

Neely, Mark E., Jr., Harold Holzer, and Gabor S. Boritt, eds. *The Confederate Image: Prints of the Lost Cause.* Chapel Hill: University of North Carolina Press, 1987.

Neff, John R. *Honoring the Civil War Dead: Commemoration and the Problem of Reconciliation.* Lawrence: University Press of Kansas, 2005.

Noe, Kenneth W. *Reluctant Rebels: Confederates Who Joined the Army after 1861.* Chapel Hill: University of North Carolina Press, 2010.

Paradis, James M. *African Americans and the Gettysburg Campaign.* Lanham, Md.: Scarecrow Press, 2005.

Parkinson, Robert G. *The Common Cause: Creating Race and Nation in the American Revolution.* Chapel Hill: University of North Carolina Press, 2016.

Parsons, Elaine Frantz. *Ku-Klux: The Birth of the Klan during Reconstruction.* Chapel Hill: University of North Carolina Press, 2015.

Pfanz, Donald C. *Richard S. Ewell: A Soldier's Life.* Chapel Hill: University of North Carolina Press, 1998.

Poole, W. Scott. *Never Surrender: Confederate Memory and Conservatism in the South Carolina Upcountry.* Athens: University of Georgia Press, 2004.

Power, J. Tracy. *Lee's Miserables: Life in the Army of Northern Virginia from the Wilderness to Appomattox.* Chapel Hill: University of North Carolina Press, 1998.

Quarles, Benjamin. *The Negro in the Civil War.* New York: Little, Brown, 1953.

Robertson, James I., Jr. *Soldiers Blue and Gray.* Columbia: University of South Carolina Press, 1988.

Robinson, Armistead L. *Bitter Fruits of Bondage: The Demise of Slavery and the Collapse of the Confederacy, 1861–1865.* Charlottesville: University Press of Virginia, 2005.

Rollins, Richard, ed. *Black Southerners in Gray: Essays on Afro-Americans in Confederate Armies.* Redondo Beach, Calif.: Rank and File, 1994.

Rubin, Anne Sarah. *A Shattered Nation: The Rise and Fall of the Confederacy, 1861–1868.* Chapel Hill: University of North Carolina Press, 2005.

————. *Through the Heart of Dixie: Sherman's March and American Memory.* Chapel Hill: University of North Carolina Press, 2014.

Segars, J. H., and Charles Kelly Barrow. *Black Southerners in Confederate Armies: A Collection of Historical Accounts.* Gretna, La.: Pelican Publishing, 2007.

Silber, Nina. *The Romance of Reunion: Northerners and the South, 1865–1900.* Chapel Hill: University of North Carolina Press, 1993.

Stone, DeWitt Boyd, Jr. *Wandering to Glory: Confederate Veterans Remember Evans' Brigade.* Columbia: University of South Carolina Press, 2002.

Sutton, Robert K., ed. *Rally on the High Ground: The National Park Service Symposium on the Civil War.* Washington, D.C.: Eastern National, 2001.

Symonds, Craig L. *Stonewall of the West: Patrick Cleburne and the Civil War.* Lawrence: University Press of Kansas, 1997.

Thompson, Jerry, ed. *Civil War in the Southwest: Recollections of the Sibley Brigade.* College Station: Texas A&M University Press, 2001.

Toplin, Robert B. *Ken Burns's "The Civil War": Historians Respond.* New York: Oxford University Press, 1996.

Wallenstein, Peter, and Bertram Wyatt-Brown, eds. *Virginia's Civil War.* Charlottesville: University Press of Virginia, 2005.

Ward, Andrew. *The Slaves' War: The Civil War in the Words of Former Slaves.* Boston: Houghton Mifflin, 2008.

Wiley, Bell I. *The Life of Johnny Reb: The Common Soldier of the Confederacy.* Baton Rouge: Louisiana State University Press, 1943.

————. *Southern Negroes, 1861–1865.* New Haven: Yale University Press, 1938.

Wilkinson, Warren, and Steven E. Woodworth. *A Scythe of Fire: A Civil War Story of the Eighth Georgia Infantry Regiment*. New York: Morrow, 2002.

Williams, Chad L. *Torchbearers of Democracy: African American Soldiers in the World War I Era*. Chapel Hill: University of North Carolina Press, 2010.

Wilson, Charles Reagan. *Baptized in Blood: The Religion of the Lost Cause, 1865–1920*. Athens: University of Georgia Press, 1980.

Woodward, Colin. *Marching Masters: Slavery, Race, and the Confederate Army during the Civil War*. Charlottesville: University Press of Virginia, 2014.

Wright, Ben, and Zachary W. Dresser, eds. *Apocalypse and the Millennium in the American Civil War Era*. Baton Rouge: Louisiana State University Press, 2013.

Articles, Essays, and Papers

Bohannon, Keith S. "'These Few Gray-Haired, Battle-Scarred Veterans': Confederate Army Reunions in Georgia, 1885–95." In *The Myth of the Lost Cause and Civil War History*, edited by Gary W. Gallagher and Alan T. Nolan, 89–110. Bloomington: Indiana University Press, 2000.

Carmichael, Peter S. "We Were 'Men': The Ambiguous Place of Confederate Slaves in Southern Armies." Unpublished paper presented at the 2005 Southern Historical Association, Atlanta, Ga.

Coleman, Christy. "Among the Ruins: Creating and Interpreting the American Civil War in Richmond." In *Interpreting the Civil War at Museums and Historic Sites*, edited by Kevin M. Levin, 1–12. Lanham, Md.: Rowman and Littlefield, 2017.

Dabney, Emmanuel, Beth Parnicza, and Kevin M. Levin. "Interpreting Race, Slavery and United States Colored Troops at Civil War Battlefields." *Civil War History* 62 (June 2016): 131–48.

Davis, Steve. "'That Extraordinary Document': W. H. T. Walker and Patrick Cleburne's Emancipation Proposal." *Civil War Times Illustrated* December 1977, 14–20.

Dukes, Jesse, and Jonno Rattman. "Lost Causes: Confederate Reenactors Take Pride in Their Southern Heritage, but Struggle with the Centrality of Slavery and Racism to the Confederacy." *Virginia Quarterly Review* 90, no. 3 (Summer 2014): 88–105.

Emerson, W. Eric. "Commemoration, Conflict, and Constraints: The Saga of the Confederate Flag at the South Carolina State House." In *Interpreting the Civil War at Museums and Historic Sites*, edited by Kevin M. Levin, 77–92. Lanham, Md.: Rowman and Littlefield, 2017.

Gallagher, Gary W. "Blueprint for Victory: Northern Strategy and Military Policy." In *Writing the Civil War: The Quest to Understand*, edited by James M. McPherson and William J. Cooper Jr., 8–35. Columbia: University of South Carolina Press, 1998.

Gallagher, Gary W., and Kathryn Shively Meier. "Coming to Terms with Civil War Military History." *Journal of the Civil War Era* 4 (December 2014): 487–508.

Goldfield, David. "Segregation and Racism: Taking Up the Dream Again." In *Understanding the Little Rock Crisis: An Exercise in Remembrance and Reconciliation*, edited by Elizabeth Jacoway and C. Fred Williams, 29–44. Fayetteville: University of Arkansas Press, 1999.

Groce, W. Todd. "New Wine in Old Bottles: Using Historical Markers to Reshape Public Memory of the Civil War." In *Interpreting the Civil War at Museums and Historic Sites*, edited by Kevin M. Levin, 45–60. Lanham, Md.: Rowman and Littlefield, 2017.

Hackethan, Lucinda H. "Reading Marlboro Jones: A Georgia Slave in Civil War Virginia." In *Virginia's Civil War*, edited by Peter Wallenstein and Bertram Wyatt-Brown, 164–75. Charlottesville: University Press of Virginia, 2005.

Helsley, Alexia J. "Notes and News from the Archives: Black Confederates." *South Carolina Historical Magazine* 74 (July 1973): 184–88.

Hollandsworth, James G., Jr. "Looking for Bob: Black Confederate Pensioners after the Civil War." *Journal of Mississippi History* 69 (Winter 2007): 295–324.

Krick, Robert E. L. "Repairing an Army: A Look at the New Troops in the Army of Northern Virginia in May and June 1864." In *Cold Harbor to the Crater: The End of the Overland Campaign*, edited by Gary W. Gallagher and Caroline E. Janney, 33–72. Chapel Hill: University of North Carolina Press, 2015.

Levin, Kevin M. "Black Confederates out of the Attic and into the Mainstream." *Journal of the Civil War Era* 4 (December 2014): 627–35.

———. "Confederate Like Me." *Civil War Monitor* 3 (Spring 2013): 60–67, 78–79.

———. "'When Johnny Comes Marching Home': The Demobilization of Lee's Army." In *Virginia at War, 1865*, edited by William C. Davis and James I. Robertson Jr., 85–102. Lexington: University Press of Kentucky, 2012.

Rudy, John M. "From Tokenism to True Partnership: The National Park Service's Shifting Interpretation at the Civil War's Sesquicentennial." In *Interpreting the Civil War at Museums and Historic Sites*, edited by Kevin M. Levin, 61–76. Lanham, Md.: Rowman and Littlefield, 2017.

Sampson, Myra Chandler, and Kevin M. Levin. "The Loyalty of Silas Chandler." *Civil War Times* 51 (February 2012): 30–34.

Theses and Dissertations

Deserino, Frank. "Wearing the Gray Suit: Black Enlistment and the Confederate Military." Ph.D. diss., University of London, 2001.

Elliott, Brian A. "Peculiar Pairings: Texas Confederates and Their Body Servants." M.A. thesis, University of North Texas, 2016.

O'Sullivan, Bryna Claire. "Why Pension? Establishing the Reasons for Body Servant Pensions Using Newspaper and Magazine Depiction." M.A. thesis, University of North Carolina at Chapel Hill, 2011.

Woodward, Colin Edward. "Marching Masters: Slavery, Race, and the Confederate Army, 1861–1865." Ph.D. diss., Louisiana State University, 2005.

Online Sources

Abbeville Institute: The Abbeville Blog, https://www.abbevilleinstitute.org/.

Ancestry.com. *1850 United States Federal Census*. Provo, Utah: Ancestry.com, Operations, Inc., 2010.

———. *1860 United States Federal Census*. Provo, Utah: Ancestry.com, Operations, Inc., 2010.

———. *1860 United States Federal Census — Slave Schedules*. Provo, Utah: Ancestry.com, Operations, Inc., 2010.

Antiques Roadshow, http://www.pbs.org/wgbh/roadshow/.

The Atlantic, https://www.theatlantic.com/.

"Black Confederates." http://www.florida-scv.org/Camp1316/Black%20Confederates
   .htm.
"Black Heroes in Gray: The Forgotten Heroes of the Confederate States of America." Bog
   Bit, https://bogbit.com/.
"Black Rebels in the C.S.A." Texas Confederate Veterans, http://www.texasconfederate
   veterans.com/.
Bradley Schmehl, http://bradleyschmehl.com.
Civil War Memory: The Online Home of Kevin M. Levin (blog), http://cwmemory.com.
Civil War Talk, https://civilwartalk.com/.
"Commemorative Landscapes." Documenting the American South, http://docsouth.unc
   .edu/.
Confederate American, http://confederateblog.com/.
C-SPAN, https://www.c-span.org/.
Daily Beast, https://www.thedailybeast.com/.
Dead Confederates: A Civil War Era Blog, http://deadconfederates.com.
Disunion: The Civil War (blog). New York Times, https://www.nytimes.com/interactive
   /2014/opinion/disunion.html.
Dixie Outfitters, https://dixieoutfitters.com/.
DixieSCV.org, http://dixiescv.org/.
Encyclopedia Virginia, https://www.encyclopediavirginia.org/.
Finding Your Roots, http://www.pbs.org/weta/finding-your-roots/home/.
Handler, Jerome S., and Michael L. Tuite Jr. "Retouching History: The Modern
   Falsification of a Civil War Photograph," http://people.virginia.edu/~jh3v
   /retouchinghistory/essay.html.
Historical Encounters: A Journal of Historical Consciousness, Historical Cultures, and History
   Education, http://hej.hermes-history.net/index.php/HEJ.
History Detectives, http://www.pbs.org/opb/historydetectives/.
Journal of the American Revolution, https://allthingsliberty.com/.
Jubilo! The Emancipation Century, https://jubiloemancipationcentury.wordpress.com/.
Kelly, Michael. "Black Confederate Combat Soldiers." Latin American Studies, http://
   www.latinamericanstudies.org/.
Last Seen: Finding Family after Slavery, http://informationwanted.org/.
Laurens County African American History, http://laurenscountyafricanamericanhistory
   .blogspot.com/.
Mississippi History Now, http://www.mshistorynow.mdah.ms.gov/.
Petersburg Express, http://www.petersburgexpress.com/.
The Root, http://www.theroot.com/.
Slate, https://slate.com/.
Sons of Confederate Veterans, http://www.scv.org/.
Southern Poverty Law Center, https://www.splcenter.org/.
Talking Points Memo, http://talkingpointsmemo.com/.

Index

Virginia Sesquicentennial of the American Civil War Commission, 164
Volck, Adalbart, 76

Waddell, Charles E., 50
Walker, William H. T., 60
Washington, Booker T., 10, 83–84
Washington, Denzel, 130
Washington, George, 55–56
Washington, John, 164
Way, Tony, 166
Wells, Edward L., 21
White, Samuel Elliot, 97
White, Wash (camp slave) 116
Wilderness, battle of, 52, 94, 118
Williams, Henson (camp slave), 105

Williams, Shane, 158
Williams, Walter, 156, 160
Williamsburg, battle of, 75
Willis (camp slave), 50
Wilson, John Andrew, 66
Wilson, Woodrow, 99
Wilson's Creek, battle of, 23
Winbush, Nelson, 159–60
Winsmith, John Christopher, 19–20, 25, 34
World's Columbian Exposition, 82
World War I, 102, 110–12
Wright, Hettie Byrd, 167

Yopp, Bill "Ten-Cent Bill" (camp slave), 25, 82, 132